MENTALIZATION

Psychoanalytic Inquiry Book Series

Volume 29

Psychoanalytic Inquiry
Book Series

MENTALIZATION

Theoretical Considerations, Research Findings,

and Clinical Implications

Edited by Fredric N. Busch

The Analytic Press

Taylor & Francis Group

New York   London

Cover image: Rembrandt, Aristotle with a Bust of Homer, 1653, Oil on canvas; 56 1/2 x 53 3/4. The Metropolitan Museum of Art, Purchase, special contributions and funds given or bequeathed by friends of the Museum, 1961 (61.198). Image © The Metropolitan Museum of Art.

The Analytic Press
Taylor & Francis Group
270 Madison Avenue
New York, NY 10016

The Analytic Press
Taylor & Francis Group
27 Church Road
Hove, East Sussex BN3 2FA

© 2008 by Taylor & Francis Group, LLC

Printed in the United States of America on acid-free paper
10 9 8 7 6 5 4 3 2

International Standard Book Number-13: 978-0-88163-485-3 (Softcover) 978-0-88163-484-6 (Hardcover)

Library of Congress Cataloging-in-Publication Data

Busch, Fredric, 1958-
   Mentalization : theoretical considerations, research findings, and clinical implications / Fredric N. Busch.
        p. ; cm. -- (Psychoanalytic inquiry book series ; v. 29)
      Includes bibliographical references and index.
      ISBN 978-0-88163-484-6 (alk. paper) -- ISBN 978-0-88163-485-3 (alk. paper)
      1. Psychoanalysis. 2. Borderline personality disorder. 3. Interpersonal relations. I. Title. II. Series.
      [DNLM: 1. Psychoanalytic Therapy. 2. Mental Processes. 3. Psychoanalytic Theory. 4. Self Concept. W1 PS427F v.29 2008 / WM 460.6 B9775m 2008]

RC506.B873 2008
616.89'17--dc22   2007049162

Visit the Taylor & Francis Web site at
http://www.taylorandfrancis.com

and The Analytic Press Web site at
http://www.analyticpress.com

Contents

Part III Clinical

Acknowledgment

I would like to thank Diana Diamond for her editorial assistance in the creation of this book.

Editor

Fredric N. Busch, M.D., is a clinical associate professor at Weill Cornell Medical College and a faculty member of the Columbia University Center for Psychoanalytic Training and Research. He is on the editorial board of *Psychoanalytic Inquiry*. Dr. Busch has authored over 30 publications as well as 10 books or book chapters. His writing and research has focused on the links between psychoanalysis and psychiatry, including psychodynamic approaches to specific disorders, psychoanalytic research, and psychoanalysis and medication. He has coauthored three books on the psychoanalytic approach to specific disorders: *Manual of Panic Focused Psychodynamic Psychotherapy, Psychodynamic Approaches to the Adolescent with Panic Disorder*, and *Psychodynamic Treatment of Depression*.

He has been involved in research on panic focused psychodynamic psychotherapy, including the first study to demonstrate efficacy of psychodynamic treatment of panic disorder, recently published in the *American Journal of Psychiatry*. Additionally, Dr. Busch has written on integrating the theoretical conceptualizations and clinical approaches of psychoanalytic treatments and medication, including coediting an issue of *Psychoanalytic Inquiry* on this topic, and coauthoring two seminal papers on treatment triangles, addressing the complex interactions of the psychotherapist, psychopharmacologist, and patient. He is also the author, along with Larry Sandberg, of *Psychotherapy and Medication* (Analytic Press, 2007).

Contributors

Andrew Aronson, M.D., is associate professor of psychiatry at the Mount Sinai School of Medicine and medical director for Ambulatory Psychiatry Services at the Mount Sinai Medical Center. A member of the New York Psychoanalytic Society and Institute, Dr. Aronson is curriculum director of psychotherapy training and co-chair of the Psychotherapy Competencies Committee for the Mount Sinai Department of Psychiatry residency training program. He is a collaborating investigator, consultant, and supervisor in several federally funded psychotherapy research projects.

Marc-André Bouchard, Ph.D., is a clinical psychologist and psychoanalyst (member of the Canadian Psychoanalytic Society) in private practice. Also a full professor in the Département de Psychologie, Université de Montréal, he is currently director of the program in Clinical Psychology.

John F. Clarkin, Ph.D., is co-director of the Personality Disorders Institute at the New York Presbyterian Hospital, and clinical professor of psychology in psychiatry at the Weill Medical College of Cornell University in New York City. He is the author of numerous publications on the nature and treatment of personality disorders, and is the past president of the International Society for Psychotherapy Research.

Diana Diamond, Ph.D., is associate professor in the doctoral program in clinical psychology at the City University of New York, and adjunct assistant professor of psychiatry in the Department of Psychiatry at the Weill Medical Center of Cornell University, where she is also a senior fellow at the Personality Disorders Institute. She is one of the co-editors, with Sidney Blatt and Joseph Lichtenberg, of *Attachment and Sexuality* (Analytic Press, 2008).

Peter Fonagy, Ph.D., F.B.A., is Freud Memorial Professor of Psychoanalysis and Director of the Sub-department of Clinical Health Psychology at University College, London. He is a clinical psychologist and a training and supervising analyst in the British Psycho-Analytical Society in child and adult analysis, and has published over 300 chapters and articles and has authored or edited several books.

György Gergely, Ph.D., is the head of the Department of Developmental Research at the Hungarian Academy of Sciences, and a professor at the Cognitive Neuroscience Doctoral Program of the Budapest University of Technology and Economics in Hungary. He has been the recipient of numerous awards, including the IPA Committee's Award for Exceptional Contribution to Research (2001) and the Kardos Memorial Prize of the Hungarian Academy of Sciences for Outstanding Scientific Achievements in Psychological Research (2002).

Otto F. Kernberg, M.D., F.A.P.A., is director of the Personality Disorders Institute at The New York Presbyterian Hospital, Westchester Division, and Professor of Psychiatry at the Weill Medical College of Cornell University. He is the author of 12 books and co-author of 11 others, including *Contemporary Controversies in Psychoanalytic Theory, Techniques and their Applications* (Yale University Press, 2004).

Serge Lecours, Ph.D., is associate professor at the Psychology Department of the Université de Montréal. He is a clinical psychologist and does research on verbal manifestations of the mentalization and regulation of affect in psychopathology and psychotherapy. He is also on the North American Editorial Board of the *International Journal of Psychoanalysis*.

Kenneth N. Levy, Ph.D., is an assistant professor in the Department of Psychology at Pennsylvania State. He is also an adjunct assistant professor of psychology and psychiatry in the Department of Psychiatry at Weill Medical College of Cornell University. He conducts research on child and adult attachment, affect regulation, borderline personality disorder, and psychotherapy process and outcome. In

2000–2001, Dr. Levy was selected as an Early Career Fellow of the American Psychoanalytic Association and is the 2007 recipient of the Outstanding Scientific Paper Prize by the Committee on Scientific Activities of the American Psychoanalytic Association.

Barbara Milrod, M.D., is associate professor of Psychiatry at Weill Medical College of Cornell University and faculty at The New York Psychoanalytic Institute. The author of over 50 publications, she has also been awarded the Heinz Hartmann Junior Award from the New York Psychoanalytic Institute for significant contribution to the field of psychoanalysis, as well as the Norbert and Charlotte Rieger Award for Psychodynamic Psychotherapy from the American Academy of Child and Adolescent Psychiatry.

Marie G. Rudden, M.D., is assistant clinical professor of psychiatry at Weill Medical School, Cornell University, and a training and supervising Analyst at Berkshire Psychoanalytic Institute, a new training facility of the American Psychoanalytic Association.

Arietta Slade, Ph.D., is professor of clinical and developmental psychology at the City University of New York and associate research scientist at the Yale Child Study Center. She is the author of numerous publications, and contributing author to *Handbook of Mentalization Based Treatment* and *Psychoanalytic Study of the Child, Enhancing Early Attachments: Theory, Research, Intervention, and Policy*, as well as the editor of *Children at Play: Reflecting on the Future of Psychoanalysis* (in press). She is also in private practice with children and adults.

Howard Steele, Ph.D., is associate professor of psychology at the New School for Social Research in New York City. At the New School, he is director of graduate studies in psychology and co-director (with M. Steele) of the Center for Attachment Research. He is also the founding and senior editor of the international quarterly journal, *Attachment & Human Development*.

Miriam Steele, Ph.D., is associate professor of psychology at the New School for Social Research in New York City. At the New School, she is assistant director of doctoral training in clinical psychology. Miriam is a Child Psychoanalyst, having trained at the Anna Freud

Centre, London. At the New School, Miriam Steele is co-director (with H. Steele) of the Center for Attachment Research.

Mary Target, Ph.D., is professional director of the Anna Freud Centre, chair of the British Psychological Society Psychotherapy Section, and a member of the Research Committee (Conceptual Research) of the International Psychoanalytic Association. She has active research collaborations in many countries in the areas of developmental psychopathology, attachment, and psychotherapy outcome.

Zsolt Unoka, M.D., is assistant professor of psychiatry and psycho-therapy at the Department of Psychiatry and Psychotherapy, Semmelweis University, and faculty of General Medicine, Budapest, Hungary. Dr. Unoka is also a member of the teaching faculty of the Postgraduate Psychotherapy Training Program at Semmelweis University, and is a psychoanalytic candidate finishing his analytic training at the Hungarian Psychoanalytic Association.

Frank E. Yeomans, M.D., Ph.D., is clinical associate professor of psychiatry at the Weill Medical College of Cornell University, director of training at the Personality Disorders Institute of Weill-Cornell, lecturer in psychiatry at the Columbia University Center for Psychoanalytic Training and Research, and director of the Personality Studies Institute. He has authored and co-authored numerous articles and books, including *A Primer on Transference-Focused Psychotherapy for the Borderline Patient* and *Psychotherapy for Borderline Personality*, with John Clarkin and Otto Kernberg.

Preface

Mentalization is the capacity to perceive and interpret behavior in terms of intentional mental states, to imagine what others are thinking and feeling. Although it has been argued that mentalization is old wine in new bottles, the chapters in this book, written by a variety of experts in this area, illustrate a new perspective for understanding the human psyche and interpersonal relationships. Those involved in identifying mentalization have also employed a new approach to investigating psychoanalytic ideas by making consistent efforts to measure and research the concept. Thus, in addition to expanding the theoretical basis and implications of mentalization and identifying clinically useful applications, the authors describe research that scientifically grounds the concept. Despite the division of the book into sections, differentiation into theoretical, research and clinical papers proved difficult, as most of the investigators pursued each of these goals.

This volume addresses and expands upon a number of implications of mentalization. These include: What are the broader implications for mentalization with regard to social and evolutionary development? How does mentalization interdigitate with other psychoanalytic models, including libido and object relations theory? How is mentalization systematically assessed? What clinical correlates have been found? How do we understand variations in the capacity for mentalization? What are the applications of mentalization in the clinical arena, including specific disorders?

The volume begins with Fonagy's description of the evolutionary role of social collaboration, and the brain areas and functions likely linked to mentalization. Anticipating and interpreting mental and emotional states and behavior permits cooperation and offers competitive advantage. Looking at evidence from recent studies of the brain, he proposes a model in which attachment trauma hyperactivates the attachment system, inhibiting mentalization. This inhibition aids adaptation to traumatic attachment, protecting the psyche from acknowledging the mental states of a traumatizing caretaker, but undermines the capacity for mentalization. This disruption has broad implications for the development of psychopathology.

Gergely and Unoka describe the development of self to other and other to self models of the caretaker. The developing child monitors how the other responds to his own mental states and behavior, and how to adjust his response to those of the other. A sensitive caretaker aids in the development of appraisal processes that can inhibit automatic emotional arousal and behavioral expressions. With a problematic caretaker, automatic inhibition of parts of the emotion response system will leave the self helplessly overwhelmed by an uncontrolled state of high physiological arousal. Mentalizing about the intentions and emotions of the other allows for an increased repertoire of coping strategies. The individual can also learn to detect internal cues about emotional reactions to others. They describe a case in which the patient's emotional states are kidnapped by concerns about an adverse impact on and reaction of the other, leading to affective freezing, and discuss what analytic approaches may be of value or potentially worsen symptoms.

Bouchard and Lecours believe that mentalization can best be described by combining Freudian-French instinctual models with the intersubjective view described by Fonagy, Target, and colleagues. The former view focuses on the role of developing thought activity in binding instinctual demands, preventing discharge in action. In contrast, Fonagy, Target, and colleagues emphasize developing mental representations gained through mirroring from significant others. The authors compare Fonagy, Target, and colleagues' model with an instinctual view as employing "a developmental and intersubjective approach, as opposed to a psychogenetics of mental structures, dyadic preoedipal intersubjective relationships, rather than a focus on mental elaboration of (and defensive activity against) the imperious urgencies of instinctual life, the mother's (and the analyst's) role in helping the infant (and the patient) develop more efficient affect tolerance and regulation within the dyad, in contrast to an analysis of affect regulation in terms of the life and death drives and pressures." Ultimately, the authors find Kernberg's conception of affects as useful in bridging these models. The authors also identify four components of poor mentalization found with different models: (a) trauma, neglect, and psychic pain; (b) mental rejection and dissociation mechanisms; (c) the persistence of primitive modes of thinking and poor symbolization; and (d) affect dysregulation.

In the first of two papers in the research section, the Steeles describe the development of the concept and measurement of reflective functioning. After developing the reflective functioning scale as a measure of mentalizing capacity, they found that parental RF during pregnancy correlated with infant-parent attachment security, and maternal RF was linked with the 5-year-old child's ability to correctly identify an emotional state on a task. Prebirth paternal RF was found to correlate negatively with the parent's estimate of behavior problems in his child at age 5 and with the children's self report at age 11 of emotional, behavioral, and peer problems. In mothers who had suffered high-deprivation during childhood those with high RF were found to have securely attached infants, but not those with low RF. They describe how poor reflective function and unmet attachment needs in parents lead to the potential for ruptures between parent and child that are not repaired, leaving them vulnerable to feelings of isolation, anger, and despair. The authors conclude that one important role of psychoanalytic work should be the facilitation of reflective functioning in the patient. RF may be an appropriate measure of outcome, and may potentially be rated in interviews concerning patients' experiences of the patient–analyst relationship.

Yeomans and colleagues explore the role of reflective functioning in the understanding and treatment of borderline personality disorder. Borderline patients are viewed as either shutting down reflecting on or hypermentalizing the mental states of others (to the neglect of focus on self states) as a defense against the experience of abuse and neglect. The therapist works to encourage mentalization by identifying the experience of patient and therapist in the transference. In addition, the therapist helps the patient to clarify conflicting affects in relation to others. In a randomized clinical trail (Clarkin, Levy, Lenzenweger, & Kernberg, 2007) comparing dialectic behavioral therapy, transference focused psychotherapy (TFP) and a psychodynamic supportive therapy for borderline patients, preliminary data analysis indicated that while all treatments were effective in symptom reduction and functional improvement, only mean RF score of the patients treated with TFP increased significantly. According to the authors, these results attest to the value of transference interpretation in borderline patients in improving RF.

Like Yeomans and colleagues, Rudden and colleagues explore how RF may function in a specific disorder, in this case panic disorder. As with Yeomans and colleagues and borderline personality, Rudden and colleagues posit that disruptions in RF can occur secondary to defensive function in an effort to avert painful affects or conflicts, and that these disruptions can be resolved through psychodynamic treatment. However, in panic disorder, the impact is viewed as being limited to those areas of conflict that can trigger panic attacks, leaving general RF intact. To test these hypotheses, Rudden and colleagues developed a measure of panic specific reflective functioning (PSRF). The authors provide case material from patients in panic focused psychodynamic psychotherapy to demonstrate improvements in PSRF. Patients show both increased awareness of their conflicted feelings and fantasies, as well as a reduction in panic symptoms.

Slade delineates how the RF concept helps to clarify what child therapists are doing when they work with children. She describes how parental RF, the parent's capacity to hold in her own mind a representation of her child as having feelings, desires, and intentions, has been found to be related to positive caregiving and the development of multiple capacities in the child. She suggests that work with parents can best be conceptualized as an effort to enhance their reflective functioning about the child. Therapists model a reflective stance for parents, viewing the child's behavior as based on feelings and meaning, and hope that the parents learn to take a similar stance.

These chapters provide the reader with a multifaceted understanding of the concept of mentalization and its uses. Clinicians of all theoretical persuasions will view their work through a new lens and find their techniques in working with patients broadened and enhanced. Psychoanalysts will gain a sense of how their efforts can be substantiated by careful delineation and systematic assessment of their concepts and approaches.

Fredric N. Busch, M.D.

References

Clarkin, J. F., Levy, K. N., Lenzenweger, M. F., & Kernberg, O. F. (2007). Evaluating three treatments for borderline personality disorder: A multiwave study. *American Journal of Psychiatry, 164,* 922–928.

Part I

Theory

1

The Mentalization-Focused Approach to Social Development

Peter Fonagy

Introduction

Reflective function refers to a quantified index of attachment-related mentalization, that is, the capacity to conceive of mental states as explanations of behavior in oneself and in others. We assume that the capacity to mentalize is a key determinant of self-organization that, along with contributory capacities of affect regulation and attention control mechanisms, is acquired in the context of early attachment relationships. Disturbances of attachment relationships will therefore disrupt the normal emergence of these key social-cognitive capacities and create profound vulnerabilities in the context of social relationships. Unusually, for what is fundamentally a psychoanalytic approach, we elaborated our model of social development on the basis of empirical observations as well as clinical work.

In the 1980s an extremely active research program in developmental psychology investigated when children begin to understand that people are capable of having false beliefs about the world (Perner & Lang, 2000; Wellman, 1990). Yet a number of researchers consider the resulting construct of theory of mind and its false-belief paradigm to be too narrow (Carpendale & Chandler, 1996) as it fails to encapsulate the relational and affect regulative aspects of interpreting behavior in mental state terms. Developmentalists have started to use the term *mentalizing* as an alternative, because it is not limited either to specific tasks or particular age groups (Morton & Frith, 1995; O'Connor & Hirsch, 1999).

We define mentalization as a form of mostly preconscious imaginative mental activity, namely, interpreting human behavior in terms of intentional mental states (e.g., needs, desires, feelings, beliefs, goals, purposes, and reasons). Mentalizing is imaginative because we have to imagine what other people might be thinking or feeling; an important indicator of high quality of mentalization is the awareness that we do not and cannot know absolutely what is in someone else's mind. We suggest that a similar kind of imaginative leap is required to understand one's own mental experience, particularly in relation to emotionally charged issues. In order to conceive of others as having a mind, the individual needs a symbolic representational system for mental states and also must be able to selectively activate states of mind in line with particular intentions, which requires attentional control.

The ability to understand the self as a mental agent grows out of interpersonal experience, particularly primary object relationships (Fonagy, 2003). The baby's experience of himself as having a mind or self is not a genetic given; it evolves from infancy through childhood, and its development critically depends upon interaction with more mature minds, assuming these are benign, reflective, and sufficiently attuned. Mentalization involves both a self-reflective and an interpersonal component. It is underpinned by a large number of specific cognitive skills, including an understanding of emotional states, attention and effortful control, and the capacity to make judgments about subjective states as well as thinking explicitly about states of mind—what we might call mentalization proper. In combination, these functions enable the child to distinguish inner from outer reality and internal mental and emotional processes from interpersonal events.

This paper provides an overview of the mentalization-focused approach to social development. We address the complex relation of attachment and mentalization and summarize contemporary neurobiological research bearing on the cognitive, affective, and relational aspects of mentalizing. This biological perspective underpins our discussion of the role of mentalizing in the development of the agentive sense of self, followed by a broader consideration of the role of interpersonal relationships in the maturation of mentalizing capacities. Finally we discuss the contribution of attachment trauma to the development of psychopathology by virtue of undermining mentalizing capacity.

Evolutionary and Neurobiological Links Between Attachment and Mentalization

The Selective Advantages of Attachment

As our understanding of the interface of brain development and early psychosocial experience increases, we can see that the evolutionary role of the attachment relationship goes far beyond giving physical protection to the human infant. Attachment ensures that the brain processes that come to subserve social cognition are appropriately organized and prepared to equip the individual for the collaborative and cooperative existence with others for which the brain was designed.

In our view the major selective advantage conferred by attachment to humans is the opportunity to develop social intelligence that nearness to concerned adults affords. Alan Sroufe (1996) and Myron Hofer (2004) played a seminal role in extending attachment theory from a concern with the developmental emergence of a complex set of social expectancies to a far broader conception of attachment as an organiser of physiological and brain regulation. More recent work has begun to articulate the associated biological pathways (e.g., Champagne et al., 2004; Jaworski, Francis, Brommer, Morgan & Kuhar, 2005; Plotsky et al., 2005; Zhang, Chretien, Meany, & Gratton, 2005). This body of work illustrates how processes as fundamental as gene expression or changes in receptor densities are influenced by the infant's environment. The brain is experience–expectant (Siegel, 1999).

The Selective Advantages of Mentalization

Mentalization is arguably the evolutionary pinnacle of human intellectual achievement. But what has driven the selection processes of the two million or so years of human evolution toward a consciousness of mental states in self and others? Was it to meet the periodic challenges the physical environment presented to our ancestors who were presumably only somewhat more agile and strong than we are?

Surprisingly, leaps forward in human brain size in the course of evolution do not correspond to what we know about ecological demands on our hominid ancestors (e.g., climatic variability, threat of predation, and availability of prey).

The evolutionary biologist Richard Alexander (1989) proposed a widely accepted model of how humans evolved their minds. He suggested that our exceptional intelligence evolved not to deal with the hostile forces of nature but rather to deal with competition from other people. This further evolution occurred only after our species had already achieved relative dominance over their environment. At that point we became our "own principal hostile forces of nature" (Alexander, 1989, p. 469). And to meet this challenge to the survival of our genes, those with common genetic material had to cooperate.

All species face competition from conspecifics but humans are special in the role that social groups play in achieving success in this regard. A kind of evolutionary arms race probably took place among ever more effective social groups. Competition with intelligent conspecifics requires skill in understanding and outsmarting other people. As the intelligence of the opposition increased so too did the requirement for ever-greater mentalizing ability. The construction and manipulation of mental scenarios (of thoughts about thoughts and feelings) acquired a major reproductive advantage. The assumption that the mind governs actions and the possibility of interpreting and anticipating behavior permits cooperation, offers competitive advantage, and continually selects for increasingly higher levels of social interpretive capacity.

The Interpersonal Interpretive Function

The capacity to interpret human behaviour (see Bogdan, 1997) requires the intentional stance: "treating the object whose behaviour you want to predict as a rational agent with beliefs and desires" (Dennett, 1987 p. 15). We label the capacity to adopt this stance the interpersonal interpretive function (IIF), an evolutionary-developmental function of attachment. Unlike Bowlby's internal working model concept, its function is not to encode representations of attachment experiences, nor is it a repository of personal encounters as in Stern's (1998) concept of schemata-of-ways-of-being-with. Rather, the IIF is a cluster of mental functions for processing and interpreting new interpersonal experiences that includes mentaliza-tion and the cluster of psychological processes on which effective mentalizing depends (Fonagy, 2003).

The emphasis on interpretation is helpful because we are par-ticularly concerned with the possibility of misinterpretations and misperceptions of others' thoughts, feelings, and intentions. Inter-pretive function also underscores the perspective-taking facet of mentalization that equips us to recognize how individuals can come to different conclusions with the same set of facts at their disposal (Carpendale & Chandler, 1996). We suggested, following Baron-Cohen's (2003) distinction between theory of mind and empa-thy, that a cognition-oriented interpersonal interpretive function (IIF-C) is complemented by an emotion or affect oriented set of processes (IIF-A). Earlier, Henry Wellman proposed a related devel-opmental transition from a desire psychology of toddlers to a belief–desire psychology of 3–4-year-olds (Bartsch & Wellman, 1995). We also include in IIF-A the notion of mentalized affectivity which refers to the simultaneous experiencing and knowing of a feeling.

Three Neural Systems of Social Cognition

Four emotional processing and control mechanisms contribute to the developmental unfolding of interpretative function: labelling and understanding affect, arousal regulation, effortful control, and specific mentalizing capacities (Fonagy & Target, 2002). We propose that these interpretive functions are subserved by three separate but interconnected and interacting nodes within the brain that are related to social detection, affect regulation, and cognitive regulation (Adolphs, 2003; Nelson, Leibenluft, McClure, & Pine, 2005).

The first node consists of a hard-wired set of structures that catego-rizes stimuli as social and deciphers or detects their social purpose. The brain regions that make up this social-detection node include the fusiform face area, the superior temporal sulcus, and the anterior temporal cortex. These regions have been shown to be involved in carrying out basic perceptual processes on social stimuli.

The second node is concerned with affect and encompasses regions of the brain engaged by reward and punishment. The gen-eration of affect imbues social stimuli with emotional significance and modulates emotional arousal. The system has a significant role in mediating attachment experience and is activated by attachment-related stimuli. Brain regions that make up the affect-regulation node include the amygdala, hypothalamus, nucleus accumbens, and bed nucleus of the stria terminalis. These regions interact with the social-detection node to imbue social stimuli with emotional significance.

Our primary concern, the third node, is devoted to cognitive regulation. Its key functions include inhibiting prepotent responses (effortful control), mediating goal-directed behavior, and mentalizing (as exemplified in perspective taking and theory-of-mind tasks). The brain regions that make up the cognitive-regulation node include the dorsomedial prefrontal cortex and the ventral prefrontal cortex. There are several systems within these structures that mediate different aspects of regulation and control, including integrating emotion with cognitive processing and making accurate social judgements. Each of these aspects of social intelligence subserves different aspects of interpersonal interpretation.

The foundations of mentalization are present in nonhuman species. Recent work on the mirror neuron system (Gallese, Keuseers, & Rizzolatti, 2004; Rizzolatti & Craighero, 2004) claims that understanding others' actions requires the activation of the mirror neuron system, and understanding others' emotions requires the activation of viscero-motor centres. Motor neurons, originally found in the ventral premotor cortex of the macaque monkey, respond both when the monkey performs a particular goal directed act and when it observes another individual performing a similar action (Gallese, Fadiga, Fogassi, & Rizzolatti, 1996). Action observation automatically activates the same neural mechanism triggered by action execution or even by the sound produced by the same action (Kohler et al., 2002). The mirror neuron system also encompasses communicative actions, both in monkeys (Ferrari, Gallese, Rizzolatti, & Fogazzi, 2003) and in humans (Rizzolatti & Craighero, 2004). In a recent fMRI study, participants observed communicative mouth actions in humans, monkeys, and dogs which led to the activation of different cortical foci corresponding to the different observed species; actions in the motor repertoire of the observer (e.g., biting and speech reading) were mapped accordingly on the observer's motor system (Buccino et al., 2004).

Extrapolating from mirror neuron research, we might conceive of a two-level system underpinning mentalization: a frontal-cortical system that invokes declarative representations and a mirror-neuron system subserving a more immediate and direct understanding of the other. In the anterior insula, visual information concerning the emotions of others is directly mapped onto the same viscero-motor neural structures that determine the experience of that emotion in the observer (Wicker et al., 2003). This direct mapping can occur even when the emotion of others is merely imagined (Singer et al., 2004). Gallese and Goldman hypothesize a shared subpersonal neural mapping between what is enacted and what is perceived that can be used to predict the actions of others (Gallese, 2003; Goldman & Sripada, 2005). This automatically established link between agent and observer may not be the only way in which the emotions of others can be understood, but the simulation of actions by means of the activation of parietal and premotor cortical networks may constitute a basic level of experiential understanding that does not entail the explicit use of any theory or declarative representation.

Mentalization also involves the capacity to represent affects in others (perhaps the limbic circuits including the amygdala), to inhibit the prepotent response of assuming that others think exactly the same as we do (the anterior cingulate) and representing and reasoning about beliefs and also desires in others (the orbitofrontal and prefrontal areas of the cortex). We should remember that mentalizing pertains to interpreting mental states in both self and others. Representing the contents of one's own mind taps into the same meta-representational capacity required for representing the contents of another's mind (Frith & Frith, 2003). Self-awareness and awareness of the mental states of others are closely linked in terms of the brain areas involved. Mentalization does not just facilitate collaboration and positive relationships but also facilitates social survival through competition. Self-awareness enables us to modify the way we present ourselves to others and to mislead them. The right prefrontal cortex may "allow us to see ourselves as others see us so that we may cause competitive others to see us as we wish them to" (Alexander, 1990, p. 7).

The Evolutionary Psychology of Mentalization

Because the mind needs to adapt to ever more challenging competitive conditions, the capacity for mentalization cannot be fixed by genetics or constitution. The social brain must continuously reach higher and higher levels of sophistication to stay on top. Evolution has charged attachment relationships with ensuring the full development of the social brain. The capacity for mentalization, along with many other social-cognitive capacities, evolves out of the experience of social interaction with caregivers. Increased sophistication in social cognition evolved hand in hand with apparently unrelated aspects of development, such as increased helplessness in infancy, a prolongation of childhood, and the emergence of intensive parenting.

We have proposed a mechanism for this process rooted in dialectic models of self-development (Cavell, 1991; Davidson, 1983). Our approach explicitly rejects the classical Cartesian assumption that mental states are apprehended by introspection; on the contrary, mental states are discovered through contingent mirroring interactions with the caregiver (Gergely & Watson, 1999). Psychoanalysts have long assumed that the child's capacity to represent mental states symbolically is acquired within the primary object relationship. Therefore early disruption of affectional bonds will not only set up maladaptive attachment patterns (e.g., Waters, Merrick, Treboux, Crowell, & Albersheim, 2000) but will also undermine a range of capacities vital to normal social development. Understanding minds is difficult if one does not know what it is like to be understood as a person with a mind.

Our argument may seem to place an excessive burden upon the caregiver-infant relationship, but we must remember that placing the social development of a human infant in the hands of one adult is a recent phenomenon compared to the previous average of four relatives who had a genetic stake in the child's survival (Hrdy, 2000). Recent neurobiological evidence discussed next buttresses the ecological view of attachment relationships as pivotally linked to mentalizing capacities.

The Neurobiology of Attachment

The neurobiology of attachment is now fairly well understood. It is linked to the mesocorticolimbic dopaminergic reward circuit, which also plays a key role in mediating the process of physical (as well as emotional) addiction. It is highly unlikely that nature created a brain system specifically to subserve cocaine and alcohol abuse. It is more likely that addictions are the accidental by-product of the activation of a biological system underpinning the crucial evolutionary function of attachment (Insel, 1997; MacLean, 1990; Panksepp, 1998). Attachment can be thought of as an "addictive disorder" (Insel, 2003). Changes in attachment behavior, such as falling in love, which are stimulated by social/sexual activity, entail the activation of an oxytocin and vasopressin sensitive circuit within the anterior hypothalamus (MPOA) linked to the VTA and the nucleus accumbens (Insel, 2003). fMRI studies indicate specific activation of the same pathways in the brain of somebody seeing their own baby or partner, compared to another familiar baby or other people's partners (Nitschke et al., 2004).

In two separate imaging studies, Bartels and Zeki (2000, 2004), reported that the activation of areas mediating maternal and/or romantic attachments appeared simultaneously to suppress brain activity in several brain regions in two systems, both responsible for different aspects of cognitive regulation and control, but also including those associated with making social judgements and mentalizing. Bartels and Zeki (2004) suggest grouping these reciprocally active areas into two functional regions. The first (let us refer to it as system A) includes the middle prefrontal, inferior parietal and middle temporal cortices mainly in the right hemisphere, as well as the posterior cingulate cortex. These areas are specialised for attention and long-term memory (Cabeza & Nyberg, 2000), and have variable involvement in both positive (Maddock, 1999) and negative (Mayberg et al., 1999) emotions. Their role in both cognition and emotion suggests that these areas may be specifically responsible for integrating emotion and cognition (e.g., emotional encoding of episodic memories). Further, these areas may play a role in recalling emotion-related material and generating emotion-related imagery that may be relevant to understanding the typology of attachment (Maddock, 1999).

The second set of areas deactivated by the activation of the attachment system includes the temporal poles, parietotemporal junction, amygdala, and mesial prefrontal cortex (let us call this system B). Activation of these areas is consistently linked to negative affect, judgements of social trustworthiness, moral judgements, theory of mind tasks, attention to one's own emotions, and in particular, they constitute the primary neural network underlying our ability to identify mental states (both thoughts and feelings) in other people (Frith & Frith, 2003; Gallagher & Frith, 2003). Mentalization pertains not just to states of mind in others but also reflecting on one's own emotional and belief states and consequently such tasks appear to be associated with activation in the same neural system (Gusnard, Akbudak, Shulman, & Raichle, 2001). Making judgements that involve mental states has been shown to be associated with activation of the same system. Thus intuitive judgements of moral appropriateness (rather than moral reasoning) are linked (Greene & Haidt, 2002) as is assessment of social trustworthiness based on facial expressions (Winston et al., 2002).

This suggests that being in an emotionally attached state inhibits or suppresses aspects of social cognition, including mentalizing and the capacity to accurately see the attachment figure as a person. (Currently we are working to perform an independent replication of this study.) If confirmed by further studies, the pattern of activation of these three systems (the attachment system, and the two overlapping cognitive information processing control systems) has important implications for our understanding of the nature of individual differences in attachment, the relationship of attachment and mentalization and consequently our understanding of dysfunctions associated with deficits in mentalization. The activation of the attachment system, mediated by dopaminergic structures of the reward system in the presence of oxytocin and vasopressin inhibits neural systems that underpin the generation of negative affect. This is to be expected because a key function of the attachment system is to moderate negative emotions in the infant and presumably to continue to do so in later development (Sroufe, 1996). The overwhelming negative affect associated with the loss of attachment figures (perhaps triggering a dramatic deactivation of the attachment system), the need for attachment figures at times of sadness (to activate the attachment system and reduce ahedonia), and the hedonic effect of finding love are obvious common observations in line with these findings. Equally consistent with expectations, is the suppression of social and moral judgements (probably mediated by the second of the two regulatory systems) associated with the activation of the attachment system. Judgements of social trustworthiness and morality serve to distance us from others but become less relevant and may indeed interfere with our relationships with those to whom we are strongly attached (Belsky, 1999a; Simpson, 1999).

The configuration described by Bartels and Zeki has critical developmental implications. Attachment has been selected by evolution as the principal training ground for the acquisition of mentalization because attachment is a marker for shared genetic material, reciprocal relationships and altruism. It is a noncompetitive relationship in which the aim is not to outsmart and thus learning about minds can be safely practiced. Missing out on early attachment experience (as for the Romanian orphans) creates a long term vulnerability from which the child may never recover—the capacity for mentalization is never fully established, leaving the child vulnerable to later trauma and unable to cope fully with attachment relationships (e.g., Rutter & O'Connor, 2004). More importantly, trauma, by activating attachment,will often decouple the capacity for mentalization. This of course is further exacerbated when the trauma is attachment trauma.

Implications of Attachment-Mentalization Reciprocity

The apparently reciprocal relationship of mentalization and attachment may at first appear to contradict our earlier assumption that mentalization and secure attachment are positively correlated. Further scrutiny suggests greater complexity but no inconsistency. The neural association between attachment and mentalization confirms the link we have identified between the two systems at a behavioural level. We have demonstrated how the parent's capacity to mentalize in the context of an attachment relationship facilitates the development of secure attachment in the infant (Fonagy, Steele, Moran, Steele, & Higgitt, 1991). It is possible, taking an evolutionary perspective, that the parent's capacity to mentalize the infant or child serves to reduce the child's experienced need to monitor the parent for trustworthiness. This relaxation of the interpersonal barrier facilitates the emergence of a strong attachment bond. We have seen that theory of mind emerges precociously in children who were securely attached in infancy (e.g., Meins, 1997). While at first sight this finding may seem inconsistent with the inverse relationship between attachment and mentalization, it is to be expected that in individuals whose attachment is secure, there are likely to be fewer calls over time for the activation of the attachment system. This in turn, given the inhibitory effect of the activation of the attachment system on mentalization related brain activity, might account for the precocious development of mentalization.

The capacity for mentalization in the context of attachment is likely to be in certain respects independent of the capacity to mentalize about interpersonal experiences outside the attachment context (Fonagy & Target, 1997). Our specific measure of mentalization in the attachment context, reflective function (Fonagy, Target, Steele, & Steele, 1998) is predictive of behavioral outcomes that other measures of mentalization do not correlate with. For example, in a quasi-longitudinal study based on interviews and chart reviews with young adults some of whom had suffered trauma, we found that the impact of trauma on mentalization in attachment contexts mediated outcome measured as the quality of adult romantic relationships but mentalization measured independently of the attachment context using the Reading the Mind in the Eyes test did not (Fonagy, Stein, Allen, & Fultz, 2003a). It seems that measuring mentalization in the context of attachment might measure a unique aspect of social behavior.

If we grant some or all of these considerations then the positive association between secure attachment and mentalization would still be predicted. The key consideration is probably that securely attached children do not need to activate their attachment system as often and have greater opportunity to practice mentalization in the context of the child-caregiver relationship. Belsky's (1999b) evolutionary model of attachment classification is helpful here. When resources are scarce and insecure attachment strategies are possibly most adaptive, children probably need to monitor the unpredictable caregivers' mental states quite carefully, are forced to find alternative social contexts to acquire social cognitive capacities, and thus they deprive themselves of some developmental learning opportunities of understanding minds in abstract ways independent of physical reality.

The model as described at this point may appear to present two alternative views about the relationship of the attachment system to mentalization. On the one hand we strongly believe that secure attachment enhances the capacity to envision mental states in self and other and there is considerable empirical evidence to support this contention. On the other hand crucial to the current model is the notion that at least at the level of brain function but also behaviorally attachment inhibits the capacity to mentalize. Partly this paradox is rooted in our understanding of the nature of the attachment system. It was John Bowlby's contention that attachment was a distinct behavioral system protected by evolution to regulate parent-child and romantic relationships. Thus for example, as we have seen, seeing pictures of one's partner activated a particular set of pathways associated with reward but also implicated in maintaining addiction behaviour. The activation of these pathways has been shown to inhibit specific areas of the brain related to mentalizing as well as long-term memory, social judgements, and other higher order cognitive functions.

These pathways, however, should not be conflated with attachment as a behavioral system. Attachment as a behavioral system is activated in infants by anxiety. It brings with it an urgent need for physical and later psychological proximity and generates a sense of wellbeing that counteracts a prior state of tension. The central place of this process in infant development ensures that affect regulation in general and also the organization of interpersonal relationships at least of a relatively intimate kind are powerfully influenced by the quality of parental responding to infant anxiety. We do not yet know how such individual differences serve to define characteristic patterns of activation of the brain structures mediating attachment (the mesocorticolimbic dopaminergic reward system). We speculate that secure attachment defined as a relative sense of certainty about the availability of the attachment figure will imply that anxiety is not as generally pervasive and the instances that require the activation of the attachment system are perhaps fewer in number. This might explain why a secure attachment relationship is associated with a precocious acquisition of mentalization in securely attached individuals.

More generally, however, the attachment relationship serves as the context within which mentalization can be acquired because in this context the child can relatively safely explore the mind of the other feeling relatively certain that the latter will harbor few if any hostile intentions toward the self. Attachment trauma is pernicious because while trauma generates anxiety and thus activates the attachment system and inhibits the child's capacity to acquire mentalization skills, the biological drive is toward proximity-seeking and increased closeness with the caregiver, but not in a context either psychologically or in terms of brain activation that might permit the free exploration of minds.

In summary, secure attachment and attachment trauma are at two extremes of the relationship of mentalization and attachment. In secure attachment the development of mentalization is facilitated by the attachment system being activated relatively less and the safe exploration of the mind of the caregiver. The robust establishment of a capacity to mentalize means that the individual is more likely to be able to retain a mentalizing capacity even when the attachment system is activated by powerful relational concerns. By contrast, in individuals with insecure attachment histories, mentalization is less firmly established. In those with attachment trauma it will be undermined by the chronic activation of the attachment system, by high levels of arousal and a fear of minds all adding up to what may become a terror of exploring the mental world. In extreme cases, clinical as well as research evidence suggests that a vicious cycle is generated by proximity seeking exposing the child to further threats, generating an increased sense of abandonment that in turn drives further proximity seeking. Such cases may be thought of as hyperactivating the attachment system, generating a dramatic inhibition of the capacity of that system to serve as the context for the acquisition of mentalizing function.

Mentalization and Attachment Classification

From an evolutionary perspective, mentalization may be less relevant in the attachment context than in competitive social contexts; nevertheless mentalizing accurately in attachment relationships is also highly desirable. Individuals who are able to mentalize while thinking about romantic partners or offspring will manage these relationships better; they may have less turbulent attachment relationships; and they may be particularly effective in resolving inevitable conflicts and arguments. Hence secure attachment is marked by a relatively good capacity to generate coherent narratives of turbulent interpersonal episodes (Main, 2000). From a neurobiological perspective, we would predict that individuals who are able to retain a relatively high activation of the parieto-temporal junction together with the mesial prefrontal cortex in the presence of the activation of the reward-sensitive dopaminergic mesolimbic pathways are most likely to be classified as secure in their attachment.

The two principal insecure attachment strategies may also be interpretable in terms of the relative state of activation of attachment-related brain systems. Insecure-dismissing individuals, because of their adverse past attachment experiences, become particularly effective in inhibiting both reciprocal systems outlined above. This deactivation would reduce the availability of long-term memories imbued with either positive or negative emotion, resulting in the typical narrative pattern of inability to recall attachment experiences in interviews aimed at activating the attachment system (George, Kaplan, & Main, 1996). By contrast, in insecure-preoccupied individuals, the attachment system may be less effective in suppressing the activity of the two reciprocal systems, resulting in greater negativity in attachment narratives and unusually good access to past attachment experience, giving the impression of current preoccupation with past events (Main, 2000). In sum, insecurity may entail either too little or too much deactivation of emotional memory, negative affect, moral and social judgments, and mentalizing.

The Development of an Agentive Self: The Social Acquisition of Social Cognition

An Overview of the Model of Contingent Mirroring

The evolutionary neurobiological speculations mentioned earlier imply that children's caregiving environments play a key role in the development of their social cognitive capacities. How are we to conceive of the actions of these environmental influences? Our model relies on the child's inbuilt capacity to detect aspects of the world that react contingently to its own actions. In his first months the child begins to understand that he is a physical agent whose actions can bring about changes in bodies with which he has immediate physical contact (Leslie, 1994). Developing alongside this is the child's understanding of himself as a social agent. Through interactions with the caregiver (from birth) the baby learns that his behavior affects his caregiver's behavior and emotions, that is, that he is a social agent whose communicative displays can produce effects at a distance in the social environment (Neisser, 1988). Both these early forms of self-awareness probably evolve through the workings of an innate contingency detection mechanism that enables the infant to analyze the probability of causal links between his actions and stimulus events (Watson, 1994). The child's initial preoccupation with perfectly response-contingent stimulation (provided by the proprioceptive sensory feedback that the self's actions always generate) allows him to differentiate his agentive self as a separate entity in the environment and to construct a primary representation of the bodily self.

At about 3–4 months, infants switch from preferring perfect contingency to preferring high-but-imperfect contingencies thereafter (Bahrick & Watson, 1985)—the level of contingency that is characteristic of an attuned caregiver's empathic mirroring responses to the infant's displays of emotion. Repeated experience of such affect-reflective caregiver reactions is essential for the infant to begin to be able to differentiate his/her internal self-states: a process we termed *social biofeedback* (Gergely & Watson, 1996). It is through providing such a state-reflective scaffolding environment that a congenial and secure attachment relationship can vitally contribute to the emergence of early mentalization capacities, allowing the infant to discover or find his/her psychological self in the social world (Gergely, 2001). The discovery of the representational or psychological self (what we may think of as full mentalization) is probably based in the same mechanism.

Coming to Understand and Regulate Emotion and Be Securely Attached

Let us take the development of an understanding of affects as an example. We assume that at first infants are not introspectively aware of different emotional states. Rather, their representations of these emotions are primarily based on stimuli received from the external world. Babies learn to differentiate the internal patterns of physiological and visceral stimulation that accompany different emotions by observing their caregivers' facial or vocal mirroring responses to these (e.g., Legerstee & Varghese, 2001; Mitchell, 1993). First, the baby comes to associate his control over the parents' mirroring displays with the resulting improvement in his emotional state, leading, eventually, to an experience of the self as a regulating agent. Second, the establishment of a second order representation of affect states creates the basis for affect regulation and impulse control: affects can be manipulated and discharged internally as well as through action, they can also be experienced as something recognizable and hence shared. If the parent's affect expressions are not contingent on the infant's affect, this will undermine the appropriate labeling of internal states which may, in turn, remain confusing, experienced as unsymbolized and hard to regulate.

If the capacity to understand and regulate emotion is to develop, two conditions need to be met: (a) reasonable congruency of mirroring whereby the caregiver accurately matches the infant's mental state and (b) *markedness* of the mirroring, whereby the caregiver is able to express an affect while indicating that she is not expressing her own feelings (Gergely & Watson, 1999). Consequently two difficulties may arise: (a) in the case of incongruent mirroring the infant's representation of his internal state will not correspond to a constitutional self state (nothing real) and a predisposition to a narcissistic structure might be established perhaps analogous to Winnicott's notion of false-self (Winnicott, 1965) and (b) in cases of unmarked mirroring the caregiver's expression may be seen as externalisation of the infant's experience and a predisposition to experiencing emotion through other people (as in a borderline personality structure) might be established (Fonagy, Gergely, Jurist, & Target, 2002). An expression congruent with the baby's state, but lacking markedness, may overwhelm the infant. It is felt to be the parent's own real emotion, making the child's experience seem contagious and escalating rather than regulating his state.

The secure caregiver soothes by combining mirroring with a display that is incompatible with the child's feelings (thus implying contact with distance and coping). This formulation of sensitivity has much in common with Bion's (1962) notion of the role of the mother's capacity to mentally contain the affect state that feels intolerable to the baby, and respond in a manner that acknowledges the child's mental state, yet serves to modulate unmanageable feelings (see following). Well-regulated affect in the infant parent couple is thought to be internalized by the child to form the bases of a secure attachment bond and internal working model (Sroufe, 1996). Ratings of the quality of reflective function of each parent during pregnancy were found independently to predict the child's later security of attachment in the London Parent-Child Project (Fonagy, Steele, Moran, Steele, & Higgitt, 1992). However, this finding is somewhat limited because only the AAI RF measure was examined in relation to infant attachment (Fonagy, Steele, Moran, Steele, & Higgitt 1991; Fonagy, Steele, Steele, Higgitt, & Target, 1994). Thus the parents' capacity to mentalize was measured in relation to their own childhood and their capacity to do likewise with their child had been assumed rather than observed.

Evidence Linking Parental Mentalization to the Development of Well-Regulated Affect (Secure Attachment)

Three programs of work, by Elizabeth Meins (Meins, Ferryhough, Fradley, & Tuckey, 2001), David Oppenheim (Koren-Karie, Oppenheim, Dolev, Sher, & Etzion-Carasso, 2002; Oppenheim & Koren-Karie, 2002) and Arietta Slade and their respective groups (Grienenberger, Kelly, & Slade, 2005; Schechter et al., 2005; Slade, 2005; Slade, Grienenberger, bernbach, Levy, & Locker, 2005) took this forward, all looking at aspects of interactional narratives between parents and children. In the Meins study mentalization was assessed on the basis of the mothers' verbalization to a 6 month old infant. One measure of maternal mind-mindedness (MMM) repeatedly used in Meins's studies was developed based on the question "Can you describe [child] for me?" with the codified categories of mental, behavioral, physical, general (Meins & Fernyhough, 1999; Meins, Fernyhough, Russel, & Clark-Carter, 1998): This is an off-line measure of mentalizing, but Meins and colleagues have also developed a more on-line measure of MMM based on 20 minutes of free play between mothers and their 6-month-old babies, which are coded for appropriate mind-related comments, amongst other parameters. Mind-related comments were shown to be predictive of attachment security at 6 months (Meins, Ferryhough, Fradley, & Tuckey, 2001), mentalizing capacity at 45 and 48 months (Meins et al., 2002) and Stream of Consciousness performance at 55 months (Meins et al., 2003). In the Oppenheim studies, the mothers provided commentaries on their own previously recorded playful interaction with their child. Both studies found that high levels of mentalization of the child in the mothers' narratives were associated with secure infant-mother attachment. Although both studies demonstrated that mentalization of the child in the context of the mother-child relationship, rather than global measures of sensitivity, was likely to predict the security of the attachment relationship, the studies assessed the quality of mentalization rather differently. The measure used in the Meins study aimed to assess the quality of the parents' thinking about the child in real time in the course of an interaction. The measure used in the

Oppenheim studies was focused on a more reflective, off-line mentalizing capacity. Both measures were however episodic, giving an indication of the parent's quality of mentalization of a particular moment of interaction. Neither was designed to measure the extent that mothers generally mentalize their relationship with their child (or rather their idea of their relationship with their idea of their child).

The Slade, Grienenberger, Bernbach, Levey, and Locker (2005) study extends previous observations by using an AAI-like autobiographical memory focused measure, the Parent Development Interview (PDI), rather than an episode of observed interaction as an index of mentalizing capacity. Strong relationships were found between attachment in the infant and the quality of mentalizing in the parent about the child. A measure such as the PDI estimates mentalization as an aggregate across many episodes of interaction and what might be assumed to be a prototype is drawn from the mother's autobiographical memory (Conway, 1996). In a structural model of autobiographical memory Conway (1992) proposed that two types of autobiographical memories exist within a hierarchical autobiographical memory system: unique, specific events and repeated, general memories. The PDI gives access to these latter types of general autobiographical memories that are assumed to have a preferred level of entry to the autobiographical memory system (Conway & Holmes, 2004).

As commentary on the events remembered is part of the content scrutinized for level of mentalization, the PDI measure probably also incorporates an indication of the mother's off-line reflective mentalizing capacity picking up the mother's predominant stance toward the child as more or less an intentional being, perhaps reflecting many hundreds of interactions and thus providing greater accuracy of prediction. In this way it is able to index more than simple mind-mindedness (Meins, Ferryhough, Fradley, & Tuckey, 2001), measured as the complexity of mental state terms and concepts used. High scorers on the PDI-RF scale are aware of the characteristics of mental functioning in their infants and grasp the complex interplay between their own mental states and the child's inner experience.

The Slade, Grienenberger, Bernbach, Levy, & Locker (2005) study includes 10 infants with disorganized attachment classification, whose mothers' RF scores are a standard deviation below those who are secure. What do low RF parents do that might disorganize the infant's attachment classification? Grienenberger, Kelly, and Slade

(2005) rated the Strange Situations collected as part of the study on Karlen Lyons-Ruth and colleagues' AMBIANCE (Atypical Maternal Behavior Instrument for Assessment and Classification, Bronfman, Parsons, & Lyons-Ruth 1999) coding system. AMBIANCE is particularly sensitive to atypical behaviors associated with the disorganization of infant-mother attachment. Parents of disorganized infants were almost a standard deviation higher on this measure than parents of secure ones. There is a substantial correlation between AMBIANCE codings and RF—again, an effect size greater than one. The size of the effect is somewhat surprising given the disparity of the domains of measurement; the AMBIANCE is a behavioral measure based on a single interaction and RF is coded from a narrative. There appears to be a strong relationship between the observed frequency of behaviors such as demanding a show of affection from the infant, fearful behavior or intrusive or negative behaviors such as mocking or criticizing and narratives that, for example, show little appreciation that the infant's mind cannot be directly read, or depict her as having no feelings, thoughts or wishes. This suggests that the same control mechanism may be responsible for the inhibitory regulation of certain aspects of the mother's behavior with the infant, and her organization of narratives about her. It is conceivable that the correlation is accounted for by the common neural basis that might underpin both tasks. The mentalizing system might provide input for the organisation of both social interaction and person-centered autobiographical narrative.

This suggests that possibly Slade and her colleagues have closed the transmission gap identified a decade ago by Marinus van Ijzendoorn (1995). A somewhat simplistic restatement of our current knowledge might go like this. Secure attachment history of the mother permits and enhances her capacity to explore her own mind and liberates and promotes a similar enquiring stance toward the mental state of the new human being who has just joined her social world. This stance of open, respectful enquiry makes use of her awareness of her own mental state to understand her infant, but not to a point where her understanding would obscure a genuine awareness of her child as an independent being. The awareness of the infant in turn reduces the frequency of behaviors that would undermine the infant's natural progression toward evolving its own sense of mental self through the dialectic of her interactions with the mother. In this context, then, disorganization of attachment is implicitly seen by Arietta Slade and her group as the consequence of an undermining of a mental self, or the disorganization of the self.

Affect regulation, the capacity to modulate emotional states, is closely related to mentalization, which plays a fundamental role in the unfolding of a sense of self and agency. In this account, affect regulation is a prelude to mentalization; yet, once mentalization occurs, the nature of affect regulation is transformed: not only does it allow adjustment of affect states, but more fundamentally it is also used to regulate the self. This is an instance of the general principle that the child's capacity to create a coherent image of mind depends on an experience of being perceived as a mind by the attachment figure. Social understanding is an emergent property of the child's experience of referential interactions with the caregiver about an object, which will inevitably generate the discovery that others have differing beliefs about the world from one's own.

Jurist's concept of "mentalized affectivity" (Fonagy, Gergely, Jurist, & Target, 2002) marks a mature capacity for the regulation of affect, and denotes the capacity to discover the subjective meanings of one's own feelings. Mentalized affectivity, we suggest, lies at the core of many psychosocial treatments. It represents the experiential understanding of one's feelings in a way that extends well beyond intellectual understanding. It is in this realm that we encounter resistances and defenses, not just against specific emotional experiences, but against entire modes of psychological functioning; not just distortions of mental representations standing in the way of therapeutic progress but also inhibitions of mental capacities or processes (Fonagy, Edgecumbe, Moran, Kennedy, & Target, 1993). Thus we can misunderstand what we feel, thinking that we feel one thing while truly feeling something else. More seriously, we can deprive ourselves of the entire experiential world of emotional richness. For example, the inability to imagine psychological and psychosocial causation may be the result of the pervasive inhibition and/or developmental malformation of the psychological processes that underpin these capacities.

Establishing Attentional Control

The capacity for attentional control, the ability to inhibit a dominant response to perform a subdominant response, is termed *effortful control by attention* by Posner and Rothbart (2000). Early attachment, which allows the child to internalize the mother's ability to divert the child's attention from something immediate to something else (Fonagy, 2001), serves to equip children with this capacity. Longitudinal studies of self-regulation demonstrate that the capacity for effortful control is strongly related to a child's observed willingness to comply with maternal wishes (committed compliance), that is, the degree to which they apparently willingly embrace the maternal agenda (Kochanska, Coy, & Murray, 2001). Withholding an impulsive response is a prerequisite for mentalizing, as this requires the foregrounding of a distal second-order nonvisible stimulus (mental state) in preference to what immediately impinges on the child (physical reality). The successful performance of theory of mind tasks, for example, must involve the inhibition of the child's prepotent responses to directly perceived aspects of current reality in favor of generating a response on the basis of less salient representations of reality attributed to other minds. Alan Leslie, one of the pioneers in the field, has come to consider theory of mind "as a mechanism of selective attention. Mental state concepts simply allow the brain to attend selectively to corresponding mental state properties of agents and thus permit learning about these properties" (Leslie, 2000, p. 1245).

Attentional control is also linked to attachment. The major function of attachment is the control of distress and attentional processes must play a key role if the attachment system is to achieve this objective (Harman, Rothbart, & Posner, 1997). Michael Posner, amongst others, suggests that the interaction between infant and caregiver is likely to train the infant to control his distress through orienting the infant away from the source of distress by soothing and involving him in distracting activities. Self-regulation is taught (or more accurately, modelled) by the caregiver's regulatory activity. It has been suggested that joint-attention with caregiver serves a self-organizing function in early development (Mundy & Neal, 2001). Indeed we have long known that intelligence remains related to early attachment security (e.g., Cicchetti, Rogosch, & Toth, 2000; e.g., Jacobsen & Hofmann, 1997). More recently, Jay Belsky and Pasco Fearon have drawn our attention to early attachment relationships as a possible organizer of attentional systems (Belsky & Fearon, 2002; Fearon & Belsky, 2004). In a study of almost 1,000 children a positive relationship was found between attachment and attentional performance using a Continuous Performance Test (CPT) to measure attentional capacity at 54 months. Findings indicated that children with secure attachment appeared to be protected from the effects of cumulative social contextual risk (and male gender) on CPT attentional performance relative to their insecure counterparts. A further study of infants who were disorganized in their attachment found that these infants also had difficulties with social attention coordination in interactions with their caregiver (Schölmerich, Lamb, Leyendecker, & Fracasso, 1997). Cocaine-exposed children with disorganized attachment at 12 months showed the greatest dysfunctions of social attention coordination not only with the caregiver but also with an experimenter (e.g., they initiated joint attention less often) (Claussen, Mundy, Mallik, & Willoughby, 2002). Evidence from late-adopted Romanian orphans with profound disorganizations of attachment suggests that quite severe attention problems are more common in this group than would be expected both in relation to other forms of disturbance and epidemiological considerations (e.g., Chugani et al., 2001).

From the point of view of our model of the development of mentalization we argue that an enfeebled attentional control system is a likely consequence of attachment disorganization, perhaps linked with enfeebled affect representation, and serves to undermine the development of mentalization as well as its appropriate functioning in later development. The prepotent response is to attribute one's own mental state to the other. Attentional control is essential if the child is to arrive at a differentiation of their own and others' thoughts, feelings, beliefs, and desires. The disruption of attentional control is likely to account for many instances where we encounter temporary and selective disruptions of mentalization. It is probable that trauma further undermines attention regulation and is associated with chronic failures of inhibitory control (Allen, 2001).

The Stages of Acquiring Mentalization (a Theory of Mind)

The emergence of mentalizing function follows a well-researched developmental line that identifies *fixation points*:

(a) During the second half of the first year of life, the child begins to construct causal relations that connect actions to their agents on the one hand and to the world on the other. From about 6 months infants recognize that animate objects are self-propelled (Spelke, Philips, & Woodward, 1995) and can distinguish between biological and mechanical movement (Woodward, 1998). Joint attention (Tomasello, 1999b) and social referencing (Moses, Baldwin, Rosicky, & Tidball 2001) emerge at this time. Also around this time, infants begin to differentiate actions from their outcomes and to think about actions as means to an end (Tomasello, 1999a). Infants around 9 months begin to look at actions in terms of the actor's underlying intentions (Baldwin, Baird, Saylor, & Clark, 2001). This is the beginning of their understanding of themselves as teleological agents who can choose the most efficient way to bring about a goal from a range of alternatives (Csibra & Gergely, 1998). At this stage agency is understood in terms of purely physical actions and constraints. Infants expect actors to behave rationally, given physically apparent goal states and the physical constraints of the situation that are already understood by the infant (Gergely & Csibra, 2003). There is no implication here that the infant has an idea about the mental state of the object. He/she is simply judging rational behavior in terms of the physical constraints that prevail and that which is obvious in terms of the physical end state which the object has reached. We have suggested a connection between the focus on understanding actions in terms of their physical as opposed to mental outcomes (a teleological stance) and the mode of experience of agency that we often see in the self-destructive acts of individuals with borderline personality disorder (BPD) (Fonagy, Target, & Gergely 2000). Thus slight changes in the physical world can trigger elaborate conclusions concerning states of mind. Patients frequently cannot accept anything other than a modification in the realm of the physical as a true index of the intentions of the other.

(b) During the second year, children develop a mentalistic understanding of agency. They understand that they and others are intentional agents whose actions are caused by prior states of mind such as desires (Wellman & Phillips, 2000) and that their actions can bring about changes in minds as well as bodies (e.g., by pointing Corkum & Moore, 1995). Shared imaginative play is enjoyable and exciting for toddlers and may be the basis for the development of collaborative, cooperative skills (Brown, Donelan-McCall, & Dunn, 1996). Fifteen-month old children can distinguish between an action's intended goal and its accidental consequences (Meltzoff, 1995). At this stage the capacity for emotion regulation comes to reflect the prior and current relationship with the primary caregiver (Calkins & Johnson, 1998). Most importantly, children begin to acquire an internal state language and the ability to reason non-egocentrically about feelings and desires in others (Repacholi & Gopnik, 1997). Paradoxically, this becomes evident not only through the increase in joint goal directed activity but also through teasing and provocation of younger siblings (Dunn, 1988). However, functional awareness of minds does not yet enable the child to represent mental states independent of physical reality and therefore the distinction between internal and external, appearance and reality is not yet fully achieved (Flavell & Miller, 1998), making internal reality sometimes far more compelling and at other times inconsequential relative to an awareness of the physical world. We have referred to these states as psychic equivalence and pretend modes respectively (see the following).

(c) Around three to four years of age, understanding of agency in terms of mental causation begins to include the representation of epistemic mind states (beliefs). The young child thus understands himself as a representational agent, he knows that people do not always feel what they appear to feel, they show emotional reactions to an event that are influenced by their current mood or even by earlier emotional experiences which were linked to similar events (Flavell & Miller, 1998). The preschool child's mental states are representational in nature (Wellman, 1990). This transforms their social interactions so their understanding of emotions comes to be associated with empathic behavior (Zahn-Waxler, Radke-Yarrow, Wagner, & Chapman, 1992) and more positive peer relations (Dunn & Cutting, 1999). Most children come to understand that human behavior can be influenced by transient mental states (such as thoughts and feelings) as well as by stable characteristics (such as personality or capability) and this creates the basis for a structure to underpin an emerging self-concept (Flavell, 1999). They also come to attribute mistaken beliefs to themselves and to others, which enriches their repertoire of social interaction with tricks, jokes and deception (Sodian & Frith, 1992; Sodian, Taylor, Harris, & Perner, 1992). A meta-analytic review of in excess of 500 tests showed that by and large children younger than three fail the false-belief task and as the child's age increases they are increasingly likely to pass (Wellman, Cross, & Watson, 2001), suggesting that mentalizing abilities take a quantum leap forward around age four. The early acquisition of false belief is associated with more elaborate capacity for pretend play (Taylor & Carlson, 1997), greater connectedness in conversation (Slomkowski & Dunn, 1996) and teacher rating of social competence (Lalonde & Chandler, 1995). Notably, also at this time the child shifts from a preference for playing with adults to playing with peers (Dunn, 1994). We understand this shift as bringing to a close the time when mentalization was acquired through the agency of an adult mind and opening a lifelong phase of seeking to enhance the capacity to understand self and others in mental state terms through linking with individuals who share one's interest and humor.

(d) In the sixth year, we see related advances such as the child's ability to relate memories of his intentional activities and experiences into a coherent causal-temporal organisation, leading to the establishment of the temporally extended self (Povinelli & Eddy, 1995). Full experience of agency in social interaction can emerge only when actions of the self and others can be understood as initiated and guided by assumptions concerning the emotions, desires, and beliefs of both. Further theory of mind skills that become part of the child's repertoire at this stage include second order theory of mind (the capacity to understand mistaken beliefs about beliefs), mixed emotions (e.g., understanding being in a conflict), the way expectations or biases might influence the interpretation of ambiguous events, and the capacity for subtle forms of social deceptions (e.g., white lies). As these skills are acquired the need for physical violence begins to decline (Tremblay, 2000; Tremblay, Japel, & Perusse, 1999) and relational aggression increases (Cote, Tremblay, Nagin, Zoccolillo, & Vitaro, 2002; Nagin & Tremblay, 2001).

Relationship Influences on the Acquisition of Mentalization

Our claim that attachment relationships are vital to the normal acquisition of mentalization challenges nativist assumptions. The nativistic position assumes that children's social environments can trigger but cannot determine the development of theory of mind (Baron-Cohen, 1995; Leslie, 1994). There is some evidence that the timetable of theory of mind development is fixed and universal (Avis & Harris, 1991). However, the bulk of the evidence is inconsistent with the assumption of a universal timetable. More recent studies find ample evidence for substantial cultural differences, not just in the rate of emergence of theory of mind skills but also the order of their emergence (Wellman, Cross, & Watson, 2001). Many findings suggest that the nature of family interactions, the quality of parental control (e.g., Vinden, 2001), parental discourse about emotions (e.g., Meins et al., 2002), the depth of parental discussion involving affect (Dunn, Brown, & Beardsall, 1991) and parents' beliefs about parenting (e.g., Ruffman, Perner, & Parkin, 1999) are all strongly associated with the child's acquisition of mentalization. The role of family members in this developmental achievement is further highlighted by the finding that the presence of older siblings in the family appears to improve the child's performance on a range of false-belief tasks (e.g., Ruffman, Perner, Naito, Parkin, & Clements, 1998). In sum, the ability to give meaning to psychological experiences evolves as a result of our discovery of the mind behind others' actions, which develops optimally in a relatively safe and secure social context.

Much is known about correlates and predictors of early ToM development that is consistent with the assumption that the attachment relationship plays an important role in the acquisition of mentalization. For example, family-wide talk about negative emotions, often precipitated by the child's own emotions, predicts later success on tests of emotion understanding (Dunn & Brown, 2001). The capacity to reflect on intense emotion is a marker of secure attachment (Sroufe, 1996). Similar considerations may explain the finding that the number of references to thoughts and beliefs and the relationship specificity of children's real-life accounts of negative emotions correlate with early ToM acquisition (false belief performance) (Hughes & Dunn, 2002). Similarly, parents whose disciplinary strategies focus on mental states (e.g., a victim's feelings, or the nonintentional nature of transgressions) have children who succeed in ToM tasks earlier (e.g., Charman, Ruffman, & Clements, 2002).

Relationship influences on the development of mentalization are probably limited and specific rather than broad and unqualified. Three key limitations to simplistic linking of mentalization and positive relationship quality should be kept in mind (Hughes & Leekham, 2004): (a) The acquisition of the capacity to mentalize may, for example, open the door to more malicious teasing (e.g., Dunn, 1988), increase the individual's sensitivity to relational aggression (Cutting & Dunn, 2002), or even mean that they take a lead in bullying others (Sutton, Smith, & Swettenham, 1999). The possession of the capacity to mentalize is neither a guarantee that it will be used to serve prosocial ends, nor a guarantee of protection from malign interpersonal influence. (b) Although, as we have seen, broadly, positive emotion promotes the emergence of mentalization (Dunn, 1999), negative emotion can be an equally powerful facilitator. For

example, children engage in deception that is indicative of mentalizing in emotionally charged conflict situations (Newton, Reddy,
& Bull, 2000). (c) The impact of relationships on the development
of mentalization is probably highly complex, involving numerous
aspects of relational influences (e.g., quality of language of mental
states, quality of emotional interaction, themes of discourse, amount
of shared pretend play, negotiations of conflict, humor in the family, discourse with peers, etc.) probably affecting several components
of the mentalizing function (joint attention, understanding of affect
states, capacity for emotion regulation, language competence, competence with specific grammatical structures such as sentential com-
plements, etc.) (Hughes & Leekham, 2004).

Understanding the Relationship Influences on Mentalization

Intersubjectivity Beyond Infancy

The basic assumption of modern developmental theory is of a primary
intersubjectivity—that knowledge about the world is shared knowledge. To paraphrase this, the evolutionary underpinnings of human
culture require that the infant turns to others for essential information about the world (Gergely & Csibra, 2005). The idea of a shared
consciousness in infancy is not new. A number of developmentalists have emphasized the key functions of such sharing (e.g., Hobson, 2002; Rochat & Striano, 1999). The sharing of minds established
at this early stage is considered by many philosophers of mind (e.g.,
Cavell, 1994) and relational psychoanalysts (e.g., Mitchell, 2000) to
be a stable characteristic of mental function. We have argued that the
evidence for relational influences on mentalization is best explained
by the assumption that the acquisition of theory of mind is part of an
intersubjective process between the infant and caregiver (see Gopnik,
1993 for an elegant elaboration of such a model). In our view, the
caregiver helps the child create mentalizing models, through complex linguistic and quasi-linguistic processes that involve nonverbal
as well as verbal aspects of social interaction within an attachment
context (Brown, Hobson, Lee, & Stevenson 1997).

Infants by 12 months of age do not just participate in joint attention, they also actively attempt to establish it, often apparently simply to share interest in something. For example, a study (Liszkowski,

Carpenter, Henning, Striano, Tomasello, 2004), observed the impact of an adult reacting to the pointing behavior of 12-month-olds. Infants were not happy when the adult simply followed the infant's pointing and looked to the object, or looked to the infant with positive affect, or did nothing. But they were satisfied when she responded by looking back and forth from the object to the infant and commented positively—implying that this sharing of attention and interest was indeed their goal. Infants of 12 months happily point just to inform an adult of the location of a misplaced object they have no direct interest in. Such declarative and informing motives are apparently "purely social" in their aims.

The small child assumes that his knowledge is shared by all. What he knows is known by others and vice versa. That is, that the world is shared between all of us and only slowly does the uniqueness of our own perspective differentiate so that a sense of mental self can develop. We noted earlier that infants possess by three months or so at the latest a distinct sense of their integrity as physical beings. But in relation to what we know and understand about reality we start with the assumption that knowledge is common and there is nothing unique about our own thoughts or feelings. Just how deeply rooted our expectations about shared knowledge are, is indicated by what has been called the *curse of knowledge bias* explored in a developmental context by Susan Birch and Paul Bloom (Birch & Bloom, 2004). Originally formally described by three economists (Camerer, Lowenstein, & Weber, 1989), the *curse of knowledge bias* describes the common observation that if one knows something about the world one tends to assume that everyone else knows it too. So, young children report that other children will know facts that they themselves have just learned (Taylor, Esbensen, & Bennett, 1994). It seems clear and unsurprising that 3-year-olds are more likely than older children to assume this (Birch & Bloom, 2003). We assume that everyone has the same knowledge as ours, because most of the beliefs that we have about the world were someone else's beliefs before we made them our own.

Children do not know fully that they are separate, that their internal world is something private and individual, of which they will eventually take ownership or at least claim privileged access. This developmental configuration shapes unconscious fantasy and primes desire for oneness and merger. They do not know that they can choose whether—for example—to share their thoughts and feelings with their parents, or their therapist. Perhaps one reason that toddlers are so prone to outbursts of rage and frustration is that as the world and individual minds are not yet clearly demarcated, they expect other people to know what they are thinking and feeling, and to see situations in the same way they do. Thus frustration of their wishes seems malign or wilfully obtuse, rather than the result of a different point of view, alternative priorities, and so forth. A developmental perspective on the narcissistic blow of Oedipus is the recognition forced upon the little boy by development that mother does not share his wish that they should marry. The illusion of shared consciousness has distinct advantages.

Mentalization evolves out of the child's biological predisposition to assume that his knowledge is shared by all. The child naturally turns to the caregiver to learn from her about the nature of the world, internal and external. Unconsciously and pervasively, the caregiver ascribes a mental state to the child with her behavior, treating the child as a mental agent. Ultimately, the child concludes that the caregiver's reaction to him makes sense given internal states of belief or desire within himself. This conclusion enables him to elaborate mental models of causation, and facilitates the development of a core sense of selfhood organized along these lines. We assume that this is mostly a mundane process, and that it is preconscious to both infant and parent—inaccessible to reflection or modification. Parents, however, execute this natural human function in different ways. Some are alert to the earliest indications of intentionality, while others may need stronger clues before they can perceive the child's mental state and modify their behavior accordingly. Yet other parents consistently misread the infant's internal state; their expectations, based on past experience or reactions to these dominate their mentalization of their infants and preclude accurate identification of intention. These biases preclude the possibility of contingent mirroring, and an emotional experience is mirrored which is incongruent with the child's constitutional experience. Yet other parents, as we have seen, fail to mark their mirroring.

Subjectivity Before Mentalization

How does the child experience subjectivity before he recognizes that internal states are representations of reality? In describing the normal development of mentalizing in the child of 2 to 5 years (Fonagy & Target, 1996; Target & Fonagy, 1996), we suggest that there is a transition from a split mode of experience to mentalization. We hypothesize that the very young child equates the internal world with the external. What exists in the mind must exist out there and what exists out there must also exist in the mind. At this stage there is no room yet for alternative perspectives. "How I see it is how it is." The toddler's or young preschool child's insistence that "there is a Tiger under the bed" is not allayed by parental reassurance. This psychic equivalence, as a mode of experiencing the internal world, can cause intense distress, because the experience of a fantasy as potentially real can be terrifying. The acquisition of a sense of pretend in relation to mental states is therefore essential. While playing, the child knows that internal experience may not reflect external reality (e.g., Bartsch & Wellman, 1989; Dias & Harris, 1990), but then the internal state is thought to have no implications for the outside world (pretend mode).

Normally at around 4-years-old, the child integrates these modes to arrive at mentalization, or reflective mode, in which mental states can be experienced as representations. Inner and outer reality can then be seen as linked, yet differing in important ways, and no longer have to be either equated or dissociated from each other (Gopnik, 1993). The child discovers that seeing-leads-to-knowing; if you have seen something in a box, you know something about what's in the box (Pratt & Bryant, 1990). They can begin to work out from gaze direction what a person is thinking about, thus making use of the eyes of another person to make a mentalistic interpretation (Baron-Cohen & Cross, 1992). There are, however, circumstances under which prementalistic forms of subjectvity re-emerge to dominate social cognition years after the acquisition of full mentalization. We shall consider these in section 5.

Mentalization normally comes about through the child's experience of his mental states being reflected on, prototypically through secure play with a parent or older child, which facilitates integration of the pretend and psychic equivalence modes. This interpersonal process is perhaps an elaboration of the complex mirroring the parent offered earlier. In playfulness, the caregiver gives the child's ideas and feelings (when he is only pretending) a link with reality, by indicating an alternative perspective outside the child's mind. The parent or older child also shows that reality may be distorted by acting upon it in playful ways, and through this playfulness a pretend but real mental experience may be introduced.

If the child's capacity to perceive mental states in himself and others depends on his observation of the mental world of his caregiver, clearly children require a number of adults with an interest in their mental state, who can be trusted (i.e. with whom an attachment bond exists), to support the development of their subjectivity from a prementalizing to a fully mentalizing mode. In this regard, in past initiatives, perhaps we have placed too much emphasis on parents (particularly mothers). It follows from the evolutionary model presented in section 2 and here that the child's brain is experience expectant from a range of benign adults willing to take the pedagogic stance toward their subjectivity. Thus, teachers, neighbors, older siblings, as well as parental figures could play important roles in optimizing the child's capacity for mentalization. Children can perceive and conceive of their mental states to the extent that the behavior of those around them has implied that they have them. This can happen through an almost unlimited set of methods ranging from shared pretend playing with the child (empirically shown to be associated with early mentalization), and many ordinary interactions (such as conversations and peer interaction) will also involve shared thinking about an idea.

Disorganized Attachment and the Unmentalized (Alien) Self

In children whose attachment is disorganized mentalization may be evident, but it does not play the positive role in self-organization that it does in securely or even in insecurely attached children. The child with disorganized attachment is forced to look not for the representation of his own mental states in the mind of the other, but the mental states of that other which threaten to undermine his agentive sense of self. These mental states can create an alien presence within his self-representation, so unbearable that his attachment behavior becomes focused on re-externalising these parts of the self onto attachment figures, rather than on the internalization of a capacity for containment of affects and other intentional states.

Disorganized infants, even if interpersonally perceptive, fail to integrate this emotional awareness with their self-organization. There may be a number of linked reasons for this: (a) the child needs to use disproportionate resources to understand the parent's behavior, at the expense of reflecting on self-states; (b) the caregiver of the disorganized infant is likely to be less contingent in responding to the infant's self-state, and further to show systematic biases in her perception and reflection of his state; (c) the mental state of the caregiver of the disorganized infant may evoke intense anxiety through either frightening or fearful behavior toward the child, including inexplicable fear of the child himself. These factors combine, perhaps, to make children whose attachment system is disorganized become keen readers of the caregiver's mind under certain circumstances, but (we suggest) poor readers of their own mental states.

The Decoupling of Mentalization in the Presence of Attachment Trauma

Trauma-Related Loss of the Capacity to Conceive of Mental States

Adults with a history of childhood attachment trauma often seem unable to understand how others think or feel. We have hypothesized that childhood maltreatment undermines mentalization. When combined with the sequelae of a deeply insecure early environment, with enfeebled affect representation and poor affect control systems as well as a disorganized self structure, trauma has profound effects on the development of such vulnerable individuals: (a) It inhibits playfulness which is essential for the adequate unfolding of the interpersonal interpretive function (Dunn, Davies, O'Connor, & Sturgess, 2000); (b) it interferes directly with affect regulation and attentional control systems (Arntz, Appels, Sieswerda, 2000); (c) most importantly, in vulnerable individuals, it can lead to an unconsciously motivated failure of mentalization. This failure is a defensive adaptive manoeuvre: the child seeks to protect himself from the frankly malevolent and dangerous states of mind of the abuser by decoupling his capacity to conceive of mental states, at least in attachment contexts (Fonagy, 1991); (d) we believe that adult social functioning is impaired by childhood and adolescent adversity to the extent that adversity causes a breakdown of attachment related mentalization (Fonagy, Stein, Allen, & Fultz, 2003a). There is considerable evidence that maltreated children have specific mentalization deficits and that individuals with BPD are poor at mentalization following severe experiences of maltreatment (Fonagy et al., 1996).

The difficulty of traumatized patients in understanding themselves and others struck us forcibly over 15 years ago while treating borderline women and violent men (Fonagy, 1989). A later study of the psychoanalytic treatment of 30 young adults with similar behavior, led by Anne-Marie Sandler at the Anna Freud Centre, reinforced these conclusions (Gerber, 2004; Perelberg, 1999). Research has shown that the capacity for mentalization is undermined in most people who have experienced trauma. Children cannot learn words for feelings (Beeghly & Cicchetti, 1994), and adults have more difficulty recognizing facial expressions, the more severe their childhood maltreatment (Fonagy, Stein, Allen, & Fultz 2003a). What is the clinical picture like when trauma brings about a partial and temporary collapse of mentalization? We observed an apparent lack of imagination about the mental world of others, a naiveté or cluelessness about what others think or feel that can verge on confusion, and a corresponding absence of insight into the way that the traumatized person's own mind works.

Many maltreated children grow up into adequately functioning adults. Although maltreatment places children at increased risk for developing psychopathology, only a small proportion will prospectively need mental health services (Widom, 1999). It is possible that early maltreatment (early experience in an interpersonally hostile environment) reduces the individual's opportunity fully to develop mentalizing skills, leaving them with inadequate capacities to identify and avoid risks for further interpersonal trauma. In dysfunctional attachment contexts, particularly when children are victims of abuse, they may learn to interpret parental initiation of communicative attention-directing behaviors as a cue that potentially harmful interactions are likely to follow. In consequence, they may defensively inhibit the mentalistic interpretation of such cues; this may finally lead to the defensive disruption of their own metacognitive monitoring procedures in all subsequent intimate relationships (Fonagy, Target, Gergely, Allen, & Bateman, 2003b).

The Equation of Inner and Outer

The collapse of mentalization in the face of trauma entails a loss of awareness of the relationship between internal and external reality (Fonagy & Target, 2000). Modes of representing the internal world re-emerge that developmentally precede awareness that thoughts, feelings, and wishes are part of the mind. The 2–3-year-old as we saw, not yet experiencing his mind as truly representational, assumes in the mode of psychic equivalence that what he thinks also exists in the physical world. Post-traumatic subjective experience (the flashback) is similarly compelling, resistant to argument and feels dangerous until it becomes mentalized. Often survivors of trauma simply refuse to think about their experience because thinking about it means reliving it. Aspects of the notion of psychic equivalence evidently overlap with descriptions of paranoid-schizoid forms of thinking particularly as formulated by Wilfred Bion in the *Elements of Psychoanalysis* (Bion, 1963), and symbolic equation as formulated by Hanna Segal (1957).

Separation from Reality

As we saw, the pretend mode is a developmental complement to psychic equivalence. Not yet able to conceive of internal experience as mental, the child's fantasies are dramatically divided off from the external world. Small children cannot simultaneously pretend (even though they know it is not real) and engage with normal reality; asking them if their pretend gun is a gun or a stick spoils the game. Following trauma and the constriction of mentalization we see the intrusion of the pretend mode, particularly in dissociative experiences. In dissociated thinking, nothing can be linked to anything— the principle of the pretend mode, in which fantasy is cut off from the real world, is extended so that nothing has implications (Fonagy & Target, 2000). Patients report blanking out, clamming up, or remembering their traumatic experiences only in dreams. The most characteristic feature of traumatization is the oscillation between psychic equivalence and pretend modes of experiencing the internal world.

I Believe It When I See It

A third prementalistic aspect of psychic reality is the re-emergence of a teleological mode of thought. This mode of understanding the world antedates even language. Infants as young as 9 months are able to attribute goals to people and to objects that seem to behave purposefully, but these goals are not yet truly mental, they are tied to what is observable. The return of this teleological mode of thought is perhaps the most painful aspect of a subjectivity stripped of mentalization.

Following trauma, verbal reassurance means little. Interacting with others at a mental level has been replaced by attempts at altering thoughts and feelings through action. Trauma, certainly physical and sexual abuse, is by definition teleological. It is hardly surprising that the victim feels that the mind of another can only be altered in this same mode, through a physical act, threat, or seduction. Following trauma we all need physical assurances of security. A man severely physically maltreated described his feelings about being sent to live in a hostel at the age of eleven as follows: "I tried to make them understand that I was upset so I was throwing things quite a lot, I threw my bed out of the window, I broke all the windows in the room. It was the only way I could make them understand that I did not like it."

Attachment trauma may result in the hyperactivation of attachment which may impact upon mentalization. Attachment is normally the ideal training ground for the development of mentalization because it is safe and noncompetitive. This biological configuration, which is so adaptive in the context of normal development, becomes immensely destructive in the presence of attachment trauma. Attachment trauma hyperactivates the attachment system because the person to whom the child looks for reassurance and protection is the one causing fear. The devastating psychic impact of attachment trauma is the combined result of the inhibition of mentalization by attachment and the hyperactivation of the attachment system by trauma. This context demands extraordinary mentalizing capacities from the child, yet the hyperactivation of the attachment system will have inhibited whatever limited capacity he has.

The coincidence of trauma and attachment creates a biological vicious cycle. Trauma normally leads a child to try to get close to the attachment figure. Where the child depends on an attachment figure who maltreats him, there is a risk of an escalating sequence of further maltreatment, increased distress and an ever-greater inner need for the attachment figure. The inhibition of mentalization in a traumatizing, hyperactivated attachment relationship is always likely to lead to a prementalistic psychic reality, largely split into psychic equivalence, and pretend modes. Because the memory of the trauma feels currently real there is a constant danger of retraumatization from inside. The traumatized child often begins to fear his own mind. The inhibition of mentalization is also clearly an intrapsychic adaptation to traumatic attachment. The frankly malevolent mental state of the abuser terrifies the helpless child. The parent's abuse undermines the child's capacity to mentalize, because it is no longer safe for the child, for example, to think about wishing, if this implies recognizing his parent's wish to harm him. Because he cannot use the model of the other to understand himself, diffusion of identity and dissociation often follows.

The Impact of Attachment Trauma on Mentalization: The Biology of Being Frazzled

The impact of trauma on mentalization is intermittent. As previously stated, sometimes mentalization disappears because an attachment relationship intensifies, for example in the course of an analysis. At other times, being stressed (for example touching on a sensitive issue) can trigger what feels like wild, unjustified reactions. Six years ago, in a hallmark paper entitled "The biology of being frazzled," Amy Arnsten (1998) explained why (see also Arnsten, Mathew, Ubriani, Taylor, & Li 1999; Mayes, 2000). At the risk of simplifying highly complex pioneering neuroscientific work, Arnsten's Dual Arousal Systems Model delineates two complementary, independent arousal systems: the prefrontal and posterior cortical and subcortical systems. The system that activates frontal and prefrontal regions inhibits the second arousal system that normally kicks in only at quite high levels of arousal, when prefrontal activity goes offline and posterior cortical and subcortical functions (e.g., more automatic or motor functions) take over.

The switch-point between the two arousal systems may be shifted by childhood trauma. Undoubtedly, as mentalization is located in the prefrontal cortex, this accounts for some of the inhibition of mentalization in individuals with attachment trauma, in response to increases in arousal that would not be high enough to inhibit mentalization in most of us. Anticipating some of the clinical implications of our thinking, in the light of this phenomenon it is important for analysts to monitor the traumatized patient's readiness to hear comments about thoughts and feelings. As arousal increases, in part in response to interpretative work, traumatized patients cannot process talk about their minds. Interpretations of the transference at these times, however accurate they might be, are likely to be way beyond the capacity of the patient to hear. The clinical priority has to be work to reduce arousal so that the patient can again think of other perspectives (mentalize).

The Impact of Attachment Trauma on Mentalization: Projective Identification as a Matter of Life and Death

Bion's (1963) first element in his elements of psychoanalysis is "the essential feature of Melanie Klein's conception of projective identification…the dynamic relationship between container and contained" (p. 3). Edith Jacobson (1954) and Donald Winnicott (Winnicott, 1956) independently noted that the internalisation of the representation of another before the boundaries of the self are fully formed undermines the creation of a coherent sense of self. The infant is forced to internalize the other not as an internal object but as a core part of his self. If the caregiver fails to contain the infant's anxieties, metabolise them, and mirror the self state, the infant, rather than gradually constructing a representation of his internal states, is forced to accommodate the object, an alien being, within his self representation. Such incoherencies in self-structure are not only features of profoundly neglected children. Because even the most sensitive caregiver is insensitive to the child's state of mind over 50% of the time, we all have alien parts to our self-structure. The illusion of self-coherence is normally maintained by the continuous narrative commentary on behavior that mentalization provides, preconsciously. This weaves our experiences together so that they make sense. In the absence of a robust mentalizing capacity, in the wake of trauma, alien fragments in the self-structure are likely to be clearly revealed in all of us.

Of course these introjections in traumatized individuals are colored by the traumatic context in which they occur. What is internalized as part of the self is a caregiver with terrifying intentions. This can generate momentary experiences of unbearable psychic pain when in the mode of psychic equivalence the self feels attacked literally from within and almost overwhelmed by an experience of badness that reassurance cannot mitigate and from which, in a teleological mode of functioning, self-destruction might appear the only escape. In our view, this state is commonly the trigger for acts of self-harm and suicide.

The only way the person can deal with such introjects is by constantly externalizing these alien parts of the self-structure into an other. Through projective identification the persecutory parts are experienced as outside. It is then essential that the alien experiences are owned by another mind, so that another mind is in control of the parts of the self set upon its own destruction. Paradoxically, then, the need for projective identification is a matter of life and death for those with a traumatizing part of the self-structure, but the constellation creates a dependence on the object that has many features of addiction. Neuroscience is helpful here, in explaining that the triggering of the attachment system (by the need to find a container for traumatized, alien parts of the self) will once again inhibit mentalization. This reduces the chance of either alternative solutions being accepted or a nonteleological (nonphysical) solution being found.

Maltreatment, or more broadly trauma, is seen as interacting with the domain- and situation-specific restrictions upon mentalization at two levels. First, maltreatment makes the young child reluctant to take the perspective of others, because of the actual threat within the intentional stance of the abuser, as well as the constraints upon self-development imposed by the parent's failure to understand and acknowledge the child's budding intentionality. Second, the child is deprived of the later resilience provided by the capacity to understand interpersonal situations (Fonagy, Steele, Steele, Higgitt, & Target, 1994). Thus individuals traumatized by their family environment are vulnerable in terms of the long-term impact of the trauma, their reduced capacity to cope with it, and their difficulty in finding better relationships later. The outcome may be severe developmental psychopathology, ultimately entrenched personality disorder.

Conclusion

We considered the development of mentalization from both a phylo-genetic and ontogenetic perspective. We argued that mentalization has a selective advantage in enhancing collaboration in the context of attachment and competition with conspecifics in all other contexts. Against this evolutionary background we argued that the preferred context for the ontogenetic development of mentalization is one where the child can have trust in the person who has the child's mind in mind. The child's sense of an agentive self, underpinned by the capacity for mentalization, takes shape in this interpersonal context. Some of the brain mechanisms underpinning mentalization are inhibited when the mesocorticolimbic dopaminergic system that mediates attachment and social affiliation is activated. We argued that this is likely to be part of the evolutionary design that privileges close relationships for the safe exploration of intersubjective space.

Mentalization is acquired alongside a range of associated cognitive capacities necessary for conceptualizing mental states, Affect representation and regulation and attentional control are important aspects of this development. The quality of children's relationships with those from whom they acquire an understanding of minds is likely to be crucial to all these. The creation of an integrated sense of agentive self depends upon a contingently, but not too accurately, mirroring relational context. Incongruent and poorly marked mirroring is assumed by us to create the kind of incoherence and disorganization within the self-structure that could account for the controlling disturbed behavior of kindergarten-aged children with a history of disorganized attachment. Before mentalization is fully acquired subjectivity is dominated by the equation of internal and external and the complement of this state, an experience of dissociation between internal and external. Disturbed attachment organization is likely to be associated with persistence of these nonmentalized ways of representing subjectivity.

We suggested that the psychological consequences of trauma, in an attachment context and perhaps beyond, entail a decoupling of mentalization and a re-emergence of nonmentalizing modes of representing internal reality. This is pernicious because the immediacy of a memory experienced in the nonmentalizing mode of psychic equivalence has the capacity to re-traumatize again and again. This further inhibits mentalization and makes the experience ever more real. Trauma in the attachment context is most pernicious because the biological basis of attachment assumes trust. Part of this is the safety of not having to mentalize, of knowing that others are thinking for us, that we need not monitor our own or others' thinking. Trauma inevitably activates the attachment system. This activation (probably for evolutionary reasons) temporarily inhibits areas of the brain concerned with both remembering and mentalization. This is why mentalization comes to be so readily abandoned in the face of trauma, particularly attachment trauma. Unmentalized trauma endures and compromises mental function. Of course it also interferes with new relationships. The self being destroyed from within, by identification with the aggressor, is an imperative for projective identification, drawing the other closer and selecting relationships that will retraumatize. To escape from the grip of trauma, the individual needs help to recover mentalization.

References

Adolphs, R. (2003). Cognitive neuroscience of human social behaviour. *Nature Reviews, 4,* 165–178.

Alexander, R. D. (1989). Evolution of the human psyche. In P. Mellars & C. Stringer (Eds.), *The human revolution: Behavioural and biological perspectives on the origins of modern humans* (pp. 455–513). Princeton, NJ: Princeton University Press.

Alexander, R. D. (1990). How did humans evolve? Reflections on the uniquely unique species. *Museum of Zoology* (Special publication no. 1). Ann Arbor, MI: University of Michigan.

Allen, J. G. (2001). Interpersonal trauma and serious mental disorder. Chichester, UK: Wiley.

Arnsten, A. F. T. (1998). The biology of being frazzled. *Science, 280,* 1711–1712.

Arnsten, A. F. T., Mathew, R., Ubriani, R., Taylor, J. R., & Li, B.-M. (1999). Alpha-1 noradrenergic receptor stimulation impairs prefrontal corical cognitive function. *Biological Psychiatry, 45,* 26–31.

Arntz, A., Appels, C., & Sieswerda, S. (2000). Hypervigilance in borderline disorder: A test with the emotional Stroop paradigm. *J Personal Disord, 14*(4), 366–373.

Avis, J., & Harris, P. (1991). Belief-desire reasoning among Baka children: Evidence for a universal conception of mind. *Child Development, 62,* 460–467.

Bahrick, L. R., & Watson, J. S. (1985). Detection of intermodal proprio-
    ceptive-visual contingency as a potential basis of self-perception in
    infancy. *Developmental Psychology, 21,* 963–973.
Baldwin, D. A., Baird, J. A., Saylor, M. M., & Clark, M. A. (2001). Infants
    parse dynamic action. *Child Development, 72*(3), 708–717.
Baron-Cohen, S. (1995). *Mindblindness: An Essay on Autism and Theory of
    Mind.* Cambridge, MA: Bradford, MIT Press.
Baron-Cohen, S. (2003*). The essential difference: The truth about the male
    and female brain.* New York: Basic Books.
Baron-Cohen, S., & Cross, P. (1992). Reading the eyes: Evidence for the
    role of perception in the development of a theory of mind. *Mind and
    Language, 6,* 173–186.
Bartels, A., & Zeki, S. (2000). The neural basis of romantic love. *Neurore-
    port, 11*(17), 3829–3834.
Bartels, A., & Zeki, S. (2004). The neural correlates of maternal and roman-
    tic love. *Neuroimage, 21*(3), 1155–1166.
Bartsch, K., & Wellman, H. M. (1989). Young children's attribution of
    action to beliefs and desires. *Child Development, 60,* 946–964.
Bartsch, K., & Wellman, H. M. (1995). *Children talk about the mind.* Oxford,
    NY: Oxford University Press.
Beeghly, M., & Cicchetti, D. (1994). Child maltreatment, attachment, and
    the self system: Emergence of an internal state lexicon in toddlers at
    high social risk. *Development and Psychopathology, 6,* 5–30.
Belsky, J. (1999a). Interactional and contextual determinants of attach-
    ment security. In J. Cassidy & P. R. Shaver (Eds.), *Handbook of
    attachment: Theory, research and clinical applications* (pp. 249–264).
    New York: Guilford.
Belsky, J. (1999b). Modern evolutionary theory and patterns of attachment.
    In J. Cassidy & P. R. Shaver (Eds.), *Handbook of attachment: Theory,
    research and clinical applications.* (pp. 141–161). New York: Guilford.
Belsky, J., & Fearon, R. M. (2002). Infant-mother attachment security, con-
    textual risk, and early development: A moderational analysis. *Devel-
    opment and Psychopathology, 14,* 293–310.
Bion, W. R. (1962). A theory of thinking. *International Journal of Psycho-
    analysis, 43,* 306–310.
Bion, W. R. (1963). *Elements of psycho-analysis.* London: Heinemann.
Birch, S. A., & Bloom, P. (2003). Children are cursed: an asymmetric bias in
    mental-state attribution. *Psychol Sci, 14*(3), 283–286.
Birch, S. A., & Bloom, P. (2004). Understanding children's and adults' limi-
    tations in mental state reasoning. *Trends Cogn Sci, 8*(6), 255–260.
Bogdan, R. J. (1997). *Interpreting minds.* Cambridge, MA: MIT Press.

Bronfman, E., Parsons, E., & Lyons-Ruth, K. (1999). Atypical Maternal Behavior Instrument for Assessment and Classification (AMBIANCE): Manual for coding disrupted affective communication, version 2. Unpublished manuscript, Cambridge, MA: Harvard Medical School.

Brown, J. R., Donelan-McCall, N., & Dunn, J. (1996). Why talk about mental states? The significance of children's conversations with friends, siblings, and mothers. *Child Development, 67,* 836–849.

Brown, R., Hobson, R. P., Lee, A., & Stevenson, J. (1997). Are there "autistic-like" features in congenitally blind children? *J Child Psychol Psychiatry, 38*(6), 693–703.

Buccino, G., Lui, F., Canessa, N., Patteri, I., Lagravinese, G., Benuzzi, F., et al. (2004). Neural circuits involved in the recognition of actions performed by nonconspecifics: An FMRI study. *J Cogn Neurosci, 16*(1), 114–126.

Cabeza, R., & Nyberg, L. (2000). Neural bases of learning and memory: Functional neuroimaging evidence. *Curr Opin Neurol, 13*(4), 415–421.

Calkins, S., & Johnson, M. (1998). Toddler regulation of distress to frustrating events: Temperamental and maternal correlates. *Infant Behavior & Development, 21,* 379–395.

Camerer, C., Lowenstein, A., & Weber, B. (1989). The curse of knowledge in economic settings: an experimental analysis. *Journal of Political Economy, 97,* 1232–1254.

Carpendale, J., & Chandler, M. J. (1996). On the distinction between false-belief understanding and subscribing to an interpretive theory of mind. *Child Development, 67,* 1686–1706.

Cavell, M. (1991). The subject of mind. *International Journal of Psycho-Analysis, 72,* 141–154.

Cavell, M. (1994). *The Psychoanalytic Mind.* Cambridge, MA: Harvard University Press.

Champagne, F. A., Chretien, P., Stevenson, C. W., Zhang, T. Y., Gratton, A., & Meaney, M. J. (2004). Variations in nucleus accumbens dopamine associated with individual differences in maternal behavior in the rat. *J Neurosci, 24*(17), 4113–4123.

Charman, T., Ruffman, T., & Clements, W. (2002). Is there a gender difference in false belief development? *Social Development,* (11), 1–10.

Chugani, H. T., Behen, M. E., Muzik, O., Juhasz, C., Nagy, F., & Chugani, D. C. (2001). Local brain functional activity following early deprivation: a study of postinstitutionalized Romanian orphans. *Neuroimage, 14*(6), 1290–1301.

Cicchetti, D., Rogosch, F. A., & Toth, S. L. (2000). The efficacy of toddler-parent psychotherapy for fostering cognitive development in offspring of depressed mothers. *J Abnorm Child Psychol, 28*(2), 135–148.

Claussen, A. H., Mundy, P. C., Mallik, S. A., & Willoughby, J. C. (2002). Joint attention and dosrganised atachment status in infants at risk. *Development and Psychopathology, 14,* 279–291.

Conway, M. A. (1992). A structural model of autobiographical memory. In M. A. Conway, H. Spinnler & W. A. Wagenaar (Eds.), *Theoretical Perspectives on Autobiological Memory.* (pp. 167–194). Dordrecht, The Netherlands: Kluwer Academic Publishers.

Conway, M. A. (1996). Autobiographical knowledge and autobiographical memories. In D.C.Rubin (Ed.), *Remembering our past: Studies in autobiographical memory* (pp. 67–93). New York: Cambridge University Press.

Conway, M. A., & Holmes, A. (2004). Psychosocial stages and the accessibility of autobiographical memories across the life cycle. *J Pers, 72*(3), 461–480.

Corkum, V., & Moore, C. (1995). Development of joint visual attention in infants. In C. Moore & P. Dunham (Eds.), *Joint Attention: Its Origins and Role in Development* (pp. 61–83). New York: Erlbaum.

Cote, S., Tremblay, R. E., Nagin, D., Zoccolillo, M., & Vitaro, F. (2002). The development of impulsivity, fearfulness, and helpfulness during childhood: patterns of consistency and change in the trajectories of boys and girls. *Journal of Child Psychology and Psychiatry and Allied Disciplines, 43*(5), 609–618.

Csibra, G., & Gergely, G. (1998). The teleological origins of mentalistic action explanations: A developmental hypothesis. *Developmental Science, 1*(2), 255–259.

Cutting, A. L., & Dunn, J. (2002). The cost of understanding other people: social cognition predicts young children's sensitivity to criticism. *J Child Psychol Psychiatry, 43*(7), 849–860.

Davidson, D. (1983). *Inquiries into Truth and Interpretation.* Oxford, UK: Oxford University Press.

Dennett, D. (1987). *The intentional stance.* Cambridge, MA: MIT Press.

Dias, M. G., & Harris, P. L. (1990). The influence of the imagination on reasoning by young children. *British Journal of Developmental Psychology, 8,* 305–318.

Dunn, J. (1988). *The Beginnings of Social Understanding.* Oxford: Basil Blackwell Ltd and Cambridge, MA: Harvard University Press.

Dunn, J. (1994). Changing minds and changing relationships. In C. Lewis & P. Mitchell (Eds.), *Children's Early Understanding of Mind: Origins and Development* (pp. 297–310). Hove, UK: Lawrence Erlbaum.

Dunn, J. (1999). Making sense of the social world: Mindreading, emotion and relationships. In P. D. Zelazo, J. W. Astington & D. R. Olson (Eds.), *Developing theories of intention: Social understanding and self control.* (Vol., pp. 229–242). Mahwah, NJ: Lawrence Erlbaum Associates.

Dunn, J., & Brown, J. (2001). Emotion, pragmatics and developments in emotion understanding in the preschool years. In D. Bakhurst & S. Shanker (Eds.), *Jerome Bruner: Language, culture, self.* Thousand Oaks: CA: Sage.

Dunn, J., Brown, J., & Beardsall, L. (1991). Family talk about feeling states and children's later understanding of others' emotions. *Developmental Psychology, 27,* 448–455.

Dunn, J., & Cutting, A. (1999). Understanding others, and individual differences in friendship interactions in young children. *Social Development., 8,* 201–219.

Dunn, J., Davies, L. C., O'Connor, T. G., & Sturgess, W. (2000). Parents' and partners' life course and family experiences: Links with parent-child relationships in different family settings. *J Child Psychol Psychiatry, 41*(8), 955–968.

Fearon, R. M., & Belsky, J. (2004). Attachment and attention: protection in relation to gender and cumulative social-contextual adversity. *Child Dev, 75*(6), 1677–1693.

Ferrari, P. F., Gallese, V., Rizzolatti, G., & Fogassi, L. (2003). Mirror neurons responding to the observation of ingestive and communicative mouth actions in the monkey ventral premotor cortex. *Eur J Neurosci, 17*(8), 1703–1714.

Flavell, J., & Miller, P. (1998). Social cognition. In D. Kuhn & R. Siegler (Eds.), *Cognition, perception, and language. Handbook of child psychology.* (5 ed., Vol. 2, pp. 851–898). New York: Wiley.

Flavell, J. H. (1999). Cognitive development: Children's knowledge about the mind. *Annu Rev Psychol, 50,* 21–45.

Fonagy, P. (1989). On tolerating mental states: Theory of mind in borderline patients. *Bulletin of the Anna Freud Centre, 12,* 91–115.

Fonagy, P. (1991). Thinking about thinking: Some clinical and theoretical considerations in the treatment of a borderline patient. *International Journal of Psycho-Analysis, 72,* 1–18.

Fonagy, P. (2001, August). Early intervention and the development of self-regulation. Paper presented at the Keynote address at the meeting of the Australian Association for Infant Mental Health, Perth, Australia.

Fonagy, P. (2003). The development of psychopathology from infancy to adulthood: The mysterious unfolding of disturbance in time. *Infant Mental Health Journal, 24*(3), 212–239.

Fonagy, P., Edgcumbe, R., Moran, G. S., Kennedy, H., & Target, M. (1993). The roles of mental representations and mental processes in therapeutic action. *The Psychoanalytic Study of the Child, 48,* 9–48.

Fonagy, P., Gergely, G., Jurist, E., & Target, M. (2002). *Affect Regulation, Mentalization and the Development of the Self.* New York: Other Press.

Fonagy, P., Leigh, T., Steele, M., Steele, H., Kennedy, R., Mattoon, G., et al. (1996). The relation of attachment status, psychiatric classification, and response to psychotherapy. *Journal of Consulting and Clinical Psychology, 64,* 22–31.

Fonagy, P., Steele, H., Moran, G., Steele, M., & Higgitt, A. (1991). The capacity for understanding mental states: The reflective self in parent and child and its significance for security of attachment. *Infant Mental Health Journal, 13,* 200–217.

Fonagy, P., Steele, M., Moran, G. S., Steele, H., & Higgitt, A. (1992). The integration of psychoanalytic theory and work on attachment: The issue of intergenerational psychic processes. In D.Stern & M.Ammaniti (Eds.), *Attaccamento E Psiconalis* (pp. 19–30). Bari, Italy: Laterza.

Fonagy, P., Steele, M., Steele, H., Higgitt, A., & Target, M. (1994). Theory and practice of resilience. *Journal of Child Psychology and Psychiatry, 35,* 231–257.

Fonagy, P., Stein, H., Allen, J., & Fultz, J. (2003a). The relationship of mentalization and childhood and adolescent adversity to adult functioning. Paper presented at the Biennial Meeting of the Society for Research in Child Development, Tampa, FL.

Fonagy, P., & Target, M. (1996). Playing with reality: I. Theory of mind and the normal development of psychic reality. *International Journal of Psycho-Analysis, 77,* 217–233.

Fonagy, P., & Target, M. (1997). Attachment and reflective function: Their role in self-organization. *Development and Psychopathology, 9,* 679–700.

Fonagy, P., & Target, M. (2000). Playing with reality III: The persistence of dual psychic reality in borderline patients. *International Journal of Psychoanalysis, 81*(5), 853–874.

Fonagy, P., & Target, M. (2002). Early intervention and the development of self-regulation. *Psychoanalytic Inquiry, 22*(3), 307–335.

Fonagy, P., Target, M., & Gergely, G. (2000). Attachment and borderline personality disorder: A theory and some evidence. *Psychiatric Clinics of North America, 23,* 103–122.

Fonagy, P., Target, M., Gergely, G., Allen, J. G., & Bateman, A. (2003b). The developmental roots of borderline personality disorder in early attachment relationships: A theory and some evidence. *Psychoanalytic Inquiry, 23,* 412–459.

Fonagy, P., Target, M., Steele, H., & Steele, M. (1998). Reflective-Functioning Manual, version 5.0, for Application to Adult Attachment Interviews. London: University College London.

Frith, U., & Frith, C. D. (2003). Development and neurophysiology of mentalizing. *Philosophical Transactions of the Royal Society of London B, Biological Sciences, 358,* 459–473.

Gallagher, H. L., & Frith, C. D. (2003). Functional imaging of 'theory of mind'. *Trends Cogn Sci, 7*(2), 77–83.

Gallese, V. (2003). The roots of empathy: the shared manifold hypothesis and the neural basis of intersubjectivity. *Psychopathology, 36*(4), 171–180.

Gallese, V., Fadiga, L., Fogassi, L., & Rizzolatti, G. (1996). Action recognition in the premotor cortex. *Brain, 119*(Pt 2), 593–609.

Gallese, V., Keysers, C., & Rizzolatti, G. (2004). A unifying view of the basis of social cognition. *Trends Cogn Sci, 8*(9), 396–403.

George, C., Kaplan, N., & Main, M. (1996). *The Adult Attachment Interview Protocol,* 3rd Edition. Unpublished manuscript, Department of Psychology, University of California at Berkeley.

Gerber, A. J. (2004). Psychodynamic psychotherapy for severe personality disorders: A quantitative study of treatment process and outcome. PhD Thesis, University of London.

Gergely, G. (2001). The obscure object of desire: 'Nearly, but clearly not, like me. Contingency preference in normal children versus children with autism. In J. Allen, P. Fonagy & G. Gergely (Eds.), *Contingency Perception and Attachment in Infancy, Special Issue of the Bulletin of the Menninger Clinic* (pp. 411–426). New York: Guilford.

Gergely, G., & Csibra, G. (2003). Teleological reasoning in infancy: The naive theory of rational action. *Trends in Cognitive Sciences, 7,* 287–292.

Gergely, G., & Csibra, G. (2004). The social construction of the cultural mind: Imitative learning as a mechanism for social pedagogy. *Interaction Studies: Social and Behavioral Communication in Biological and Artificial Systems,* Vol 6 (3), pp. 463–481.

Gergely, G., & Watson, J. (1996). The social biofeedback model of parental affect-mirroring. *International Journal of Psycho-Analysis, 77,* 1181–1212.

Gergely, G., & Watson, J. (1999). Early social-emotional development: Contingency perception and the social biofeedback model. In P. Rochat (Ed.), *Early social cognition: Understanding others in the first months of life* (pp. 101–137). Hillsdale, NJ: Erlbaum.

Goldman, A. I., & Sripada, C. S. (2005). Simulationist models of face-based emotion recognition. *Cognition, 94*(3), 193–213.

Gopnik, A. (1993). How we know our minds: The illusion of first-person knowledge of intentionality. *Behavioral and Brain Sciences, 16,* 1–14, 29–113.

Greene, J., & Haidt, J. (2002). How (and where) does moral judgment work? *Trends Cogn Sci, 6*(12), 517–523.

Grienenberger, J., Kelly, K., & Slade, A. (2005). Maternal reflective function-
    ing, mother-infant affective communication, and infant attachment:
    Exploring the link between mental states and observed caregiv-
    ing behaviour in the intergenerational transmission of attachment.
    Attachment and Human Development, 7(3), 299–311.
Gusnard, D. A., Akbudak, E., Shulman, G. L., & Raichle, M. E. (2001).
    Medial prefrontal cortex and self-referential mental activity: relation
    to a default mode of brain function. Proc *Natl Acad Sci USA, 98*(7),
    4259–4264.
Hardy, S. B. (2000). *Mother nature.* New York: Ballentine Books.
Harman, C., Rothbart, M. K., & Posner, M. I. (1997). Distress and intention
    interactions in early infancy. *Motivation and Emotion, 21,* 27–43.
Hobson, P. (2002). *The cradle of thought: Explortions of the origins of think-
    ing.* Oxford, UK: Macmillan.
Hofer, M. A. (2004). The Emerging Neurobiology of Attachment and Sepa-
    ration: HowParents Shape Their Infant's Brain and Behavior. In S.
    W. Coates & J. L. Rosenthal (Eds.), *September 11- "When the Bough
    Broke", Attachment Theory, Psychobiology, and Social Policy: An Inte-
    grated Approach to Trauma.* New York: Analytic Press.
Hughes, C., & Dunn, J. (2002). When I say a naughty word. Children's
    accounts of anger and sadness in self, mother and friend: Longitudi-
    nal findings from ages four to seven. *British Journal of Developmental
    Psychology, 20,* 515–535.
Hughes, C., & Leekham, S. (2004). What are the links between theory of
    mind and social realtions? Review, reflections and new directions
    for studies of typical and atypical development. *Social Behavior, 13,*
    590–619.
Insel, T. (1997). A neurobiological basis of social attachment. *American
    Journal of Psychiatry, 154,* 726–735.
Insel, T. R. (2003). Is social attachment an addictive disorder? *Physiol
    Behav, 79*(3), 351–357.
Jacobsen, T., & Hofmann, V. (1997). Children's attachment representations:
    longitudinal relations to school behavior and academic competency
    in middle childhood and adolescence. *Dev Psychol, 33*(4), 703–710.
Jacobson, E. (1954). The self and the object world: Vicissitudes of their
    infantile cathexes and their influence on ideational affective develop-
    ment. *The Psychoanalytic Study of the Child, 9,* 75–127.
Jaworski, J. N., Francis, D. D., Brommer, C. L., Morgan, E. T., & Kuhar, M. J.
    (2005). Effects of early maternal separation on ethanol intake, GABA
    receptors and metabolizing enzymes in adult rats. *Psychopharmacol-
    ogy, 181*(1), 8–15.

Kochanska, G., Coy, K. C., & Murray, K. T. (2001). The development of self-regulation in the first four years of life. *Child Development, 72,* 1091–1111.

Kohler, E., Keysers, C., Umilta, M. A., Fogassi, L., Gallese, V., & Rizzolatti, G. (2002). Hearing sounds, understanding actions: action representation in mirror neurons. *Science, 297*(5582), 846–848.

Koren-Karie, N., Oppenheim, D., Dolev, S., Sher, S., & Etzion-Carasso, A. (2002). Mother's insightfulness regarding their infants' internal experience: Relations with maternal sensitivity and infant attachment. *Developmental-Psychology, 38,* 534–542.

Lalonde, C., & Chandler, M. J. (1995). False belief understanding goes to school: On the social-emotional consequences of coming early or late to a first theory of mind. *Cognition and Emotion, 9,* 167–185.

Legerstee, M., & Varghese, J. (2001). The role of maternal affect mirroring on social expectancies in 2–3 month-old infants. *Child Development, 72,* 1301–1313.

Leslie, A. M. (1994). TOMM, ToBy, and agency: Core architecture and domain specificity. In L. Hirschfeld & S. Gelman (Eds.), *Mapping the mind: Domain specificity in cognition and culture* (pp. 119–148). New York: Cambridge University Press.

Leslie, A. M. (2000). "Theory of Mind" as a mechanism of selective attention. In M. S. Gazzaniga (Ed.), *The new cognitive neurosciences* (2nd ed., pp. 1235–1247). Cambridge, Massachusetts: The MIT Press.

Liszkowski, U., Carpenter, M., Henning, A., Striano, T., & Tomasello, M. (2004). Twelve-month-olds point to share attention and interest. *Developmental Science, 7,* 297–307.

MacLean, P. (1990). *The triune brain in evolution: Role in paleocerebral functions.* New York: Plenum.

Maddock, R. J. (1999). The retrosplenial cortex and emotion: new insights from functional neuroimaging of the human brain. *Trends Neurosci, 22*(7), 310–316.

Main, M. (2000). The organized categories of infant, child and adult attachment: Flexible vs. inflexible attention under attachment-related stress. *Journal of the American Psychoanalytic Association, 48*(4), 1055–1096.

Mayberg, H. S., Liotti, M., Brannan, S. K., McGinnis, S., Mahurin, R. K., Jerabek, P. A., et al. (1999). Reciprocal limbic-cortical function and negative mood: Converging PET findings in depression and normal sadness. *Am J Psychiatry, 156*(5), 675–682.

Mayes, L. C. (2000). A developmental perspective on the regulation of arousal states. *Seminars in Perinatology, 24,* 267–279.

Meins, E. (1997). *Security of attachment and the social development of cognition.* London: Psychology Press.

Meins, E., & Fernyhough, C. (1999). Linguistic acquisitional style and mentalising development: The role of maternal mind-mindedness. *Cognitive Development, 14,* 363–380.

Meins, E., Fernyhough, C., Russel, J., & Clark-Carter, D. (1998). Security of attachment as a predictor of symbolic and mentalising abilities: a longitudinal study. *Social Development, 7,* 1–24.

Meins, E., Fernyhough, C., Wainwright, R., Clark-Carter, D., Das Gupta, M., Fradley, E., et al. (2003). Pathways to understanding mind: construct validity and predictive validity of maternal mind-mindedness. *Child Development, 74*(4), 1194–1211.

Meins, E., Fernyhough, C., Wainwright, R., Das Gupta, M., Fradley, E., & Tuckey, M. (2002). Maternal mind-mindedness and attachment security as predictors of theory of mind understanding. *Child Development, 73,* 1715–1726.

Meins, E., Ferryhough, C., Fradley, E., & Tuckey, M. (2001). Rethinking maternal sensitivity: Mothers' comments on infants mental processes predict security of attachment at 12 months. *Journal of Child Psychology and Psychiatry, 42,* 637–648.

Meltzoff, A. N. (1995). Understanding the intentions of others: Re-enactment of intended acts by 18-month-old children. *Developmental Psychology, 31,* 838–850.

Mitchell, R. W. (1993). Mental models of mirror self-recognition: Two theories. *New Ideas in Psychology, 11,* 295–325.

Mitchell, S. A. (2000). *Relationality: From attachment to intersubjectivity.* Hillsdale, NJ: Analytic Press.

Morton, J., & Frith, U. (1995). Causal modeling: A structural approach to developmental psychology. In D. Cicchetti & D. J. Cohen (Eds.), *Developmental psychopathology.* Vol. 1: Theory and methods (pp. 357–390). New York: John Wiley.

Moses, L. J., Baldwin, D. A., Rosicky, J. G., & Tidball, G. (2001). Evidence for referential understanding in the emotions domain at twelve and eighteen months. *Child Development, 72*(3), 718–735.

Mundy, P., & Neal, R. (2001). Neural plasticity, joint attention, and a transactional social-orienting model of autism. In L. Masters Glidden (Ed.), *International review of mental retardation: Autism* (Vol. 23) (pp. 139–168). San Diego, CA: Academic Press.

Nagin, D. S., & Tremblay, R. E. (2001). Parental and early childhood predictors of persistent physical aggression in boys from kindergarten to high school. *Archives of General Psychiatry, 58*(4), 389–394.

Neisser, U. (1988). Five kinds of self-knowledge. *Philosophical Psychology, 1,* 35–59.

Nelson, E. E., Leibenluft, E., McClure, E. B., & Pine, D. S. (2005). The social re-orientation of adolescence: a neuroscience perspective on the process and its relation to psychopathology. *Psychol Med, 35*(2), 163–174.

Newton, P., Reddy, V., & Bull, R. (2000). Children's everyday deception and performance on false-belief tasks. *British Journal of Developmental Psychology, 18*, 297–317.

Nitschke, J. B., Nelson, E. E., Rusch, B. D., Fox, A. S., Oakes, T. R., & Davidson, R. J. (2004). Orbitofrontal cortex tracks positive mood in mothers viewing pictures of their newborn infants. *Neuroimage, 21*(2), 583–592.

O'Connor, T. G., & Hirsch, N. (1999). Intra-individual differences and relationship-specificity of mentalising in early adolescence. *Social Development, 8*, 256–274.

Oppenheim, D., & Koren-Karie, N. (2002). Mothers' insightfulness regarding their children's internal worlds: The capacity underlying secure child-mother relationships. *Infant-Mental-Health-Journal, 23*, 593–605.

Panksepp, J. (1998). *Affective neuroscience: The foundations of human and animal emotions.* Oxford: Oxford University Press.

Perelberg, R. J. (Ed.). (1999). *Psychoanalytic Understanding of Violence and Suicide.* London: Routledge.

Perner, J., & Lang, B. (2000). Theory of mind and executive function: Is there a developmental relationship? In S. Baron-Cohen, H. Tager-Flusberg & D. J. Cohen (Eds.), *Understanding other minds: Perspectives from developmental cognitive neuroscience* (pp. 150–181). New York: Oxford University Press.

Plotsky, P. M., Thrivikraman, K. V., Nemeroff, C. B., Caldji, C., Sharma, S., & Meaney, M. J. (2005). Long-Term Consequences of Neonatal Rearing on Central Corticotropin-Releasing Factor Systems in Adult Male Rat Offspring. *Neuropsychopharmacology, 30*(12), 2192–2204.

Posner, M. I., & Rothbart, M. K. (2000). Developing mechanisms of self-regulation. *Development and Psychopathology, 12*, 427–441.

Povinelli, D. J., & Eddy, T. J. (1995). The unduplicated self. In P. Rochat (Ed.), *The Self in Infancy: Theory and Research* (pp. 161–192). Amsterdam: Elsevier.

Pratt, C., & Bryant, P. E. (1990). Young children understand that looking leads to knowing (so long as they are looking into a single barrel). *Child Development, 61*, 973–982.

Repacholi, B. M., & Gopnik, A. (1997). Early reasoning about desires: Evidence from 14- and 18-month-olds. *Developmental Psychology, 33*, 12–21.

Rizzolatti, G., & Craighero, L. (2004). The mirror-neuron system. *Annu Rev Neurosci, 27*, 169–192.

Rochat, P., & Striano, T. (1999). Social-cognitive development in the first year. In P. Rochat (Ed.), *Early social cognition.* Mahwah, NJ.: Lawrence Erlbaum.

Ruffman, T., Perner, J., Naito, M., Parkin, L., & Clements, W. (1998). Older (but not younger) siblings facilitate false belief understanding. *Developmental Psychology, 34*(1), 161–174.

Ruffman, T., Perner, J., & Parkin, L. (1999). How parenting style affects false belief understanding. *Social Development, 8,* 395–411.

Rutter, M., & O'Connor, T. G. (2004). Are there biological programming effects for psychological development? Findings from a study of Romanian adoptees. *Dev Psychol, 40*(1), 81–94.

Schechter, D. S., Coots, T., Zeanah, C. H., Davies, M., Coates, S., Trabka, K., et al. (2005). Maternal mental representations of the child in an inner-city clinical sample: Violence-related posttraumatic stress and reflective functioning. *Attachment and Human Development, 7*(3), 313–331.

Schölmerich, A., Lamb, M. E., Leyendecker, B., & Fracasso, M. P. (1997). Mother-infant teaching interactions and attachment security in Euro-American and Central-American immigrant families. *Infant Behavior and Development, 20,* 165–174.

Segal, H. (1957). Notes on symbol formation. *International Journal of Psycho-Analysis, 38,* 391–397.

Siegel, D. J. (1999). *The developing mind: Toward a neurobiology of interpersonal experience.* New York: Guilford.

Simpson, J. A. (1999). Attachment theory in modern evolutionary perspective. In J. Cassidy & P. R. Shaver (Eds.), *Handbook of attachment: Theory, research and clinical applications* (pp. 115–140). New York: Guilford.

Singer, T., Seymour, B., O'Doherty, J., Kaube, H., Dolan, R. J., & Frith, C. D. (2004). Empathy for pain involves the affective but not sensory components of pain. *Science, 303*(5661), 1157–1162.

Slade, A. (2005). Parental reflective functioning: An introduction. *Attachment and Human Development, 7*(3), 269–281.

Slade, A., Grienenberger, J., Bernbach, E., Levy, D., & Locker, A. (2005). Maternal reflective functioning, attachment and the transmission gap: A preliminary study. *Attachment and Human Development, 7*(3), 283–298.

Slomkowski, C., & Dunn, J. (1996). Young children's understanding of other people's beliefs and feelings and their connected comunication with friends. *Developmental Psychology, 32,* 442–447.

Sodian, B., & Frith, U. (1992). Deception and sabotage in autistic, retarded and normal children. *J Child Psychol Psychiatry, 33*(3), 591–605.

Sodian, B., Taylor, C., Harris, P. L., & Perner, J. (1992). Early deception and the child's theory of mind: False trails and genuine markers. *Child Development, 62,* 468–483.

Spelke, E., Philips, A., & Woodward, A. L. (1995). Infant's knowledge of object motion and human action. In D. Sperber, D. Premack & A. Premack (Eds.), *Causal cognition: A multidisciplinary debate.* (pp. 44–78). Oxford: Clarendon Press.

Sroufe, L. A. (1996). *Emotional development: The organization of emotional life in the early years.* New York: Cambridge University Press.

Stern, D. N. (1998). The process of therapeutic change involving implicit knowledge: Some implications of developmental observations for adult psychotherapy. *Infant Mental Health Journal, 19,* 300–308.

Sutton, J., Smith, P. K., & Swettenham, J. (1999). Social cognition and bullying: Social inadequacy or skilled manipulation? *British Journal of Developmental Psychology, 17,* 435–450.

Target, M., & Fonagy, P. (1996). Playing with reality II: The development of psychic reality from a theoretical perspective. *International Journal of Psycho-Analysis, 77,* 459–479.

Taylor, M., & Carlson, S. M. (1997). The relation between individual differences in fantasy and theory of mind. *Child Development, 68*(3), 436–455.

Taylor, M., Esbensen, B. M., & Bennett, R. T. (1994). Children's understanding of knowledge acquisition: the tendency for children to report that they have always known what they have just learned. *Child Development, 65*(6), 1581–1604.

Tomasello, M. (1999a). *The Cultural Origins of Human Cognition.* Cambridge, MA: Harvard University Press.

Tomasello, M. (1999b). Having intentions, understanding intentions, and understanding communicative intentions. In P. Zelazo, J. Astington & D. Olson (Eds.), *Developing theories of intention: Social understanding and self-control.* (pp. 63–75). Mahwah, NJ: Lawrence: Erlbaum Associates.

Tremblay, R. E. (2000). *The origins of violence.* ISUMA(Autumn), 19–24.

Tremblay, R. E., Japel, C., & Perusse, D. (1999). The search for the age of onset of physical aggression: Rousseau and Bandura revisited. *Criminal Behavior and Mental Health, 9,* 8–23.

van IJzendoorn, M. H. (1995). Adult attachment representations, parental responsiveness, and infant attachment: A meta-analysis on the predictive validity of the Adult Attachment Interview. *Psychological Bulletin, 117,* 387–403.

Vinden, P. G. (2001). Parenting attitudes and children's understanding of mind: A comparison of Korean American and Anglo-American families. *Cognitive Development, 16,* 793–809.

Waters, E., Merrick, S. K., Treboux, D., Crowell, J., & Albersheim, L. (2000). Attachment security from infancy to early adulthood: a 20 year longitudinal study. *Child Development, 71*(3), 684–689.

Watson, J. S. (1994). Detection of self: The perfect algorithm. In S. Parker, R. Mitchell & M. Boccia (Eds.), *Self-Awareness in Animals and Humans: Developmental Perspectives* (pp. 131–149): Cambridge University Press.

Wellman, H. (1990). *The Child's Theory of Mind*. Cambridge, Mass: Bradford Books/MIT Press.

Wellman, H. M., Cross, D., & Watson, J. (2001). Meta-analysis of theory-of-mind development: the truth about false belief. *Child Development, 72*(3), 655–684.

Wellman, H. M., & Phillips, A. T. (2000). Developing intentional understandings. In L. Moses, B. Male & D. Baldwin (Eds.), *Intentionality: A Key to Human Understanding*. Cambridge, MA: MIT Press.

Wicker, B., Keysers, C., Plailly, J., Royet, J. P., Gallese, V., & Rizzolatti, G. (2003). Both of us disgusted in My insula: the common neural basis of seeing and feeling disgust. *Neuron, 40*(3), 655–664.

Widom, C. S. (1999). Posttraumatic stress disorder in abused and neglected children grown up. *Am J Psychiatry, 156*, 1223–1229.

Winnicott, D. W. (1956). Mirror role of mother and family in child development. In D. W. Winnicott (Ed.), *Playing and reality* (pp. 111–118). London: Tavistock.

Winnicott, D. W. (1965). *The maturational process and the facilitating environment*. London: Hogarth Press.

Winston, J. S., Strange, B. A., O'Doherty, J., & Dolan, R. J. (2002). Automatic and intentional brain responses during evaluation of trustworthiness of faces. *Nat Neurosci, 5*(3), 277–283.

Woodward, A. L. (1998). Infants selectively encode the goal object of an actor's reach. *Cognition, 69*(1), 1–34.

Zahn-Waxler, C., Radke-Yarrow, M., Wagner, E., & Chapman, M. (1992). Development of concern for others. *Developmental Psychology, 28*, 126–136.

Zhang, T. Y., Chretien, P., Meaney, M. J., & Gratton, A. (2005). Influence of naturally occurring variations in maternal care on prepulse inhibition of acoustic startle and the medial prefrontal cortical dopamine response to stress in adult rats. *J Neurosci, 25*(6), 1493–1502.

2

The Development of the Unreflective Self

György Gergely and Zsolt Unoka

Introduction: Psychoanalytic Approaches to the Etiology of Affective Self Disorders

In spite of their diversity, the majority of psychoanalytic schools have historically shared two general assumptions concerning the etiology and analytic treatment of affective self disorders. The first concerns the psychosocial and developmental origins of many affective self pathologies; it is often assumed that the quality of the infant's early affective experiences with the primary caregiver play an important role in self development and that the patterns of affective attachment interactions between infant and caregiver form the foundation for primary self-object relationship representations. It is also thought that these patterns contribute significantly to the internalization of psychological processes that shape nonadaptive patterns of affective functioning in later life. The second assumption shared by most psychoanalysts is that the mechanisms employed in order to bring about therapeutic change in their treatment of affective self disorders involve the same psychological mechanisms that mediate the formation of primary affective self-object representations within the context of early attachment relationships.

Beyond these assumptions, however, the views of the different schools of psychoanalysis diverge. For example, there are various theories about the underlying processes, representations, and variable developmental time-tables offering different accounts of *how* early affective experience with caregivers influences the formation of the representational structure of the self, and how these early experiences can in later life lead to pathological affective functioning (see Fonagy, Target, & Gergely, 2004, for a review). It is possible that even theories which share specific analytically-inspired developmental models disagree on the previously mentioned because psychoanalytic reconstructions of infancy are precisely that: retrospective attributions (*re*-constructions) drawn from adult patients and the transference phenomena and intersubjective processes observed during their treatment (Gergely, 1992, 2000; Lichtenberg, 1987, Fonagy, 2001; Fonagy, Target, & Gergely, 2004); however, psychoanalytic theories have recently begun to pay more attention to the significant empirical advances in the study of early attachment, social cognitive development, developmental psychopathology, evolutionary psychology, and the cognitive neurosciences (e.g., Allen & Fonagy, 2006; Beebe, Knoblauch, Rustin, & Sorter, 2005; Bowlby, 1969; Cassidy & Shaver, 1999; Fonagy, 2001; Fonagy & Bateman, 2006; Fonagy & Target, 1997; Fonagy, Gergely, & Target, 2007; Fonagy, Target, & Gergely, 2000; Fonagy, Gergely, Jurist, Target, 2002; Fonagy, Target, Gergely, Allen, & Bateman, 2003; Gergely, 2007a; Gergely & Unoka, in press; Gergely & Watson, 1996; Gergely, Fonagy, & Target, 2002; Hobson, 2002; Sander, 1988; Sroufe, 1996; Stern, 1985, Stern, Sander, Nahum, Harrison, Lyons-Ruth, Morgan, et al., 1998). As a result, more recent psychoanalytic theories have sought to explain the nature of the analytic process and the mechanisms of therapeutic change by drawing directly upon the models of early development arising from infancy research (and this has contributed to the development of various concepts including separation-individuation, attachment security, internal working models, attachment disorganization, primary intersubjectivity, moments of meeting, mentalization, reflective self function, psychic equivalence, or contingent reactivity and affect-mirroring).

This paper similarly seeks to integrate empirical research into infancy with psychoanalytic theory. We begin this integration by outlining a new theoretical framework that helps us to conceptualize the development of the representational affective self in humans and its role in emotional self-regulation and control. We construct this social cognitive model of emotional self-development through the use of advances in several areas of contemporary developmental science. We try to integrate our proposed developmental theory into pre-existing psychoanalytic theories of the etiology of affective self disorders. We then demonstrate the clinical value of our theoretical approach, showing how it can account for the core symptomatology of a patient suffering from a severely dysfunctional and limited capacity for awareness of his feelings, and from distorted perception and awareness of the intersubjective aspects of affective relationships. Finally, we discuss the clinical implications of the theory by showing how it can help us better to understand the practical difficulties that the patient's unreflective self functioning represents for different therapeutic intervention techniques.

The Social Construction of the Representational Affective Self in Humans

The Constitutional Self

With regard to an infant, the *constitutional self* (Gergely, 2007a; Gergely & Unoka, in press; Gergely & Watson, 1966, 1999; Fonagy et al., 2002; 2007) designates a complex prewired affective structural organization. In other words, it is characterized by genetically-based individual differences in temperamental traits (Kagan, 1994; Rothbart, 1989) and it also contains innate specifications of the core physiological and motor components of a number of basic emotion programs (Ekman, 1992; Ekman, Friesen, & Ellsworth, 1972; Izard & Malatesta, 1987; Tomkins, 1995; see also Darwin, 1872). Current research suggests that these categorical basic emotions (such as fear, anger, joy/interest, or disgust) are universally recognized and shared by adult humans across all cultures. The basic emotions have evolved from similar automatic coping systems present in several nonhuman social animal species, including primates (Panksepp, 1998; Suomi, 1999).

Basic emotion programs are automatic, in that they are prewired, procedurally represented and stimulus-driven (Ekman, 1992). They have evolved to generate quick and adequate coping responses (e.g., fight or flight) in order to deal with specific types of environmental threats to survival (e.g., predators, territorial conflicts, mating competition, etc.). Two major structural components emerge from these primary emotion programs: firstly, a specific pattern of physiological arousal responses, and, secondly, prewired emotion-specific motor routines. The latter component consists of two types of fixed behavioral automatisms: (a) stereotypic action tendencies (approach/ avoidance, fight/flight, etc.) and (b) emotion-expressive facial-vocal displays and bodily postures. The evolutionary function of both components is to provide specific coping responses as well as to modify environmental conditions in order to eliminate the threat posed.

In nonhuman animal species, basic emotion responses are on the whole controlled and activated automatically by prespecified inputs. Only a small number of stereotypic outcomes can result from the execution of these fixed behavioral components such as attack, threat displays, courting behavior, distress calls. These outcomes are the innately prespecified reactions they induce in other conspecifics (e.g., flight/fight, submission, acceptance/refusal of mating approaches). The range of possible effects of such stereotyped emotional interactions on the initial emotion-triggering environmental conditions is limited. The resulting environmental changes may terminate the organism's basic emotional arousal, inhibit its behavioral expressions, or activate a different basic emotion response.

Clearly, it is only in highly stable evolutionary niches that such prewired, stereotypic, and fully stimulus-controlled emotion programs can be adaptive. Indeed, the prespecified and modular structure of these behavioral coping systems must initially have evolved under the selective pressure of such an invariant and stable environment. This kind of stability, however, has become less and less characteristic of the increasingly more complex and changing social, technological, and cultural environment of early humans. In human social interactions, different individuals will respond to the same show of emotion in different ways, depending on their personality traits, social status, current mood, and how informed they are concerning relevant aspects of the present situation. As individuals develop, they acquire a wide variety of alternative and nonstereotypic emotional responses, the context-sensitive selective activation of which is under their cognitive voluntary control at least some if not all of the time. As a result, there can be great variation in the reactions that one's own displays of emotion can induce in others in different contexts. Along with the development of a wider number of possible consequences of emotion responses and the increasing range of social environmental conditions with which humans have had to cope, we argue that correspondingly significant changes have coevolved in the capacity of humans to inhibit and control their basic emotion responses. These changes have taken place in order to ensure the continued functional role of these emotion mechanisms as functional coping systems. In order to remain adaptive in the face of the previously mentioned conditions of variable environmental reactivity, the control systems of these basic emotion programs must have evolved to incorporate two mechanisms. First, they would need to be able to anticipate, represent, and evaluate the consequences of the self's specific emotional reactions under different situational and interpersonal contexts. Second, they would need to be able to inhibit or modify the automatic emotional responses as a function of their anticipated situation-specific effects.

However, based upon the observation of young infants' affective behavior, it seems that in early life no such flexible and context-sensitive emotion-control mechanisms exist. Generally, infants are unable to modulate or inhibit the automatic motor expressions of their basic emotional arousal states. Regulation of their affective states is in fact largely under the external control of the attachment figure, whose reactions influence the baby's behavior (Gergely, 2007a; Gergely & Watson, 1996, 1999; Sroufe, 1996; Tronick, 1989; Fonagy et al., 2002; 2007). Regulating the baby's emotional arousal can be achieved by at least two different mechanisms. First, it can be realized through maternal attachment reactions, the effects of which can modify the infant's emotional state (e.g., through the innate soothing effect that gentle bodily contact or the specific intonation pattern of motherese can induce in babies; see Fernald, 1985, 1992; Hofer, 1995; Cooper & Aslin, 1990; Polan & Hofer, 1999). Second, it can be achieved by actively changing the baby's environment, thereby changing the external conditions that trigger/maintain the infant's emotional arousal.

Based on repeatedly experiencing how the automatic emotion expressions can induce emotion-regulative social responses in the attachment environment, the young child starts to develop an increasing ability to anticipate and cope with a growing variety of situations by representing the typical consequences of the self's emotion reactions. The ability to construct representations of the likely outcomes of one's emotional responses in particular contexts requires event-monitoring and representation-building mechanisms that can register, analyze, and represent the characteristic causal dependencies between the self's particular emotion responses and the specific reactions they invoke in others.

The Contingency Detection Mechanism

The so-called *contingency detection mechanism* (Gergely & Watson, 1996, 1999; Watson, 1994) is an innate information-processing and representation-building device, which can construct the required type of experience-based and context-sensitive primary emotion representations. The contingency detection mechanism not only detects but also represents the *causal contingency relations* between the infant's specific responses and consequent environmental outcomes. It does this by registering over time the likelihood with which certain stimuli provoke certain responses in certain situational contexts (for technical details and review of supporting evidence, see Gergely, 2002, 2004, 2007a; Watson, 1985, 1994, 1995, 2001; Gergely & Watson, 1996, 1999; or Fonagy et al., 2002). The contingency detection device can also be used to identify and represent both the extent to which the infant has *causal control* over different responses of the social environment, and the specific contextual factors that have an impact on these causal effects (Watson, 1995, 2001). The resulting experience-based primary representations of the degree of causal efficacy of the infant's responses reflect the young child's developing *primary sense of self-efficacy and social self-agency* (Gergely, 2002; 2007a; Gergely & Watson, 1996).

Only one property of the contingency detection mechanism is relevant for our present purposes, and that is the fact that there are *two different (and independent) aspects of the causal dependency relation*, which in order to be monitored, requires the construction of *two separate representations*. In other words, not only is there the *specific target behavior of the self*, which can induce a certain response in the other and which must be represented in order to assess its causal efficacy, but there is also the *target response of the other*, which may or may not have been provoked by the self's behavior, and which must also be represented in order to assess the degree of causal connection.

Let us use an example from Watson (1995) to clarify this point: a boy is frightened, meaning that he automatically shows fear through his facial expression (negative emotion arousal). Seeing his facial expression, the mother promptly responds by picking the boy up. Upon monitoring what happens over the course of many similar and reoccurring episodes, we discover that the boy will, thanks to his contingency detection mechanism, work out that his mother will pick him up on, say, 80% of the occasions that he shows fear;

however, this does not mean that the boy's behavior alone is what causes his mother to pick him up (i.e., this is not a true measure of the causal efficacy of the boy's behavior). In order to get a closer measure of the causal efficacy of the boy's behavior, we must also take into account the mother's behavior. Let us say that the mother is over-controlling, physically intrusive, that she has an anxious, worried, and fearful disposition, or that she is emotionally unstable and insecure with a constant need for physical proximity. Any of these traits might result in the mother picking her boy up on more occasions than those when the boy has shown fear.

In order to take into account the occasions when the mother's response was *not* brought about by the boy's frightened expression, the contingency detection mechanism needs to (and does, see Watson, 1985, 1994; Gergely & Watson, 1996, 1999) separately monitor the occurrences of the maternal target behavior (picking the boy up), and it also gauges how often this gesture is preceded by the boy's fear-expressive display. If the boy shows fear on only 20% of the occasions that the mother picks the boy up, it would be misleading to say that the boy's show of fear prompts the mother to pick the boy up 80% of the time (i.e., that it has 80% causal efficacy). In fact, *both* values are required for a more accurate estimate and representation of the *actual* degree of causal relatedness between the two target events monitored (frightened facial expression; picking the boy up; see Watson, 1994; Gergely & Watson, 1996).

The contingency detection mechanism registers both of these values in order to measure to what extent one is caused by or is the result of the other. As a result, there are two separate representations for the two behavioral events: the so-called *sufficiency index*, which represents *the monitored target behavior of the infant and its degree of causal efficacy in bringing about the target response of the other*; and the *necessity index*, which represents *the monitored target response of the other and its degree of causal dependence on the preceding occurrence of the target response of the infant* (see Watson, 1994; Gergely & Watson, 1996).

Self-to-Other Versus Other-to-Self Emotion Schemes

When the contingency detection mechanism is applied to recurring scenarios that take place between infant and caregiver, we see that the resulting primary affective self-other representations have three features that seem to play a crucial role in establishing the infant's emerging capacity for emotional self-control, particularly when interacting with its caregiver. These key features are (a) representation of the *causal properties* of emotion responses (e.g., fear, both in terms of under what conditions it is triggered and the consequences of displaying it), (b) representation of their effects in different *situational and personal contexts* (i.e., the contexts within which the monitored emotional response takes place), and (c) the creation of *separate primary emotion schemes* that on the one hand represent the effects of the self's emotion responses in different situations and on the other hand represent the responses of different caregivers (together with their causal and situational properties). It stands to reason that the better an infant is able to represent these separate conditions (i.e., the better picture an infant has of the effects of his emotional responses in different situations and how they will affect his own behavior and reactions as well as those of different caregivers), the better that infant will be at adapting to different situations involving different caregivers. This is particularly helpful when the infant finds itself in situations where a caregiver is threatening the infant's well-being, whether physically or emotionally. In such instances, the ability to represent the likely causes and outcomes of such responses in different situations helps the infant to anticipate and potentially to prevent emotionally highly charged and possibly self-endangering interactions with particular caregivers in specific attachment contexts. It similarly allows the child an opportunity to generate coping strategies in these situations.

The contingency detection mechanism provides the infant with information about emotional interactions with caregivers through *two basic kinds of experience-based primary emotion representations*. These are self-to-other causal emotion schemes and other-to-self causal emotion schemes. Self-to-other emotion schemes represent the predictable consequences of a show of emotion to a particular attachment figure/caregiver in a particular context, both in terms of the likelihood of a specific response by the caregiver and in terms of the effect that the caregiver's response is likely to have on the environmental conditions/situation themselves. Other-to-self causal emotion schemes, meanwhile, represent the causal properties of certain monitored aspects of the probable behavior of the caregiver in certain contexts. The caregiver's behavior is monitored not only because it often takes place as a result of the infant's expression of emotion, but also because it can trigger a basic emotional reaction in the infant. Other-to-Self emotion schemes enable the infant to modify its expressions of emotion in order to avoid evoking a particular response from the caregiver.

Primary Response Inhibition and Substitution Mechanisms of Automatic Emotional Self-Control

Being able to anticipate, cope with and selectively avoid certain emotional responses are aspects of the capacity to control emotional self states. Humans can achieve different levels of affective self-regulation and coping during emotionally charged interactions through the application of two basic types of emotion control processes involving primary automatic versus secondary cognitive control mechanisms. Both of these emotion control systems make use of the representational contents of the Self-to-Other and Other-to-Self emotion schemes in order to anticipate and modulate the emotional consequences of particular types of attachment interactions.

What we may call the primary response inhibitory control mechanism automatically suppresses the behavioral expression (be it facially or otherwise) of a basic emotional arousal state (such as fear). One potential condition for the response inhibitory control mechanism to be triggered is when, as per a Self-to-Other emotion scheme, the behavioral expression of the emotion (making a frightened face) is anticipated (and is likely) to lead to severe negative consequences for the self in the given attachment context. Anticipation of these negative consequences has a direct and automatic inhibitory effect, which impedes the impending motor expression of the emotion.

This primary response-inhibitory emotion control mechanism is automatic and procedural. Evidence from attachment research indicates that this mechanism becomes operational in early life—as exemplified by the separation-induced response pattern observed in the Strange Situation Test (Ainsworth, Blehar, Waters, & Wall, 1978), in which certain 1-year-olds show avoidant attachment to their caregiver. That is, they do *not* exhibit the behavioral-expressive signs of distress or protest that we might otherwise expect from infants who have been separated from their caregiver (Ainsworth et al., 1978; Cassidy & Shaver, 1999; Goldberg, Muir, & Kerr, 1995). Despite the lack of apparent expressive response to separation, physiological measures such as heart-rate and cortisol-elevation indicate that—as with infants in other attachment categories—separation from the caregiver does still cause high negative emotional arousal and stress in these infants (see Spangler & Grossmann, 1993; Cassidy & Shaver, 1999).

It is worth noting that this automatic inhibition of the expression of separation-induced distress does not become general, but is *relationship-specific*. In other words, no strong correlation has been found between the types of attachment infants exhibit toward different caregivers, and infants who show avoidant attachment toward a particular caregiver do not automatically generalize their tendency to inhibit the expression of their negative emotional arousal to other attachment figures as well (see Cassidy & Shaver, 1999; Fonagy, 2001, for reviews). It seems rather that infants are avoidant toward a particular caregiver in order to prevent (or cope with) the systematically negative emotional reaction that the caregiver is anticipated to produce in response to the infant's own expressions of negative affect (Watson, 2001).

The infant's *Other-to-Self emotion schemes* can also trigger the automatic response-inhibitory control mechanism. These represent certain behavioral patterns of the caregiver that in the past have given rise to negative emotional arousal for the infant in certain attachment contexts. If the expression of the infant's negative emotional arousal has been experienced (and is therefore represented by the infant's Other-to-Self scheme) as a likely cause that can be anticipated to trigger the threatening behavior of the other, the activation of such an arousal state in the presence of the attachment figure can trigger the primary response-inhibitory coping reaction in the infant. The resulting automatic response-inhibition process will suppress the infant's expression of emotional arousal in order to avoid the realization of its anticipated negative consequences.

This kind of automatic response-inhibitory coping reaction has its limitations when exercised in isolation. First, because this coping reaction involves the inhibition of the *expression* of an emotion, but not the inhibition of the physiological arousal reaction (e.g., the infant cannot stop its heart-rate from increasing, even if its face betrays no fear), this negative physiological arousal remains unmodified and unmodulated. Second, *not* to express an emotional reaction means that the conditions that triggered the (admittedly inhibited) response remain unchanged. In other words, to inhibit the expression of its own response can leave the infant in an uncontrolled and continued state of heightened physiological arousal and stress. The long-term toxic effects of such a condition can cause a rigid and dysfunctional organization of the physiological stress-regulation system (Francis & Meaney, 1999; Francis, Diorio, Liu, & Meaney, 1999; Fonagy et al., 2002; Pruessner, Champagne, Meaney, & Dagher, 2004; Wismer Fries, Ziegler, Kurian, Jacoris, & Pollak, 2005). In order to avoid these toxic effects, one must apply a second type of primary emotion control mechanism, which involves not just response inhibition, but *response substitution.* This mechanism *automatically activates a suitable substitute behavior* that has a high probability of changing the environmental conditions that originally triggered the infant's basic emotional arousal. It stands to reason, however, that this can only take place if the infant has a wide range of alternative and suitable substitute responses.*

Dealing With Unfamiliar Persons and Situations

In order to regulate its emotions during early affective interactions, we have argued that the infant employs a repertoire of primary emotion representations as part of its automatic primary emotion control mechanism. However, this primary emotional control mechanism has several limitations in terms of scope and flexibility, because the Self-to-Other and the Other-to-Self emotion schemes are stimulus-driven and automatic. Furthermore, especially during

---

* Watson (1995) offers a strong example of this: A young child has been put to bed, and its mother is about to leave the room. We might expect separation from the mother to induce negative emotional arousal and distress in the baby, which might then be expressed either through the baby crying or raising its arms in order to be picked up. However, if the situation is such that the baby recognizes signals of irritability and fatigue in the mother, a Self-to-Other emotion scheme might be activated in the infant, meaning that it not only inhibits its initial response (which might otherwise trigger anger and shouting in the mother, which would in turn elevate the baby's negative arousal), but it also adopts a substitute response (such as telling the mother that it loves her), which does induce the mother to pick it up, and which thereby avoids not only the mother's anger but also the potentially prolonged and unmodulated state of negative emotional arousal that a simple inhibition of the initial response might have provoked. As explained, this scheme of course requires that the infant has a repertoire of alternative reactions represented by its Self-to-Other emotion schemes.

the earlier stages of life, these primary emotion schemes represent only a limited number of recurring affective attachment interactions for the infant, meaning that there is only a limited number of circumstances in which they can be adaptively used.

However, as the infant develops, it discovers an increasing number of interpersonal contexts for affective interactions, which often involve unfamiliar persons and situations. Because the infant's primary emotion schemes are automatic and stimulus-driven, it is by definition impossible for the infant to cope with a new and unfamiliar person or situation that are not 'recognized' by (and do not trigger) its primary emotion schemes. To cope with such novel environmental challenges the infant needs to rely on an additional *secondary mechanism of emotion control*, which is not automatic and involves *cognitive reappraisal processes* (e.g., Lazarus, 1991, Lazarus and Lazarus, 1994; LeDoux, 2000; Thompson, 1994; Ellsworth & Scherer, 2003; Ochsner & Gross, 2005; Posner & Rothbart, 2000). Increasing experience with a growing variety of interpersonal situations allows the child to develop a pool of relevant knowledge that its top-down cognitive secondary appraisal processes can rely on in order to evaluate the significance that new types of input conditions represent for the self. Based upon these cognitive evaluations, the top-down executive action control systems can then activate the relevant emotion responses to cope with the situation.

A further potential problem arises when a new and unfamiliar situation has the appearance of a familiar interactive context (as represented by some of the self's primary Self-to-Other or Other-to-Self emotion schemes), and therefore automatically activates a primary and procedural emotion representation, which in turn triggers an emotion reaction that is inappropriate for the current situation. Without a secondary cognitive mechanism in place, the risk of an inappropriate response is greatly increased and so, in order to control such dysfunctional automatic activation of primary emotion schemes, the growing child must once again rely on a *top-down process of secondary cognitive re-appraisal* of current situational cues (e.g., Lazarus, 1991; Thompson, 1994; Ellsworth & Scherer, 2003; Ochsner & Gross, 2005) in order to inhibit and override an inappropriate primary response. Two related aspects of these secondary cognitive processes are key to the ontogenetically developing capacity for top-down control over one's primary and automatic emotional responses. First, the secondary cognitive processes can draw upon previous information and infer from current information in order to reinterpret the significance for the self of the *causal evoking conditions* that initially automatically activated the primary emotional reaction. This process can override the automatic and primary emotional response (LeDoux, 1995, 1996, 2000; Ochsner & Gross, 2005). Second, the secondary cognitive processes can also evaluate the likely ramifications/*causal consequences* of any spuriously activated automatic response.

We should note that, for the secondary cognitive reappraisal processes to function, several preconditions must be fulfilled. First, if top-down cognitive processes are to allow an individual to control their primary emotional responses, then the cognitive emotion control system must be able to monitor, detect and introspectively access cues that signal the onset of a basic emotional reaction. Second, internal state signals must be sufficiently differentiated to enable the correct identification and self-attribution of the particular emotion category that has been triggered. Third, the cognitive process of secondary reappraisal must have access to enough stored or inferred information about a certain situation and/or person that it can reevaluate the situation and redirect the emotional response. What is more, the secondary cognitive mechanisms must work at a fast enough rate that they can perform these tasks *before* the automatic behavioral response kicks in.

Species-Unique Features of the Human Attachment System and Its Functions

Humans are unique (differing even from our closest primate relatives) in terms of the structural organization of early attachment interactions, which possess an apparently human-specific proto-conversational *turn-taking contingency structure* (Brazelton & Tronick, 1980; Brazelton, Koslowski, & Main, 1974; Sander, 1988; Stern, 1985; Trevarthen, 1979; Trevarthen & Aitken, 2001; Tronick, 1989; Tronick & Cohn, 1989). During infancy, humans prefer *highly response-contingent stimulus events*, which are typical of the interactive style of infant-attuned social partners (Bigelow, 1999; Bigelow & De Coste, 2003; Bigelow & Rochat, 2006; Watson, 1972, 1985, 1994; Bahrick & Watson, 1985; Rochat & Morgan, 1995; Lewis, Allessandri, & Sullivan, 1990). Human infants are also especially sensitive toward so-called *ostensive-communicative cues* (Csibra & Gergely, 2006), such as *eye-contact* (Farroni, Csibra, Simion, & Johnson, 2002), *infant-directed speech/'motherese'* (Fernald, 1985, 1992; Cooper & Aslin, 1990), and *contingent reactivity* (Floccia, Christophe, & Bertoncini, 1997; Johnson, Slaughter, & Carey, 1998; Movellan & Watson, 2002; Watson, 1994, 1995, 2001). Young human infants spontaneously follow the *referential cues* of others (e.g., following someone else's gaze), but only if these cues are preceded by direct eye-contact and/or infant-contingent reactivity (Farroni et al. 2002; Johnson et al. 1998; Movellan & Watson, 2002; see Csibra & Gergely, 2006, for a review). By one year, human infants show *communicative and referential understanding* and use of *pointing* in triadic joint attention interactions—a competence that sets them apart from apes (see Behne, Carpenter, & Tomasello, 2005; Liszkowski, Carpenter, Henning, Striano, & Tomasello, 2004; Tomasello & Haberl, 2003; Tomasello, Carpenter, & Liszkowski, 2007; Southgate, van Maanen, & Csibra, 2007). There are also frequent *exchanges of an increasingly differentiated repertoire of basic emotion expressions* during the interactions between mother and infant (Camras, 1992; Gergely, 2002, 2007a; Gergely & Watson, 1996, 1999; Sroufe, 1996; Tronick, 1989; Cohn & Tronick, 1988; Izard & Malatesta, 1987; Bennett, Bendersky, & Lewis, 2004, 2005; Malatesta, Culver, Tesman, & Shepard, 1989).

Compared to other species, including primates, humans make significantly more and increasingly frequent displays of emotion during infant-caregiver interactions (see De Marco & Visalberghi, 2007). Similarly unique to human mother-infant interactions are empathic *affect-mirroring emotion displays* by the caregiver (Bigelow, 1999; Gergely, 2004, 2007a; Gergely & Watson, 1996, 1999; Tronick, 1989; Cohn & Tronick, 1988; Fonagy et al. 2002, 2007; Malatesta et al., 1989; Uzgiris, Benson, Kruper, & Vasek, 1989). Now many popular developmental and attachment theories argue that infants have a rich mentalistic interpretation of early interactions thanks to their capacity for primary intersubjectivity. These theories assume that the human infant from the first months of life has access to, recognizes in itself, and can recognize in and even share with others (especially the caregiver) a variety of mental states, including emotions, goals, intentions, or motives (see Trevarthen, 1979, 1993; Trevarthen & Aitken, 2001; Braten, 1988, 1992, 1998; Meltzoff, 2002; Meltzoff & Gopnik, 1993; Meltzoff & Moore, 1977, 1989, 1998;

Hobson, 1993, 2002; Stern, 1985; Giannino & Tronick, 1988). Such assumptions have been criticized elsewhere for attributing too rich a mentalizing capacity to young infants (see Gergely, 2002, 2007a; Gergely & Watson, 1996, 1999; Fonagy et al. 2002, 2007, for details), and at least one more parsimonious alternative model of early socio-emotional self-development has been proposed (Gergely & Watson, 1996, 1999; Fonagy et al. 2002). This alternative model hypothesizes that the child's awareness of different emotional states in itself and in others has its origins in social interaction and that this awareness is (relatively) hard-won rather than being a universally given prewired capacity.

Furthermore, this alternative model proposes that the growing infant learns to differentiate emotions through repeated experience not just of the emotion itself, but also of the caregiver's contingent mirroring reaction to that emotion. In other words, it is only through the repeated experience of anger *and* the contingent external feedback reactions that its expression evokes in others that we can learn to differentiate anger from undifferentiated negative tension. This model of *the development of introspectively accessible emotional self-representations* is based on two central assumptions: the initially *introspectively inaccessible constitutional affective self* and the *social interactive origins of affective subjectivity*.

The *introspectively inaccessible constitutional affective self* involves the assumption that the infant has a highly structured, innate constitutional self. The constitutional self is characterized by genetically based individual differences of temperament (e.g., Kagan, 1994; Rothbart, 1989). Furthermore, it contains a basic set of prewired universal categorical emotion programs, which are primary biological adaptations (Ekman, 1992; Ekman et al., 1972; Gergely & Watson, 1996). As argued earlier, these basic emotions are best understood as prewired and automatic; they are not initially conscious and cannot be voluntarily controlled. At first, it is the caregiver who is mainly responsible for regulating the infant's emotional arousal states during attachment interactions. The caregiver achieves this by reading the infant's automatic emotion expressions and reacting to them with appropriate affect-modulating interactions and emotion displays (Gergely, 2007a; Gergely & Watson, 1996, 1999; Fonagy et al. 2002). Therefore, the infant may be able to tell positive and negative emotion states apart, but, beyond this general impression, it has no initial introspective awareness of the difference between its various emotion states, and the constitutional affective self is at first deemed introspectively inaccessible (Gergely & Watson, 1996). We further hypothesize (contrary to classical approaches, such as Bruner, Olver, & Greenfield, 1966; Mahler, Pine, & Bergman, 1975; cf. Gergely, 2000) that the attention system is initially prewired to be dominantly externally oriented. It is assumed that very little introspective monitoring of internal self states takes place in the earliest months of life (see Gergely & Watson, 1996, 1999; Fonagy et al. 2002, for supporting arguments).

Now let us discuss the social interactive origins of affective subjectivity: the development of introspectively accessible emotional self-representations. Here, we assume that two basic conditions must be fulfilled before the infant can begin to introspect about and subjectively experience his internal emotion states. First, the primary and automatic emotion programs must become associated with second-order representations, which, once activated, allow the cognitive self-monitoring processes to begin. This process must also involve a change of direction in the infant's attentional system, from being outwardly directed to being partially directed toward the self's internal states, which enables the active, introspective monitoring and detection of the activation of the self's second-order emotion representations. Thereafter, the infant can perceive itself as being in a particular emotion state whenever the basic emotions are automatically aroused to which the second-order emotion representations are associatively linked.

Once this has been achieved, and the child can recognize its own emotion states, it will continuously update its emotional self representations, since the states themselves are dynamically changing. Therefore, when a basic emotional arousal state is activated, the child can anticipate its own emotion-induced behavior, and, becoming aware of its own dispositional state change *before* the automatic activation of the primary emotion-induced action-tendencies can take effect, it can control its own response (Gergely & Watson, 1996). Our ability to detect our self states, update our state representations and thereby to improve our ability for emotional self-control develops as a result of social feedback, which comes in the form of repeated and congruent reactions to the child's (initially nonconscious) emotion expressive behaviors in the attachment environment. This feedback brings the child into awareness by externally mirroring or reflecting the infant's inner emotion state, thereby facilitating the development of the infant's subjective sense and awareness of its differentiated affective self states. Of course, this mirroring would be irrelevant if infants did not have the innate capacity to detect and to represent both the automatic expression of different emotion states and the ways in which these affect the environment that provoked them. This capacity enables them to internalize the representation of any external mirroring feedback signals as a second-order representation of the primary self state whose automatic expression invokes the contingent mirroring reaction in question.

This theory ties in with previous work on the *social biofeedback theory* of parental affect-mirroring (Gergely & Watson, 1996, 1999), in which the infant's contingency detection device has the necessary structural properties to establish second-order emotion representations when applied to contingent affect-mirroring interactions. That is to say, the infant is innately capable of analyzing the degree of contingent relatedness between the infant's responses and subsequent external events (Watson, 1985, 1994). The infant simultaneously monitors three separate aspects of contingent relatedness (temporal contingency, spatial similarity, and relative intensity; see Gergely & Watson, 1999, for a review), thereby identifying those aspects of the social environment that are, to a greater or lesser extent, under the *causal control* of the infant's expressions of emotion states. The child's ability to work out the extent of its causal control over the social environment is important, because it also provides the child with a subjective experience of agency.

Marked Expressions and Knowledge Transfer

Human infant-caregiver interactions differ from other species for another reason: human caregivers can produce *marked affect-mirroring expressions* as a result of the baby's automatic emotion displays. These marked affect-mirroring expressions are *deliberately modified versions* of the automatic displays that the caregiver normally uses to express its affective states (Gergely, 2007a; Gergely & Watson, 1996, 1999; Fonagy et al., 2002). Examples include exaggerated, slowed down, schematic, abbreviated or only partial execution of the normal display of emotion, and these are often accompanied by *ostensive-communicative cues* (such as direct eye-contact, eye-brow raising, motherese vocal intonation; see Csibra & Gergely, 2006).

In the past, we emphasized the importance of this markedness as a cue to signal that the displayed emotion is not for real and that it should therefore be decoupled from the caregiver/that the attribution of the marked response as real should be inhibited (Gergely & Watson, 1996). We have also proposed (see Gergely, 2007a; Gergely & Unoka, in press) that these marked interactions constitute a form of cultural knowledge transfer (Csibra & Gergely, 2006; Gergely, 2007b; Gergely & Csibra, 2005, 2006), particularly with regard to the socialization of emotions. With this latter pedagogical function of marked interactions in mind, we can extend the theory in two directions. First, we can offer a theory as to *why* marked affect-mirroring displays become interpreted self-referentially by the infant, meaning that they become internalized as second-order emotion representations that are associatively linked to the infant's own primary emotions. Second, we explicate how marked responses help the infant to change the direction of its attention system from a predominantly external bias to an *internal* direction that enables the infant introspectively to monitor its internal affective states.

The previously mentioned theory of marked emotions forming a type of cultural knowledge transfer is a specific application of a recently developed theory arguing that humans have a species-unique social communicative learning system of natural pedagogy (Csibra & Gergely, 2006; Gergely, 2007b; Gergely, Király, & Egyed, 2007). According to this evolutionary-based theory of cultural transmission, humans have evolved so as spontaneously to manifest relevant cultural knowledge to conspecifics who are similarly inclined to notice and learn from these manifestations—thanks to a specialized cue-driven social communicative learning mechanism of mutual design. This system of natural pedagogy guarantees the intergenerational transfer of several forms of relevant cultural knowledge, including words, gestures, artifacts, social habits, rituals, and so forth (Gergely, 2007b; Gergely and Csibra, 2005, 2006; Gergely, Bekkering, & Kiraly, 2002, Gergely et al., 2007; Csibra & Gergely, 2006).

We argue that natural pedagogy is also employed in the domain of emotion socialization to teach infants to recognize in themselves those categorical emotions that are culturally universal and shared among humans. In this view, early infant-caregiver affective interactions (involving ostensively cued marked forms of contingent emotion-mirroring) constitute a special case of pedagogical knowledge transfer whereby sensitive caregivers establish second-order representations in infants that enable them to identify the categorical emotions that are culturally universal and can be communicated to other humans.

Human natural pedagogy has a *mutual design structure*, which involves a biological predisposition toward providing and receiving relevant cultural information. Caregivers transfer knowledge to juveniles through *ostensive communicative cues* (eye-contact, eyebrow flashing, motherese), which are followed by *referential cues* (such as gaze-shift), which help the infant to identify the referent object about which new information is to be demonstrated, and which trigger in the infant a specially receptive learning attitude. These ostensive referential cues prompt the infant to learn about the referent object, the new and relevant knowledge manifested by the communicating other (cf. Sperber & Wilson, 1986). These manifestations of relevant information are performed in a marked manner that involves a *modified version* of the cultural knowledge skill that is being demonstrated for the infant to learn. For example, when a caregiver shows a child how to hammer a nail for the first time, it does so in a marked manifestative form, as opposed to the standard motor execution of the same routine when it is performed simply to drive a nail in. Thanks to these cues, the child understands not only that the caregiver is manifesting relevant and culturally shared information about the referent, but they also signal that the other is doing so with the explicit communicative intent to transfer this knowledge to the child. The marked form of expression allows the mother to foreground the new and relevant informational content for the juvenile learner to identify, helping it to infer which aspects of the manifested knowledge should be encoded—by extracting and then internalizing the foregrounded/marked information (see Gergely, 2007b, for details).

Pedagogical cues lead the infant to identify the intended referent of the caregiver's marked emotion manifestation, and to link, or to anchor, the mirroring display to some referent *other* than the caregiver's actual emotion state (from which it has been decoupled due to the marking). The infant relies on cues such as eye-gaze direction to identify the referent and because the caregiver will be looking at the infant while displaying marked emotion-reflecting expressions, the infant's attention will therefore be directed toward its *own* face and body as the likely locus of the referent—not least because the caregiver mirrors the automatic facial-vocal emotion expressions that emanate from the infant's face and body. The infant's contingency detection mechanism therefore identifies its own expressions of emotion as the source of contingent control over the caregiver's mirroring response (see Gergely & Watson, 1996). These two sources of information converge, meaning that the infant will referentially anchor the representation of the marked mirroring display to its own primary emotion program, and internalize it as its second-order representation.

Through this process, we see how caregivers can naturally teach the infant about its differential categorical emotion states, establishing cognitively accessible and culturally shared and communicable second-order emotion representations by providing marked and contingent social biofeedback mirroring accompanied by ostensive communicative cues. Furthermore, as a result of such natural social biofeedback training the infant's attentional system becomes increasingly introspective and can better detect and monitor the activation of the self's affective states. Sensitivity to the internal proprioceptive cues that accompany emotional self-expressions is also heightened as a result. Further consequences include the development of subjective awareness and the subsequent deliberate/voluntary use of emotion responses in order to exert control over the social environment.

Through these processes, we see that the infant's social mirroring-environment plays a significant role in establishing the introspectively detectable subjective self by populating it with cognitively accessible second-order representations of internal affective self states. It is thanks to this representational structure that—together with the infant's introspectively socialized attentional system—the emergence of top-down cognitive emotional self-monitoring and secondary reappraisal processes become possible.

Mentalization

By increasing the efficacy and range of the secondary cognitive reappraisal processes, mentalization can play a key role in enhancing one's ability to achieve top-down cognitive emotional self-regulation and control. From the evolutionary perspective (cf. Sperber & Hirschfeld, 2004), one can speculate that the capacity for mentalization originally arose solely to infer and represent the causal intentional mental states of *other minds*. The ability to read other minds has enormous potential benefits, because it allows the mind-reader to anticipate the likely actions of other conspecifics in competitive situations (see Fonagy, this book). However, following on from the previously mentioned argument, in which humans develop the capacity to monitor their own behavior, we hypothesize that the proper evolutionary domain (cf. Sperber & Hirschfeld, 2004) of mentalization becomes ontogenetically extended to include reading not just the minds of others, but one's own mind as well. There are significant advantages to this hypothesis: reading one's own mind would result in significantly better coping strategies in both competitive and cooperative interactions and affective relationships, because the self would become able to anticipate its *own* actions and reactions as well as those of others.

If mentalization is a system based upon inference to mental states from observable cues, how is it applied introspectively in order to control one's own emotions and to help cope with affectively charged interpersonal interactions? If mentalization can provide useful information that instructs the self's secondary cognitive emotion re-appraisal mechanisms, then it would do so when top-down cognitive processes are applied to re-evaluate the significance for the self of the *causal input conditions* (which themselves involve another person's actions, reactions, or emotion expressions directed toward the self) that have induced one's primary and automatic emotional arousal reactions. In such cases, mentalization could support secondary cognitive re-appraisals by accessing and evaluating relevant stored information about the other person (their enduring mental dispositions, their self-related attitudes, their long-term aspirations, their temperamental and personality traits, their recent life events) in order to reconstruct/understand the reasons for their self-directed actions. Similarly, mentalization can help the subject to infer from others' cues what particular present desires, intentions, and (possibly false) beliefs about the situation and/or about one's own self may have induced the other's behavior, which in turn has triggered one's automatic basic emotional arousal response.

Mentalization can also help us cognitively to evaluate the likely *causal consequences* of the expression of our basic emotional arousal reactions in a given interpersonal context. Not only can mentalization help humans to predict the social consequences of their own expressions of emotion states, but it can also help predict what mental states and consequent actions the self's automatic emotion-induced responses are likely to induce in particular others. Mentalization enables the individual to take into account a wide range of potential factors that may motivate the reactions of another person in a given situation; as previously mentioned, these include temperamental features, personality traits, childhood history, current dispositional states, his or her quality of relationship with the self, how much or how little and precisely what the other knows or thinks about one's own self, and so forth. Importantly, in generating predictions about the other's likely reactions to one's own potential emotional expressions, a good mentalizer can also take into account *the other's mentalizing skills*, and the fact that the latter may also be evaluating the reasons behind the emotional reactions *of both parties* in a given situation.

The Development of Unreflective Affective Self Organization: A Clinical Application

In the following clinical case vignette we apply our model of affective self-development to shed light on the etiology of the patient's unreflective self structure.

The Case of Andy: Dysfunctions of Mentalizing About Affects and the Development of Unreflective Self Functioning.

A) Background: Andy's early attachment relationships.
   Andy is a 24-year-old male patient currently in psychoanalytic treatment three times a week on the couch.* He is an only child. His mother developed post-partum psychosis following Andy's birth. Since then she has continued to experience regular and severe psychotic episodes leading to frequent hospitalizations. Her thought processes were dominated by paranoid ideation, persecutory delusions, and hallucinatory states that persisted even when sedated due to antipsychotic medication. To control her spirits and her paranoid hallucinatory fears of being poisoned by her doctors, Andy's mother spent much of her time with a sock pulled over her head or with large dark sunglasses over her eyes. Due to her paranoid and/or sedated states, most of the time she was unable to respond to Andy's various attempts to emotionally

---

* The patient's analyst is Zsolt Unoka.

engage or relate to her. All the emotions that Andy displayed in his mother's presence (whether proximity seeking, distress signals, expressions of love, playfulness, sadness, fear, anger, rage, crying, or other signs of helplessness) were met with stress-inducing and frightening emotional reactions of often traumatizing intensity: she would become severely annoyed, agitated, fearful and frightened, or aggressive (sometimes physically threatening or actually abusing her son). Often Andy's emotional overtures (regardless of their specific affective content) could also result in immediate and severe mental and emotional disintegration and destabilization of his mother.

These episodes of his mother going crazy as a result of Andy's expressions of feelings and needs and attempts to communicate with her were traumatic, and Andy experienced them as threatening his own emotional, mental, and physical self integrity. Andy's mother's frightening psychotic episodes also occurred frequently and largely unpredictably on other occasions, induced by unknown internal or external factors that were unrelated to Andy's behavior. She often showed unpredictable rage or fright, or she became suddenly withdrawn and unresponsive. Sometimes in her hallucinatory states she perceived her son as being her persecutor. On such occasions she often threatened him physically and verbally, or sometimes went on to actually attack him and beat him up.

Andy's parents had an early divorce and so Andy was left to live mostly alone with his deranged mother. His father lived close by, however, and came to the rescue when absolutely needed. He tried to help and defend his son by teaching him many practical behavioral strategies to monitor, anticipate and cope with his mother's disintegrative psychotic states (e.g., to attend to specific behavioral signs often preceding her psychotic episodes, to monitor and modify her medication according to the perceived changes in her level of agitated emotional state, or to know when—and when not—to call the ambulance). However, he systematically dismissed his son's emotional reactions and expressions of attachment needs as useless and even harmful in relation to the ongoing task of vigilantly monitoring and controlling the ups-and-downs of his mother's disintegrative emotional states. He criticized his son's helpless and fearful feelings as "not manly" and told him that his mother's problems were "not so serious, not to be frightened of, and not worth crying about." Andy's father portrayed his ex-wife's "crazy" states as "not that big of a deal," as something to simply watch out for and "handle and solve" in a practical manner by anticipating them in time and doing what his mother wants or needs to control them. Otherwise, Andy was taught to simply wait until the "craziness" receded while keeping calm, as when he became emotional this could provoke further disintegration in his mother's state.

B) Core symptoms of Andy's affective self functioning in adulthood.

    1. Panic attacks and dread of losing emotional self-control.   Andy initially sought therapeutic help for his frequent and unpredictable severe panic attacks involving strong vegetative bodily reactions (palpitation, sweating, dyspnea). The central cognitive component of these panic attacks was the anticipation and intense fear of imminent loss of control over his overly tense, but rather unspecific and diffuse, emotional state of agitation. During his panic attacks he was terrified of "going crazy" or "becoming schizophrenic like my mother" if his uncontrollable emotions were unleashed. When asked about the causes of these attacks, he described predominantly external factors: perceiving the word "crazy" or "schizophrenic" in any context (e.g., when reading about the Hungarian economy being in a "schizophrenic state"), or perceiving (often contrary to reality) a disturbing and intensifying change in other people's (e.g., his partner's) emotional states or reactions to his own shows of feeling. (This also happened when Andy was alone fantasizing about interactive situations and imagining others' emotional reactions to his presence or behavior). His panic attacks and fear of "going crazy" are well illustrated by a dream reported in the early phase of his treatment: Andy dreamt about a lonely man in chains in the middle of the desert. The man was "crazy" and "in a terrible and terrifying rage" trying to tear off his chains. In the dream Andy sometimes experienced the crazy man as being himself, sometimes saw him from an external perspective as somebody else; however, in both cases he was terrified about what would happen if the man succeeded in breaking his chains and let loose his aggressive rage.

    2. Distorted subjective experience of emotional states of the self and others in real or fantasized object relationships.

        a) Lack of introspective awareness of affective self experiences and nonmentalistic teleological interpretation of others' behavior.   At the beginning of his treatment Andy showed a striking lack of emotional involvement when describing even the most horrifying life events from his childhood (or his present relationship difficulties). At this stage, he seemed almost completely unaware of his own feelings and rarely described how he had felt during what must have been affectively highly charged episodes. A further salient aspect of his descriptions of his object relationships was his focus on others' visible behavior. He obsessively and vigilantly monitored the other's visible state expressions and behavioral cues. He appeared to be constantly on guard to pick up minute behavioral signs that could be taken to indicate changes in the other's feelings. The focus of this vigilant attentional monitoring, however, was always highly restricted and stereotypic: He was searching for signs of emotional destabilization in the other, or signs of the other becoming irritated, discontent, or angry with him. Although he was obsessed with trying to figure out (and satisfy) what the other wanted of him, his interpretations of the other's behavior remained shallow and unreflective, lacking any mentalistic account of what intentions, motives, or beliefs might lie behind the other's perceived behavior. Elsewhere (Fonagy et al., 2002) we have called this kind of nonmentalistic externalist interpretation of others that is restricted to the goal-directed interpretation of visible behaviors, actions, and their observable effects, the *teleological mode of construal** of interactive experience.

b) The 'Causal Illusion': Confusing the anticipated effects of one's emotions with their instigating causes leading to a distorted perception of affective states in others. Andy's obsessive monitoring of the other's behavior often led to mistaken and distorted perceptions of alarming emotional changes in the other. These mistakenly attributed emotional reactions were perceived by Andy as *real external causal events* that threatened him with (anticipated and feared) disintegration of his self: losing control over his emotions and "going crazy." But what was the source of these misattributions? Our clinical observations suggested that when Andy became emotionally aroused

---

* This terminology refers to the application of an ontogenetically very early interpretational system for representing goal-directed actions of other agents, the so-called "teleological stance" (Csibra & Gergely, 1998; Gergely & Csibra, 2003). This action interpretation system is functional in human infants already during the first year of life (Gergely, Nádasdy, Csibra, & Bíró, 1995; Csibra, Bíró, Koós, & Gergely, 2003) and may not yet rely on any mentalistic constructs in representing the other's intentional actions.

in an interpersonal situation, he could not attend to the physiological cues signaling his internal emotional reaction because he was focused exclusively on monitoring the other's behavior. Therefore, he mostly remained subjectively unaware of and introspectively blind to the changes in his own feelings.

We hypothesize, however, that whenever his basic emotions were triggered, his physiological arousal automatically activated his corresponding Self-to-Other emotion schemes. These included the representations of the typical *consequences* that his automatic emotion expressions used to induce in his caregivers during early childhood. Because his mother generally reacted with undifferentiated and traumatizing rage or disintegration to the *whole range of his emotional repertoire*, most of Andy's primary Self-to-Other emotion schemes came to include the representations of such traumatizing effects as the likely outcomes of his emotional response. Therefore, whenever the primary representation of any one of these basic emotions became activated, it uniformly led to anxious anticipation of emotional disintegration or rage in the other. These traumatizing emotional reactions of his mother—which also often occurred unpredictably—must have become represented in Andy's Other-to-Self emotion schemes as well.

His mother's rages and emotional disintegration were frequently experienced as emotion triggering external events that threatened to result in the disintegration of his own affective self. As a result, Andy's attentional system remained dominantly externally focused on vigilantly monitoring for signs of these dangerous target states of emotional disintegration or rage in others. Andy's primary relationships (both with his psychotic mother and his distant father who provided Andy with only externally oriented behavioral coping strategies) were similar in that they provided him with an attachment environment that showed no differential reactivity to his displays of emotion with regard to contingent reactions or marked affect-mirroring responses, which were absent in both parents. Earlier we hypothesized that differential and contingent reactivity and marked mirroring of the infant's automatic emotion expressions are central requirements for the development of introspective access to primary affective self states. They turn the—initially dominantly externally oriented—attentional system in an introspective direction of self-monitoring and lead to the internalization of differentiated second-order representations for the self's primary emotions.

We hypothesize that the practical absence of these developmental preconditions in Andy's case must have significantly contributed to his introspective blindness to his own emotional states. The lack of a contingently reactive mirroring environment must have led to the maintenance of Andy's dominantly external attentional orientation and vigilant monitoring of others' behavior. Due to this fixation of the other-directed orientation of Andy's attention, when he was in a basic emotional arousal state, his attentional focus got kidnapped by the activated representation of the *external consequences* that his emotional response would be likely to induce in the other. The emotional content of these Self-to-Other effect representations in Andy's case happened to be largely identical with the contents of the target events represented in his Other-to-Self emotion schemes: they both represented his mother's frequent and traumatizing emotional rage or disintegration. However, in the first case these maternal emotion responses were represented as the expectable consequences, while in the latter case as the likely causes of Andy's emotional arousal reactions. As a result, the activation of his Self-to-Other affective outcome representations that were triggered by his internal emotional arousal can easily overflow and trigger his Other-to-Self emotion representations as the contents of the two representations greatly overlap. In this way his own emotional arousal could lead to the reality-distorting perception of emotional destabilization or rage in the *other person*. This is why Andy experienced his own primary emotional arousal states as *actually occurring external causal events* directed at him and threatening to result in the disintegration of his affective self.

We refer to this specific kind of reality-distorting object perception as *the causal illusion* because its occurrence is facilitated by the fact that due to their identical contents the activated representations of emotion-induced *consequences* and emotion-inducing *causes* become mixed up in the patient's subjective experience. This type of reality-distorting perceptual confusion of aspects of the activated mental representation of one's own internal emotion states with corresponding realistically perceived events in the external world is similar to the psychic equivalence mode of mental functioning described by Fonagy and Target (1996, 1997, see also Fonagy et al., 2002). It seems theoretically important to point out that the type of reality-distorting perception of affects exemplified by the "causal illusion" described above may be easily confused at the clinical or phenomenological level with classical defensively motivated projective phenomena. However, whereas both involve reality-distorting perceptual experience of object relationships, they are clearly different in psychodynamically important respects. The reality-distortion in classical projection results from the defensive operation of detaching the representation of some undesirable affective content of the self and attributing it to the other through projection. In the case of the *causal illusion* described here, however, no defensive motive is served by the reality-distorting perception of one's own emotional arousal as self-endangering affective states of the other. Rather, this phenomenon is more akin to a kind of *abnormal perceptual illusion*.

Due to the dominant external focus and other-oriented fixation of Andy's attentional affect-monitoring system, the internally activated representation of the likely external consequences of his primary emotion response prevented him from being aware of the internal physiological emotional arousal cues themselves. Andy consciously perceived only the anticipated external consequences of his emotion response, while his internal emotional arousal state remained non-conscious. In his subjective experience this perception appeared to be caused by the other's corresponding external emotion reactions. Due to their identical contents, the activated representations of the anticipated and feared consequences of his unconscious emotional reaction triggered the representations of the vigilantly monitored and feared target behaviors of the other (as these are represented in his Other-to-Self emotion schemes). They become experienced as part of actual reality out there that is threatening the self, while the internal arousal state remains largely outside of consciousness.

c) Subjective sense of emotional isolation: Affective freezing and lack of sense of emotional self-agency. One consequence of Andy's distorted or mistaken perception that the other was emotionally disintegrating or showing signs of threatening emotional reactions was his immediate inhibition of his emotional responses. This automatic reaction of total affective freezing was a central symptom that characterized Andy's experience of emotional interactions with others. Importantly, the inhibition of his own emotion expression occurred both when he actually and correctly perceived the vigilantly monitored default target state of emotional destabilization in the other, or when he himself became emotionally aroused which—due to the constellation of the causal illusion discussed earlier—led to the distorted subjective perception of the other's alarming emotional state change. We suggest that this radical inhibition of emotional expression was an automatic coping reaction induced by the activation of Andy's primary affective self-other representations which originate from his early experiences with his mother. Andy's primary Self-to-Other schemes represented the other's emotional destabilization as among the likely consequences of his own emotional arousal. Therefore, the immediate inhibition of his emotion expressive behaviors can be interpreted as an automatic attempt to cope with the other's anticipated reactions by removing their (assumed) instigating cause: namely, Andy's own shows of feeling.

This constellation, however, resulted in a subjective state of affective emptiness as well as a numbing lack of any sense of emotional self-agency in affective relationships. This subjective sense of emotional void can be interpreted as a further consequence of the extreme lack of marked affect-mirroring reactions and absence of differentiated contingent reactivity by Andy's parents in relation to his basic emotion expressions during his childhood. When during later phases of the therapy the nature and developmental origins of these automatic affective freezing reactions became cognitively more accessible to Andy, this self-reflective insight resulted in a painful and heightened conscious sense of his total emotional isolation. This, in turn, triggered a depressive reaction due to his feeling that his overriding inability to express his feelings in emotionally charged situations would forever make it impossible for him to engage in real and spontaneous intimate object relationships.

Notes on Process: The White Ball Dream

As an interesting transference by-product of the affective causal illusion phenomenon described earlier, during the earlier stages of the analysis a kind of *confusion of tongues* (Ferenczi, 1980) developed within the intersubjective construal of emotional experience between the patient and the analyst. Let us illustrate by some examples how these vicissitudes in the transference unfolded during the analytic process.

Andy's central symptoms all related to different aspects of his difficulties in mentalizing about his own and others' feelings in emotionally charged object relationships. This made psychoanalytic work a seriously challenging enterprise both for Andy and for his analyst. The analyst's interventions mainly consisted of simply mirroring the patient's current affective states or those he was likely to have felt during recalled events in the past, interpreting the re-occurring aspects and patterns of the affective relational schemes that appeared in the transference, and focusing and directing the analysand's attention to introspectively monitor, detect, and contemplate the mental contents of his internal states. Often, however, especially during the initial phases of the treatment, these interventions seemed to backfire, leading to—at first, unexpected or misunderstood—consequences, reactions, and misinterpretations by the patient. These clearly illustrate the technical difficulties encountered in analysis of patients with serious mentalization deficits.

The analyst tended to focus his attention on the patient's inner world, mirroring and naming the mental states, affects, and internal processes that he felt the patient must be—or ought to be—experiencing while relating some recent or past event from his life. This, however, often activated the patient's fear of losing emotional self-control. In such cases, his fear of losing his mind was usually triggered by the analyst's suggestions of the possible affective content, relevance or significance of the life events he described. At the early stages of the therapy, the analysand interpreted any kind of emotional mirroring from the therapist as a suggestion that his mental functioning was abnormal.

A further central symptom, however, was Andy's compulsive and vigilant monitoring of and fixation on the other's perceived and/or anticipated emotion states and their imminent changes. This manifested itself as an intense desire to keep the analyst in a calm mental state by anticipating and attempting to fulfill his perceived expectations. Andy was very frightened that the analyst would disintegrate if he did not cooperate fully. All these factors led the patient to try to stick to the analytic contract to the letter. The analyst's interventions were understood as concrete tasks that the patient needed to accomplish. For example, when the analyst asked a question about the emotions Andy might have experienced during a certain event that he described during a session, Andy understood this as a communication of a requirement that he should experience and notice such emotions. To fulfill this perceived request, he began to intensively read a large amount of psychological literature, and developed a very rich vocabulary of mental state terms. Thus, on the one hand, the analyst's emotional mirroring interventions were experienced as torturous because they were perceived as likely to lead to Andy's self-disintegration as well as endangering the analyst's mental and emotional equilibrium. On the other hand, Andy interpreted these mirroring interpretations as a task to be accomplished in order to live up to the analyst's expectations and to avoid angering or emotionally disintegrating him.

In line with his tendency for affective freezing, Andy avoided expressing the emotions that were aroused within the therapeutic setting and the transference, thereby attempting to avoid the analyst's anticipated disintegration. In the early stages of analysis this constellation created a surprisingly pleasant situation for the analyst, the illusion of positive transference (Freud, 1912; Kernberg, 2004). The analyst felt that his interventions were accepted and successful and, consequently, Andy's ability to mentalize about affects appeared to have significantly increased. It appeared that he was beginning to monitor, categorize, and name his own emotions as well as interpreting others' behaviors in terms of mental states. He also seemed able to apply adequately at a cognitive level the patterns of object relations revealed by the analyst's interpretations, and he used them as a new tool to afford a level of cognitive self-control previously unavailable to him. He showed evidence of becoming able to experience and reflect on his own intense emotions and passions as signs of madness (maternal identification), and as weakness that contrasted with his stereotypical ideas of masculine identity (paternal identification). Although many of these emerging phenomena may have represented true therapeutic progress, transference themes that emerged in the therapy raised new perspectives, suggesting the possibility of a less benevolent interpretation for them.

To summarize, the consequences of the analyst's mirroring interventions were threefold. First, they pushed Andy toward awareness of intense affective experiences that he found unbearable and dangerous and that he was trying desperately to avoid. This led to panic attacks combined with feelings of disintegration through the activation of his maternal object relations, and to experiencing intense shame and humiliation through his paternal identifications. At the same time, Andy also experienced the analyst's mirroring of his emotions in terms of the kind of problem solving strategies that he learnt from his father, and recognition of his own emotions appeared to him to be a task he was required to take on and accomplish. Finally, Andy's complex reactions to the analyst's mirroring interventions implied that in his view the analyst was unable to comprehend and identify with the level and nature of the actual internal suffering that his life experiences had caused him. Instead, the analyst's perceived instructions to attend to and face his internal affective states made Andy feel that the analyst considered these as easily resolvable matters. To Andy it was as though he was saying: "no problem, if you express and recognize your emotions then everything is going to be okay." Andy experienced this perceived attitude of the analyst as a devaluation of his inner world that made him feel still more emotionally and interpersonally isolated.

We now describe a dream that contains several aspects of the complexities of the therapeutic process described earlier. Andy had this dream in the eighth month of the therapy. In the dream he is in a park, feeling out of control and frightened. He is trying to avoid something; he recognizes that he is being pursued by something or someone that he is trying to escape from. While he is running away, his pursuer suddenly jumps on top of him. His attacker turns out to be himself. He finds himself lying on the ground on his back, while at the same time he is sitting on top of himself with a white ball in his hand. He starts to push and force the ball toward himself, and at this point he realizes that what he was trying to escape from was something horrible, perhaps schizophrenia, or some other form of madness. When he recognizes this, he begins to feel an intense fear of the ball and twitches under it. He is enveloped in the intense light emanating from the white ball, which he finally manages to push into himself. At this point, he begins to scream as loudly as he can, in total ecstasy, as though he has gone mad. He recognizes this mystical madness and aggression to be the state that he had always been afraid of during his panic attacks. When he wakes up, his first thought is to check whether he is actually shouting in reality as well, because he feels extremely worried about waking up and terrifying his girlfriend who is asleep next to him in their bed. He finds it very comforting to realize that his screaming was not real, but only a dream.

Andy brought this dream during the first session of the week, and his associations pointed to material from the previous session (on Friday). In earlier sessions his severe panic attacks had become a central topic. He started to recognize (going along with the observations made by the analyst) that most of the time these attacks were preceded by some specific emotion state: anger, fear, erotic passion, and that the inarticulate panic state was in fact triggered by these emotions. He recalled that during the previous session the therapist had suggested to him that he should face his own emotions. He interpreted his dream as showing how he was forcing himself to identify with this expectation. At this point of the therapy he started to feel that he was already becoming capable of experiencing the emotions that had originally seemed overwhelming and highly threatening and that he was becoming able to verbalize them as well. He felt that in the dream he managed to force himself to experience his previously unbearable emotions, which finally became a part of him.

However, important transference phenomena—which went beyond Andy's conscious construal of the meaning of the dream—seemed to be detectable in his associations. The analyst's interventions—which consisted mainly of naming Andy's emotions and suggesting the connection between the panic attacks and the preceding strong emotion states he was in—had been perceived by Andy as the analyst setting him a task. This, on the one hand, represented an act of violence against him in the form of the analyst's perceived demand that Andy should confront his emotions. On the other hand, Andy understood the interventions as practical advice analogous to the advice given by his father when he left Andy alone with his deranged mother. However, while being similar at a formal level, the advice differed in its actual content. Whereas the father's advice usually suggested that Andy should repress his emotions and concentrate on practical solutions to cope with his mother's problems, the analyst's interventions seemed to Andy to suggest that he should face and experience his emotions instead of repressing them.

Both pieces of advice seemed, however, to portray the task at hand as trivial and relatively easy to accomplish. In fact, while the analyst was struck by the disturbing and violent atmosphere of the dream and tried to mirror this back to him, Andy emphasized the liberating, elementary feeling of the scream. He pointed out that as he was pushing the white ball and felt himself being pushed by it, he alternately identified either with the experience of one or the other part of himself. He felt that the elementary basic anger expressed by the final scream when the white ball was eventually pushed into him became his own property at that point and lost its frightening and strange quality. Madness became energy for him that he had incorporated and felt now to be his own; a previously unmanageable emotion that now belonged to him and was under his control without leading to destruction and craziness.

At this point in the chain of associations the analyst picked up on Andy's newly emerging sense of agency, and recalled an earlier dream (reported 7 months earlier) when Andy's panic attacks were the central theme in the early days of the therapy: the dream about the chained wild being raging with madness in the desert. This was a man who was mad, filled with anger and wildly trying to break his chains. In his associations, Andy sometimes observed this person from the outside, and sometimes identified with him. In either case this person was perceived as very threatening. His uncontrollable rage made a terrifying impression on Andy as did the prospect of him breaking his chains: who knew what he might do then. His fear of his own potential aggression as well as his mother's states of losing control came to his mind. Comparing the two dreams, the analyst drew Andy's attention to the more elaborated nature of the white ball dream, and the increased experience of agency it seemed to convey. He also pointed out that the apparent increase in Andy's sense of affective agency and ability to face his dreaded feelings of intense anger and rage—as these were indicated by the white ball dream—seemed to have coincided with a notable decrease of the frequency and intensity of his panic attacks during this period.*

---

* Note that this therapeutic picture seems quite in line with some of the proposals of the psychodynamic model of panic disorder (see Busch, Cooper, Klerman, Shapiro, & Shear, 1991; Shear, Cooper, Klerman, Busch, & Shapiro, 1993) that emphasizes that panic attacks may be related to fears that acknowledging and/or expressing intense anger may threaten significant relationships involving strong dependence on the patient's part.

Andy seemed to agree and emphasized that he himself was the one pushing the ball into himself, and he indeed experienced this as a new subjective sense of agency that felt good to him. At the time when the white ball dream was reported the analyst at first tended to accept—perhaps somewhat too hastily—the positive interpretations that Andy ascribed to the dream. Andy proposed that the dream signified the disappearance of his phobic avoidance of affects, and he became the agent of his feared madness (i.e., he gained control over his affective states). Other—apparently related—positive changes that coincided with the dream seemed to be realistic and acceptable signals of positive therapeutic change: Andy's panic attacks became milder and more manageable, he seemed to become capable of providing more differentiated descriptions of his own affective experiences, and he showed an increased ability for online identification of his own desires in a relational situation. He started to be able to focus his attention inward in the presence of an important other, and showed increased ability to mentalize about and empathize with other people's motivations when they were in an emotional state.

However, the dream also clearly represented negative aspects of the therapeutic relationship and these became more apparent in the light of subsequent events in the therapy and in the transference. The violent abusive act of pushing the white ball into his face by his persecutor and associations to this part of the dream seemed to imply that it represented Andy's negative and fearful attitude toward and interpretation of the affect-mirroring activity of the analyst. These aspects of the dream and Andy's reactions raise the possibility that his somewhat over-enthusiastic collaboration may have in fact represented an effort to avoid the analyst's anticipated disintegration by fulfilling—through the dream—his perceived desire for Andy to mentalize about his affects. The most obvious sign of this was the fact that when Andy woke up, his first thought was concern that he had really cried out and terrified his girlfriend by his emotional reaction. His attention seemed to be focused on his desire to avoid screaming about the therapeutic relationship.

As time passed, it became more and more evident that Andy's readiness to satisfy the analyst's desires was covering up a painful state of affective isolation. A few weeks after the white ball dream, he became depressed and felt lonely. Rescheduling a session also caused him an unexpectedly high level of anxiety. He realized that the states of mind he feared were unavoidable, and were important parts of him. The analysis did not erase these torturing affective states, just made them more available for his self-reflective insight. This, however, resulted in a painful and conscious sense of affective isolation. This, in turn, triggered a depressive reaction due to his feeling that this overriding inability to express his affects in emotionally charged situations would forever make it impossible for him to engage in real and spontaneous intimate object relationships.

However, it seems that the very fact of having been able to talk about this by complaining about the therapeutic relationship in the presence of his analyst was itself already a kind of adaptive engagement in a real and spontaneous intimate object relationship. The initial phase of the therapy centered on the patient's inner processes and their verbal mirroring by the analyst activated Andy's fears of going mad. Repeatedly working through these issues seemed to help him to understand at a cognitive level the patterns of object relations involved and to keep his panic attacks manageable. At the same time, the analyst's repeated mirroring of Andy's affective states seemed to have succeeded in establishing a new kind of object-relational experience for Andy. The analyst focused his attention on Andy's internal mental and emotional states, and during this process Andy learned that his expressions of feeling would not have a disintegrative effect on the analyst's mind. Furthermore, he no longer anticipated that as a result of focusing on his internal affective states the analyst's behavior would change in a frightening way. These developments suggest that Andy started to acquire a new mental skill of focusing his attention on his feelings without anticipating either self-disintegration or a self-endangering change in the perceived emotional states of others. The causal illusion started to evaporate.

In cases of serious mentalizing deficits such as Andy's, the patient's reactions to interventions must be very carefully monitored. At the present state of the analytic process we cannot judge with certainty whether the applied interventions—affect mirroring, interpretation of the affective relational schema in the transference, the therapist's focus of the patient's attention on his internal states—have led to essential changes in Andy's difficult case of affective self-disorder.

Conclusion

Human beings have the arguably species-unique ability to exercise on-line introspective control over their primary emotional impulses in affectively charged interpersonal situations and relationships. However, individuals differ significantly in the degree to which this remarkable capacity is available to them or can be put to functional use. In this paper we argued that certain types of affective disorders involving deficits in mentalizing about the emotional states of the self and others in intimate and affiliative relationships can be traced back to the developmental effects of deviant patterns of early interactions with the primary caretaker.

We first outlined a social cognitive developmental theory specifying the early social environmental conditions and cognitive representation-building and attention socialization mechanisms that underlie the unfolding of the introspectively accessible representational affective self. This approach relates the variable capacity of individuals for introspective access to affective self states and emotional self-control to the differences in the availability of a contingently reactive infant-attuned attachment environment in which the infant's automatic emotion expressive responses induce contingent external feedback reactions and marked forms of affect-mirroring displays by caregivers. We argued that these human-specific features of early caregiver-infant interactions are necessary to enable the infant to establish second-order cognitively accessible representations for the initially nonconscious, stimulus-controlled, and procedural basic emotional automatisms of the innate constitutional self.

Our approach sheds new light on the functional role of the human-specific features of early affective attachment interactions (such as contingent turn-taking reactivity, marked forms of affect-mirroring, or ostensive-communicative cues of pedagogical knowledge manifestations) in early social cognitive development. It interprets ostensively cued marked affect-reflective interactions as a special case of pedagogical knowledge manifestations (Csibra & Gergely, 2006) that function to transfer relevant cultural knowledge about universally shared emotion categories through establishing second-order representations for the infant's primary emotion states. We argued that the developmentally established second-order emotion representations allow the child to extend the original domain of the innate capacity for mentalizing about other minds to include introspective mentalizing about one's own internal affective mental states and anticipated emotion-induced actions as well. As a result the introspectively accessible representational affective self can employ its innate mentalizing ability in the service of emotional self-regulation and control by anticipating and adaptively modifying its own emotion-induced action tendencies to cope more efficiently with affectively charged interpersonal interactions.

To demonstrate the clinical usefulness of our model of affective self-development we applied it to explain the core symptomatology of a patient exhibiting severe dysfunctions of mentalizing about affects. Through this case illustration we described how certain reoccuring patterns of dysfunctional affective reactivity experienced within the child's attachment environment can seriously derail the normal processes of representation–building and attention socialization leading to the establishment of an unreflective self structure characterized by dysfunctional and reality-distorting perceptions of affective states of both the self and others. Finally, we tried to show how our social cognitive developmental model can contribute to a deeper understanding of the methodological difficulties that the patient's unreflective self functioning represents for different therapeutic intervention techniques during analytic treatment.

References

Ainsworth, M. D. S., Blehar, M. C., Waters, E., & Wall, S. (1978). *Patterns of attachment: A psychological study of the strange situatio.* Hillsdale, NJ: Lawrence Erlbaum.

Allen, J. G., & Fonagy, P. (2006). *Handbook of mentalization-based treatment.* New York: John Wiley & Sons Ltd.

Bahrick, L. R., & Watson, J. S., (1985). Detection of intermodal proprioceptive-visual contingency as a potential basis of self-perception in infancy. *Developmental Psychology, 21,* 963–973.

Beebe, B., Knoblauch, S., Rustin, J., & Sorter, D. (2005). *Forms of intersubjectivity in infant research and adult treatment.* New York: Other Press.

Behne, T., Carpenter, M., & Tomasello, M. (2005). One-year-olds comprehend the communicative intentions behind gestures in a hiding game. *Developmental Science, 8,* 492–499.

Bennett, D. S., Bendersky, M., & Lewis, M. (2004). On specifying specificity: Facial expressions at 4 months. *Infancy, 6*(3), 425–429.

Bennett, D. S., Bendersky, M., & Lewis, M. (2005). Does the organization of facial expression change over time? Facial expressivity from 4 to 12 months. *Infancy, 8*(2), 167–187.

Bigelow, A. E. (1999). Infants' sensitivity to imperfect contingency in social interaction. In P. Rochat (Ed.), *Early Social Cognition*, 137–154. Hillsdale, NJ: Erlbaum.

Bigelow, A. E., & De Coste, C. (2003). Infants' sensitivity to contingency in social interactions with familiar and unfamiliar partners. *Infancy, 4*, 111–140.

Bigelow, A. E., & Rochat, P. (2006). Two-month-old infants' sensitivity to social contingency in mother-infant and stranger-infant interaction. *Infancy, 9*(3), 313–325.

Bowlby, J. (1969). *Attachment and Loss, Vol. 1: Attachment*. London: Hogarth Press and the Institute of Psycho-Analysis.

Braten, S. (1988). Dialogic mind: The infant and the adult in protoconversation. In M. Carvallo (Ed.), *Nature, Cognition, and System*, Vol. I., 187–205.Dordrecht: Kluwer Academic Publishers.

Braten, S. (1992). The virtual other in infants' minds and social feelings. In H. Wold(Ed.), *The dialogical alternative*, 77–97. Oslo: Scandinavian University Press.

Braten, S. (Ed.). (1998). *Intersubjective communication and emotion in early ontogeny*. Paris: Cambridge University Press.

Brazelton, T. B., & Tronick, E. (1980). Preverbal communication between mothers and infants. In D. R. Olson (Ed.), *The social foundations of language and thought*. 299–315. New York: Norton.

Brazelton, T. B., Koslowski, B., & Main, M. (1974). The origins of reciprocity: The early mother-infant interaction. In M. Lewis & L. Rosenblum (Eds.), *The Effect of the Infant on its Caregiver*, 49–76. New York: Wiley.

Bruner, J. S., Olver, P. R., & Greenfield, P. M. (1966). *Studies on cognitive growth*. New York: Wiley.

Busch, F. N., Cooper, A. M., Klerman, G. L., Shapiro, T., & Shear, M. K. (1991). Neurophysiological, cognitive-behavioral and psychoanalytic approaches to panic disorder: toward an integration. *Psychoanalytic Inquiry, 11*, 316–332.

Camras, L. A. (1992). Expressive development and basic emotions. *Cognition and Emotion, 6*, 269–283.

Cassidy, J. & Shaver, P. R. (1999). *Handbook of attachment: Theory, research and clinical implications*. New York: The Guilford Press.

Cohn, J. F. & Tronick, E. Z. (1988). Mother-infant face-to-face interaction: Influence is bidirectional and unrelated to periodic cycles in either partner's behavior. *Developmental Psychology, 24*, 386–392.

Cooper, R. P., & Aslin, R. N. (1990). Preference for infant-directed speech in the first month after birth. *Child Development, 61*, 1584–1595.

Csibra, G., & Gergely, G. (1998). The teleological origins of mentalistic action explanations: A developmental hypothesis. *Developmental Science, 1*(2), 255–259.

Csibra, G., & Gergely, G. (2006). Social learning and social cognition: The case of pedagogy. In M. H. Johnson & Y. M. Munakata (Eds.), Processes of change in brain and cognitive development. *Attention and Performance,* XXI, 249–274.

Csibra, G., Bíró, S., Koós, O., & Gergely, G. (2003). One-year-old infants use teleological representations of actions productively. *Cognitive Science, 27*(1), 111–133.

Darwin, C. (1872). *The expression of emotions in man and animals.* New York: Philosophical Library.

De Marco, A., & Visalberghi, E. (2007). Facial displays in young tufted Capuchin monkeys (*Cebus apella*): Appearance, Meaning, Context and Target, *Folia Primatologica, 78*(2), 118–137.

Ekman, P. (1992). Facial expressions of emotion: New findings, new questions. *Psychological Science, 3*(1), 34–38.

Ekman, P., Friesen, W. V., & Ellsworth, P. (1972). *Emotion in the human face.* New York: Pergamon Press.

Ellsworth, P. C., Scherer, K. R. (2003). Appraisal process in emotion. In R.J. Davidson, K. R. Scherer & H. H. Goldsmith (Eds.), *Handbook of Affective Sciences,* 572–595. Oxford University Press.

Farroni, T., Csibra, G., Simion, F., & Johnson, M. H. (2002). Eye contact detection in humans from birth. *Proceedings of the National Academy of Sciences of the United States of America,* 99, 9602–9605.

Ferenczi, S. (1980) Confusion of tongues between adults and the child. In Bálint, M. (Ed.), *Final contributions to the problems and methods of psychoanalysis* (156–167). London: Brunnel/Mazel.

Fernald, A. (1985). Four-month-old infants prefer to listen to motherese. *Infant Behavior and Development,* 8, 181–195.

Fernald, A. (1992). Human maternal vocalizations to infants as biological signals: An evolutionary perspective. In J. H. Barkow, J. Tooby & L.C. Cosmides (Eds.), *The adapted mind: Evolutionary psychology and the generation of culture,* 391–428. New York: Oxford University Press.

Floccia, C., Christophe, A., & Bertoncini, J. (1997). High-amplitude sucking and newborns: The quest for underlying mechanisms. *Journal of Experimental Child Psychology,* 64, 175–189.

Fonagy, P. (2001). *Attachment theory and psychoanalysis.* New York: The Other Press.

Fonagy, P. & Bateman A. W. (2006). Mechanisms of change in mentalization-based treatment of BPD. *Journal of Clinical Psychology,* 62, 41–430.

Fonagy, P., & Target, M. (1996). Playing with reality: I. Theory of mind and the normal development of psychic reality. *International Journal of Psycho-Analysis, 77,* 217–233.

Fonagy, P., & Target, M. (1997). Attachment and reflective function: Their role in self-organization. *Development and Psychopathology, 9,* 679–700.

Fonagy, P., Gergely, G., & Target, M. (2007). The parent-infant dyad and the construction of the subjective self. *Journal of Child Psychology and Psychiatry, 48:3/4,* 288–328.

Fonagy, P., Target, M., & Gergely, G. (2000) Attachment and borderline personality disorder: A theory and some evidence. *Psychiatric Clinics of North America, 23*(1), 103–123.

Fonagy, P., Target, M., & Gergely, G. (2004). Psychoanalytic perspectives on developmental psychopathology. In D. Cicchetti & D. J. Cohen (Eds.). *Developmental Psychopathology,* (2nd ed.), 504–554. New York: Guilford Press.

Fonagy, P., Gergely, G., Jurist, E., & Target, M. (2002). *Affect-regulation, mentalization and the development of the self.* New York: The Other Press.

Fonagy, P., Target, M., Gergely, G., Allen, J. G., & Bateman, A. (2003). The developmental roots of borderline personality disorder in early attachment relationships: A theory and some evidence. *Psychoanalytic Inquiry, 23,* 412–459.

Francis, D. D., & Meaney, M. J. (1999) Maternal care and the development of stress responses. *Current Opinions in Neurobiology, 9,*128–134.

Francis, D. D., Diorio, J., Liu, D., & Meaney, M. J. (1999). Variations in maternal care from the basis for a non-genomic mechanism of intergenerational transmission of individual differences in behavioral and endocrine responses to stress, *Science, 286*(5442),1155–1158.

Freud, S. (1912). *The Dynamics of Transference. Standard Edition, 12,* 97–108.

Gergely, G. (1992). Developmental reconstructions: Infancy from the point of view of psychoanalysis and developmental psychology. *Psychoanalysis and Contemporary Thought, 15*(1), 3–55.

Gergely, G. (2000). Reapproaching Mahler: New perspectives on normal autism, normal symbiosis, splitting and libidinal object constancy from cognitive developmental theory. *Journal of the American Psychoanalytic Association, 48*(4), 1197–1228.

Gergely, G. (2002). The development of understanding self and agency. In U. Goshwami (Ed.), *Blackwell Handbook of Childhood Cognitive Development,* 26–46. Malden, MA: Blackwell Publishers. Oxford: Blackwell.

Gergely, G. (2004). The role of contingency detection in early affect-regulative interactions and in the development of different types of infant attachment. *Social Development, 13*(3), 468–488.

Gergely, G. (2007a). The social construction of the subjective self: The role of affect-mirroring, markedness, and ostensive communication in self development. In L. Mayes, P. Fonagy & M. Target (Eds.), *Developmental Science and Psychoanalysi*. London: Karnac.

Gergely, G. (2007b). Learning 'about' versus learning 'from' other minds: Human pedagogy and its implications. In P. Carruthers (Ed.), *Innateness Vol. III. Foundations and Mechanisms*. Oxford, UK: Oxford University Press.

Gergely, G., & Csibra, G. (2003). Teleological reasoning about actions: The one-year-old's naïve theory of rational action. *Trends in Cognitive Sciences, 7*, 287–292.

Gergely, G., & Csibra, G. (2005). The social construction of the cultural mind: Imitative learning as a mechanism of human pedagogy. *Interaction Studies, 6*(3), 463–481.

Gergely, G., & Csibra, G. (2006). Sylvia's recipe: The role of imitation and pedagogy in the transmission of cultural knowledge. In S. Levenson & N. Enfield (Eds.), *Roots of Human Sociality: Culture, Cognition, and Human Interaction*, 229–255. New York, NY: Berg Publishers.

Gergely, G., & Watson, J. S. (1996). The social biofeedback theory of parental affect-mirroring: The development of emotional self-awareness and self-control in infancy. *The International Journal of Psycho-Analysis, 77*, 1–31.

Gergely, G., & Watson, J. S. (1999). Early social-emotional development: Contingency perception and the social biofeedback model. In P. Rochat (Ed.), *Early Social Cognition*, 101–137. Hillsdale, NJ: Erlbaum.

Gergely, G., & Unoka, Z. (in press). Attachment, affect-regulation and mentalization: The developmental origins of the representational affective self. In C. Sharp, P. Fonagy & I. Goodyer (Eds.), *Social Cognition and Developmental Psychopathology*. Oxford, NY: Oxford University Press.

Gergely, G., Bekkering, H., & Király, I. (2002, February 14). Rational imitation in preverbal infants. *Nature, 415*, 755.

Gergely, G., Fonagy, P., & Target, M. (2002). Attachment, mentalization, and the etiology of borderline personality disorder. *Self Psychology, 3*(1), 73–82.

Gergely, G., Király, I., & Egyed, K.(2007). On pedagogy. *Developmental Science, 10*(1),139–146.

Gergely, G., Nádasdy, Z., Csibra, G., & Bíró, S. (1995). Taking the intentional stance at 12 months of age. *Cognition, 56*(2), 165–193.

Gianino, A., & Tronick, E.Z. (1988). The mutual regulation model: The infant's self and interactive regulation and coping and defensive capacities. In T. M. Field, P. M. McCabe & N. Schneiderman (Eds.), *Stress and Coping Across Development*, 47–68. Hillsdale, NJ: Lawrence Erlbaum Associates.

Goldberg, S., Muir, R., & Kerr, J. (1995). *Attachment theory: Social, developmental and clinical perspectives.* Hillsdale, NJ: Analytic Press.

Hobson, R. P. (1993). *Autism and the development of mind.* Hove, UK: Lawrence Erlbaum Associates.

Hobson, P. (2002). *The cradle of thought: Exploring the origins of thinking.* Oxford: Oxford University Press.

Hofer, M. A. (1995). Hidden regulators: Implications for a new understanding of attachment, separation and loss. In S. Goldberg, R. Muir & J. Kerr (Eds.), *Attachment theory: Social, developmental and clinical perspectives,* 203–230. Hillsdale, NJ: Analytic Press.

Izard, C. E., & Malatesta, C.Z. (1987). Perspectives on emotional development. I. Differential emotions theory of early emotional development, In J. D. Osofsky (Ed.), *Handbook of Infant Development* (2nd ed.), 494–554. New York: Wiley.

Johnson, S. C., Slaughter, V., & Carey, S. (1998). Whose gaze will infants follow? The elicitation of gaze-following in 12-month-olds. *Developmental Science, 1,* 233–238.

Kagan, J. (1994). *Galen's prophecy: Temperament in human nature.* New York: Basic Books.

Kernberg, O. (2004) *Contemporary Controversies in Psychoanalytic Theory, Techniques, and their Applications.* New Haven, Conn.: Yale University.

Lazarus, R. S. (1991). *Emotion and adaptation.* New York: Oxford University Press.

Lazarus, R. S., & Lazarus, B. N. (1994). *Passion and reason: Making sense of our emotions.* New York: Oxford University Press.

LeDoux, J. E. (1995). Emotion: Clues from the brain. *Annual Review of Psychology, 46,* 209–235.

LeDoux, J. E. (1996). *The emotional brain: The mysterious underpinnings of emotional life.* New York: Simon and Schuster.

LeDoux, J. E. (2000). Emotion circuits in the brain. *Annual Review of Neuroscience, 23,* 155–184.

Lewis, M., Allessandri, S. M., & Sullivan, M. W. (1990). Violation of expectancy, loss of control and anger expressions in young infants. *Developmental Psychology, 26*(5), 745–751.

Lichtenberg, J. D. (1987). Infant studies and clinical work with adults. *Psycho-Analytic Inquiry, 7,* 311–330.

Liszkowski, U., Carpenter, M., Henning, A., Striano, T., & Tomasello, M. (2004). Twelve-month-olds point to share attention and interest. *Developmental Science, 7,* 297–307.

Mahler, M., Pine, F., & Bergman, A. (1975). *The psychological birth of the human infant: Symbiosis and individuation.* New York: Basic Books.

Malatesta, C. Z., Culver, C., Tesman, R. J., & Shepard, B. (1989). The development of emotion expression during the first two years of life. *Monographs of the Society for Research in Child Development, 54*, Serial No. 219.

Meltzoff, A.N. (2002). Imitation as a mechanism of social cognition: Origins of empathy, theory of mind, and the representation of action. In U. Goshwami (Ed.), *Blackwell Handbook of Childhood Cognitive Development*, 6–25. Oxford, UK: Blackwell.

Meltzoff, A.N., & Gopnik, A. (1993). The role of imitation in understanding persons and developing a theory of mind. In S. Baron-Cohen, H. Tager-Flusberg & D. J. Cohen (Eds.), *Understanding Other Minds: Perspectives from Autism* 335–365. Oxford Medical Publications, UK: Oxford University Press.

Meltzoff, A. N., & Moore, M.K. (1977). Imitation of facial and manual gestures by human neonates. *Science, 198*(4312), 75–78.

Meltzoff, A. N. & Moore, M. K. (1989). Imitation in newborn infants: Exploring the range of gestures imitated and the underlying mechanisms. *Developmental Psychology, 25,* 954–962.

Meltzoff, A. N., & Moore, M. K. (1998). Infant intersubjectivity: broadening the dialogue to include imitation, identity and intention. In S. Braten (Ed.), *Intersubjective communication and emotion in early ontogeny,* 47–62. Paris: Cambridge University Press.

Movellan, J.R., & Watson, J.S. (2002). The development of gaze following as a Bayesian systems identification problem. *UCSD Machine Perception Laboratory Technical Reports* 2002(1).

Ochsner, K. N., & Gross, J. J. (2005). The cognitive control of emotion. *Trends in Cognitive Sciences, 9*(5), 242–249.

Panksepp, J. (1998). *Affective neuroscience: The foundations of human and animal emotions,* Oxford, NY: Oxford University Press.

Polan, H. J., & Hofer, M.A. (1999). Psychobiological origins of attachment and separation responses. In J. Cassidy & P. R. Shaver (Eds.), *Handbook of attachment: Theory, research and clinical implications,* 162–180. New York: The Guilford Press.

Posner, M. I., & Rothbart, M. K. (2000). Developing mechanisms of self-regulation. *Development and Psychopathology, 12,* 427–441.

Pruessner, J. C., Champagne, F., Meaney, M. J., & Dagher, A.(2004). Dopamine release in response to a psychological stress in humans and its relationship to early life maternal care: A positron emission tomographystudy using [11c]raclopride. *Journal of Neuroscience, 24*(11), 2825–2831.

Rochat, P., & Morgan, R. (1995). Spatial determinants in the perception of self-produced leg movements in 3- and 5-month-old infants. *Developmental Psychology, 31,* 626–636.

Rothbart, M. K. (1989). Temperament and development. In G. A. Kohnstamm, J. E. Bates & M. K. Rothbart (Eds.), *Temperament in childhood*, 187–247. New York: Wiley.

Sander, L. (1988). The event-structure of regulation in the neonate-caregiver system as a biological background for early organisation of psychic structure. In A. Goldberg (Ed.), *Frontiers in Self Psychology*, 64–77. Hillsdale, NJ: Analytic Press.

Shear, M. K., Cooper, A. M., Klerman, G. L., Busch, F. N., & Shapiro, T. (1993). A psychodynamic model of panic disorder. *American Journal of Psychiatry, 150*,859–866.

Southgate, V., van Maanen, C., & Csibra, G. (in press). Infant pointing: Communication to cooperate or communication to learn? *Child Development, 78*(3), 735–740.

Spangler, G., & Grossmann, K. E. (1993). Bio-behavioral organization in securely and insecurely attached infants. *Child Development, 64*, 1439–1450.

Sperber, D., & Hirschfeld, L. (2004). The cognitive foundations of cultural stability and diversity. *Trends in Cognitive Sciences, 8*(1), 40–46.

Sperber, D., & Wilson, D. (1986). *Relevance: Communication and cognition.* Oxford, UK: Blackwell.

Sroufe, L. A. (1996). *Emotional development: The organization of emotional life in the early years.* Cambridge, Mass.: Cambridge University Press.

Stern, D. N. (1985). *The interpersonal word of the infant.* New York, NY: Basic Books.

Stern, D. N., Sander, L. W., Nahum, J. P., Harrison, A. M., Lyons-Ruth, K., Morgan,A. C., Bruschweiler-Stern, N., & Tronick, E. Z. (1998). Non-Interpretive mechanisms in psychoanalytic therapy. *International Journal of Psychoanalysis, 79*, 903.

Suomi, S. J. (1999). Attachment in rhesus monkeys. In J. Cassidy & P. R. Shaver (Eds.), *Handbook of attachment: Theory, research and clinical implications*, 181–197. New York: The Guilford Press.

Thompson, R. S. (1994). Emotion regulation. A theme in search of definition. *Monographs of the Society for Research on Child Development, 59*(2/3), 25–52.

Tomasello, M., & Haberl, K. (2003). Understanding attention: 12- and 18-month-olds know what's new for other persons. *Developmental Psychology, 39*, 906–912.

Tomasello, M., Carpenter, M., & Liszkowski, U. (in press). A new look at infant pointing. *Child Development, 78*(3), 705–722.

Tomkins, S. (1995). *Exploring affect: The selective writings of Silvan Tomkins.* Cambridge, Mass.: Cambridge University Press.

Trevarthen, C. (1979). Communication and cooperation in early infancy: A description of primary intersubjectivity. In M. Bullowa (Ed.), *Before Speech: The Beginning of Interpersonal Communication*, 321–347. New York: Cambridge University Press.

Trevarthen, C. (1993). The self born in intersubjectivity: an infant communicating. In U. Neisser (Ed.), *The perceived self*, 121–173. New York: Cambridge University Press.

Trevarthen, C., & Aitken, K. J. (2001) Infant intersubjectivity: Research, theory, and clinical applications. *Journal Child Psychology and Psychiatry, 42*(1), 3–48.

Tronick, E. Z. (1989). Emotions and emotional communication in infants. *American Psychologist, 44*, 112–119.

Tronick, E.Z., & Cohn, J. F. (1989). Infant-mother face-to-face interaction: Age and gender differences in coordination and the occurrence of miscoordination. *Child Development, 60*, 85–92.

Watson, J. S. (1972). Smiling, cooing, and "the game." *MerrillPalmer Quarterly, 18*, 323–339.

Watson, J. S. (1985). Contingency perception in early social development. In T. M. Field & N.A. Fox (Eds.), *Social perception in infants*, 157–176. Norwood, NJ: Ablex.

Watson, J. S. (1994). Detection of self: The perfect algorithm. In S. T. Parker, R. W. Mitchell & M. L. Boccia (Eds.), *Self-awareness in animals and humans: Developmental perspectives*, 131–148. New York: Cambridge University.

Watson, J. S. (1995). Mother-infant interaction: Dispositional properties and mutual designs. In N. S. Thompson (Ed.), *Perspectives in Ethology, Volume 11. Behavioral Design.* New York: Plenum Press.

Watson, J. S. (2001). Contingency perception and misperception in infancy: Some potential implications for attachment. *Bulletin of the Menninger Clinic, 65*(3), 296–321.

Wismer Fries, A. B., Ziegler, T. E., Kurian, J. R., Jacoris, S., & Pollak, S. D. (2005). Early experience in humans is associated with changes in neuropeptides critical for regulating social behavior. *P.N.A.S., 102*, 17237–17240.

Uzgiris, I. C., Benson, J. B., Kruper, J. C., & Vasek, M. E. (1989). Contextual influences on imitative interactions between mothers and infants. In J. J. Lockman & N. L. Hazen (Eds.), *Action in social context: Perspectives on early development*, 103–127. New York: Plenum Press.

3

Contemporary Approaches to Mentalization in the Light of Freud's *Project**

Marc-André Bouchard and Serge Lecours

Introduction

Freud did not employ the concept of mentalization as such, nor did he think of making a concept of it. But in the *Project* (1895) he put forward a detailed view of the mind, that includes a central hypothesis concerning the economic origins of thought, which remained part of his later work, and has been a continuing source of inspiration, particularly to several French psychoanalysts (Green, Luquet, Marty, de M'Uzan, Roussillon) thinking over issues of mental elaboration. Their views elaborate Freud's (1895) concepts of endogenous excitations (somatic or Q element, not yet the sexual drive) from which the organism cannot withdraw, and of the *effort* or psychical working out (*Psychische Verarbeitung*) necessary to protect from a wild and disorganizing discharge. This is achieved by creating a proportional complication through binding (*Bindung*, or linking), that is, secondary inhibitory processes allowing for the perception of the absence of the object, in order to prevent primary hallucinatory wish fulfillment and a disorganizing discharge of energy. Central to

* The authors would like to express their appreciation to Dr. Fredric Busch for his careful editorial reading of this contribution. The following colleagues also provided very helpful comments on an earlier version of the paper: J. Dauphin, M. Hudon, S. Rosenbloom, D. Scarfone, L.M. Tremblay and D. Wiethaeuper.

this Freudian tradition are the notions of effort, work, and continual alteration of the somatic element, performed by the mental apparatus in creating "contrivances", as a means to achieve at least partial mastery of an, as yet, unspecified quantum of energy through its metamorphosis into quality (Freud, 1895, p. 309).

The first explicit formulation of mentalization (Marty, 1990, 1991), based on an elaboration of the preconscious system (Freud, 1915; see review by Lecours & Bouchard, 1997), grew out of initial observations made by Marty and de M'Uzan (1963) during their investigation of psychosomatic phenomena. They were confronted with modes of psychic functioning which were quite different from those met with in neurotic subjects, and which demonstrated a characteristic lack in both "the quantity and quality of psychic representations" (Marty, 1991, p. 11). Psychosomatic patients typically showed "poor mentalization," that is, a very restricted capacity to elaborate their inner world or the thoughts of their desires; dreams and fantasies were rare or absent; and the characteristic disguised, that is neurotic and repressed, representations of infantile sexual wishes were strikingly deficient.

By contrast, a recent emerging psychoanalytic paradigm (e.g., Beebe & Lachmann, 2002; Fosshage, 2000; Stolorow, 1997) emphasizes a developmental and intersubjective approach, as opposed to a psychogenetics of mental structures, dyadic preoedipal intersubjective relationships, rather than a focus on mental elaboration of (and defensive activity against) the imperious urgencies of instinctual life, the mother's (and the analyst's) role in helping the infant (and the patient) develop more efficient affect tolerance and regulation within the dyad, in contrast to an analysis of affect regulation in terms of the life and death drives and pressures. The quality of mutual regulation, a prerequisite to self-regulation, is defined as the capacity of partners to influence and manage each other's states of affective connectedness and arousal (alertness, readiness to respond, inhibition to reduce expression, and prevent overstimulation) in response to various mutually sent and perceived nonverbal cues. Within this new paradigm, combining child-caregiver observation and Freud's method, mentalization has been redefined as the representation and understanding of self and others in terms of mental states, partly the outcome of sufficiently stable early attuned sensitive caregiving (Fonagy & Target, 1996, 2000; Target & Fonagy, 1996).

The premise for this paper stems from a recognition that a full account of mentalization in all its complexities requires a contribution from both perspectives, that is, the French-Freudian and the developmental-intersubjective. First, we briefly summarize Fonagy and Target's work on mentalization and reflective functioning. Then, we highlight key ideas contained in Freud's Project, which guides us in our review of the French-Freudian important and varied contributions. We then engage in a discussion concerning some points of convergence and divergence between the two main traditions, thus introducing contributions by Kernberg and Roussillon on the mental elaboration of affects into drives, and of self and object representation.

Fonagy, Target, and Gergely's Developmental and Intersubjective Approach

Fonagy and Target (1996, 2000, 2002) have offered a series of articulate, stimulating and original recent contributions to an understanding of mental elaboration and of its crucial role in mediating psychopathology. They are involved in developing a psychoanalytic understanding of personality disorder with influences from attachment theory, developmental psychology, the interpersonal and intersubjective outlook, recently adjoining a concept borrowed from evolutionary psychology, the interpersonal interpretive function (IIF), as a revision of the initial reflective function notion (see Bateman & Fonagy, 2004, p. 58; Fonagy, this issue). The IIF is conceived as a means of processing new experiences, interpreted in psychological terms. It integrates the following three interconnected components: (a) attentional control to selectively activate states of mind consistent with one's intentions, a key feature in the transformation of experience into thought; (b) stress regulation; (c) the mentalizing capacity itself, a core aspect of human social functioning, providing representation to the subjective world. Early attachment creates uniquely human opportunities for sharing affective experiences that, in turn, propel the development of the IIF. The quality of the affective-communicational attachment bonds precedes cognitive development (Fonagy, Target, Gergely, Allen, & Bateman, 2003), while the IIF is one of its products. Mentalization is described as "the development of representations of psychological states in the mind of the human infant" (Fonagy & Target, 2002, p. 321), while the relevant cognitive aspects are embedded in an affective-relational matrix. Normal development is presented as a series of five (the physical, social, teleologic, intentional, and representational) increasingly sophisticated phases in the emergence of an agentive self, and in the associated growing awareness concerning the nature of mental states. Several detailed descriptions of these transformations are available and may easily be consulted (e.g., Bateman & Fonagy, 2004; Fonagy & Target, 2000, 2002; Fonagy, Gergely, Jurist & Target, 2002; Gergely & Watson, 1996; Gergely, this issue; Target & Fonagy, 1996).

The capacity to experience psychic reality in terms of purposeful mental states implies the development of a second-order representation or concept that links and "integrates the actual internal experiences that constitute that state" (Fonagy et al., 2003, p. 422). Child–caregiver observation has now led to believe that this is crucially determined by the infant's learning to differentiate his or her various affective patterns of expression and internal response through observing his or her caregivers' facial or vocal mirroring responses (Gergely & Watson, 1996). Thus, the infant internalizes the caregiver's empathic expression "by developing a secondary representation of his emotional state with the mother's face as the signifier of his own emotional arousal as the signified" (Fonagy et al., 2003, p. 424). Correlatively, the caregiver's failure to produce adequate mirroring creates contradictory or frightening affective communications, the infant becoming preoccupied with the mother's moods, simultaneously turning away from his own. In situations of chronic misattunement, neglect, abuse, the child is compelled to internalize the abusive object's mental state as a central aspect of self (constituting the alien self), to split it off and to reproject it for example as a persecutor as seen in projective identification, and/or identification with the aggressor. Distortions occur because they contain within themselves representations of the other: thus, "the image of the mother comes to colonize the self" (Fonagy et al., 2003, p. 439), resulting in fragmentations. Neglected and traumatized individuals, as seen in adult borderline syndromes, featuring disorganized forms of attachment, present with defects, distortions and regressions in the interpretive mentalizing, self-regulating, and attentional mechanism (the IIF), resulting in disordered (often manipulative) behavioral strategies to maintain coherence and achieve security.

Freud's *Project* and the Economics of Thought

The *Project* (Freud, 1895) is Freud's first, neuropsychological account of both primary and secondary processes, which may also be considered as two modes of mentalization (Roussillon, 2001). In this model, the experience of satisfaction and its accompanying discharge contributes to a "reproductive remembering," via a facilitation, following the law of association by simultaneity (Freud, 1895, p. 319), therefore between the simultaneously cathected mnemic images of the state of wishful activation, of the object, and of the motor image of the discharge. When the state of urgency of *wishing* reappears, Freud envisions that the cathexis of the image of the object (which implies facilitation and the passage of quantity) will produce the same result as a perception: that is, a wishful hallucinating, typical of primary processes. The only condition that in principle can prevent memory traces from being massively recathected by the emergence of bodily pressures is the perception of the absence of the object (a secondary process).

Further, the quantitative elements, the "endogenous quantities of excitation, which must be faced without protection" constitute "the mainspring of the psychical mechanism" (Freud, 1895, p. 316; Freud, 1920, p. 29). Freud thus places the resolution of the economic pressures at the source of thought, and notes that between thought and the primary process a quantitative characteristic difference is to be observed: the secondary process of thought is a repetition of the original passage of quantity at a lower level, with smaller quantities (Freud, 1895, p. 334). Thought processes *bind* a quota of the quantity flowing through the neurone, resulting in a bound state that is a blend of high cathexis and small current. The ego itself is made of a mass of such (inhibitory) neurones holding fast to their cathexes, and running opposite to, restraining the primary (hallucinatory-wish) processes and automatic discharge. This reasoning led Freud to a well-known formulation: "Thus quantity in ϕ [here the functional equivalent of endogenous excitation leading to wishful pleasurable hallucination] is expressed by complication in ψ [the functional equivalent of perception/thought]" (Freud, 1895, p. 315). Complication by the creation of associative pathways (mentalization, or "structuralization of the ego" as Kaplan-Solms & Solms, 2000, p. 260, would put it), and modulation of somatic excitations into drives (and primary affects, see later discussion of Kernberg's revised drive theory), through some degree of binding and mastery of energy (quantity) go hand in hand.

For Freud, the activity of thought becomes interpolated between an instinctual demand and the action that satisfies it. In contemporary terms, thought inhibits stereotypical primary process and binds its psychic energy, preventing it from free motor discharge. These functions have been associated, among others, by Kaplan-Solms and Solms (2000, p. 272 & p. 269), in their sketch of a "neuro-anatomy of the mental apparatus," with Luria's (1973) programming, regulating, and verifying or third functional unit, that involves the key participation of the prefrontal lobes.

De M'Uzan: Quantity, Trauma and Perverse Structure

De M'Uzan's work (1994) perhaps most clearly illustrates the lasting influence of Freud's *Project*, and is particularly inspiring and clinically relevant through his systematic use of the concept of quantity of excitations (Simpson, 2003). De M'Uzan's (1973) approach to the understanding of some forms of perversion stresses early trauma and the consequent fact that the mental apparatus may be relatively helpless in its task to link excitations coming from instinctual life, and becomes unable to prevent the economic pressures from overriding issues of meaning. In such situations, there is a repetition of the identical (*répétition de l'identique*), the closest to pure discharge and motor expression, the subject being overwhelmed by internal or external excitations. These moments are made of a painful mixture of discharge with a sense of despair and fatality, under the grips of "sheer quantity," not tied to either conflict or underlying fantasy. In fact, the mental apparatus is consequently impoverished, the fantasy function altered. The subject lives in a world lacking in a sense of personal history. This is contrasted to situations or moments where the internal traces of one's subjective experience of the past is established within the psyche, which, in turn, allows the experience of a repetition of the same (*répétition du même*), a witness to the presence of true psychic conflict, between wishes and their opponents.

Differences in the capacity to regulate the quantity of excitation are used by de M'Uzan as a key feature to help differentiate between the neurotic and the perverse modes of mental functioning. Perverse patients may include some of the most severe personality disordered subjects belonging to the borderline spectrum, depending on their degree of grandiosity, superego pathology, and perversity (see Kernberg, 1992a, p. 274), to which criteria de M'Uzan adds the degree of mentalization. For him, the neurotic mode has the following characteristics: (a) it rests on a mentally elaborate dynamic unconscious, a structure based predominantly on repression and inner communication of symbolic meanings; (b) there is available some significant degree of the ability to bind energy in the form of word cathexes; (c) this facilitates the related capacity to elaborate fantasy in a manner that allows for subjective experience to emerge and organize psychic life; (d) therefore, enactments are "acting-outs," that is, these acts are driven by fantasies, and they are filled with meaning, because they contain and represent a message being sent to an internally significant other. By contrast, the perverse mode of functioning or structure is described as: (a) based on an often severely diminished, restricted, and atrophied unconscious psychic life, dominated by rejection (*Verwerfung*, or repudiation), a primitive means of protection against trauma, but which considerably reduces the capacity for further mental elaboration and symbolization, as the existence of a certain reality is made to be the same as it's nonexistence (Freud, 1918); (b) displaying unstable energy regulation, with major oscillations from unbearably high levels of energy to absolute discharge under the influence of the principle of inertia, a reduced capacity to bind these excitations, and a predominance of a particular form of concrete thinking (*pensée opératoire*, noted later); (c) illustrating a virtually absent sense of subjective agency and/or fantasy life, with a consequent impression of an irrevocable destiny, "constituted in actual trauma" (De M'Uzan, 2003, p. 703), taking roots in infantile helplessness (*détresse* in French, translated by Simpson as disarray), resulting in an experience whereby the psychic apparatus itself has been overwhelmed and left in a state of severe confusion; (d) pervaded with enactments that tend to take the form of *passages à l'acte*, implying that these often violent acts (toward self of others) are not driven by a fantasy, that they are thoughtless, carrying little or no meaning or symbolic value, and that their main function is to get rid of intolerable quantities of excitation by direct discharge. Finally, de M'Uzan's choice of invoking an analogy between a notion of "intolerable quantities of excitation" and a notion of unbearable psychic pain is open to critical comment, as it, nevertheless, leaves open the obscure nature of their relationship, illustrating once again the stubborn nature of the classic mind-body problem.

Concrete Thinking at the Low End of the Mentalization Spectrum

Marty and de M'Uzan (1963) first described a variety of concrete thinking (*pensée opératoire*), particularly devoid of fantasy life, and seen initially in severe psychosomatic cases. As it erects itself against the affective-sexual, concrete thinking becomes unable to establish strong links to instinctual energies, bearing witness to a disorganization and collapse of the life drive (Marty, 1968). Sadly, it thus degrades, to this same measure, the lively gratifying possibilities in the relationship with the object. De M'Uzan (2003) extends these observations to suggest that perverse structures also demonstrate this severely restricted degree of mentalization, in marked contrast to the neurotic mode operating under the stamp of the richly diversified Freudian dream-memory model (Freud, 1900). In patients whose main outlet from accumulated quantities of stimulation is somatic, the discharge, rather than involving another person via sadomasochistic transactions, is an action turned against the body itself. In one case, sex is the preferred instrument, in the other, the body itself becomes the site of the thoughtless violence. In both, however, forms of concrete thinking (poor mentalization) predominate. Although one can see in some patients a fair amount of mental sophistication in the realms of objective or technical knowledge, there is nevertheless, instead, a tendency toward an accumulating of quantities of excitations, and simultaneously, a fulfilling of what is being requested by the externally perceived situation, to the detriment of the wishing-desiring aspects of the self.

The following criteria help to recognize the occurrence of such concrete thinking and associated states: (a) associations from one topic to another are tangential, as seen in material, narrow, factual reporting, the presence of anecdotal (even if specific) and/or circumstantial affirmations, that appear as psychologically "meaningless," pointless; (b) the material only refers to itself, *words reduplicate action*, and thinking is utilitarian. It is, at best, structured as a sequential system of facts, of iterative actions-reactions, of concrete quotes and actions; (c) stereotyped expressions, "clichés," and conformism are used instead of thoughtful, particular linking; (d) thoughts and memories are generally not consciously related to one another within a coherent framework. They appear to exist in an island, isolated and fragmented. The discourse typically excludes any associative/symbolic/abstract connections. If present, connections do not seem to move much beyond the sensori-motor world; (e) Context is not used to create meaning. The patient does not rely on a strong temporal structure to bind together and establish interrelationships between thoughts/memories, or with other temporal modes (of what precedes, of what might follow). The notion of a past that might be repeated is absent; (f) There is a sense of an empty presence, of a noncontactful quality ("white relationship"), that lacks reference to an inner, alive object or self.

Marty and the Preconscious Mind

In a carefully reasoned reconsideration of Freud's concept of actual neurosis, Marty has suggested that a deficiency in representational capacity may result from genetic determinants, perhaps a depressed caretaker unable to supplement the child with enough rêverie, or from some severe occlusion (cleavage, suppression, and the like) of strategic groups of representation as a consequence of severe trauma or overwhelming conflict. This representational *deficit* creates a surplus of the quantitative element, a situation which may become impossible to integrate and transform into wish. This deficit is one key precondition to an actual neurosis, in contrast to a psychoneurosis. In poorly mentalized structures, one, therefore, observes various forms of expression through discharge in action or via the somatic field. These expressions result from an accumulation of instinctual and drive excitations which are wanting in meaning. The propensity for meaningless actions and somatic discharge over symbol formation is seen as resulting from the interplay of both the quality of mentalization and the quantity of accumulated excitations either from trauma, overstimulation, or intrusion.

Marty (1990, 1991) suggested that mentalization results from the quantity, permanence, fluidity, and nondefensive accessibility of the representational field. The preconscious mind is that which plays an intermediate role between the sensorimotor and further complexity by means of representations. To represent involves the development and use of a stable mental image of a thing, in place of the thing itself, whereas to symbolize means to connect representations with one another. Mentalization, then, subsumes all representational and symbolic operations by which the psychical apparatus comes to operate a metamorphosis of its instinctual energies as demonstrated in extended psychical regulation. It contributes to associate meaning to excitations, by allowing the subject to transform, elaborate, and integrate excitations issued from the somatic sphere into mentally usable elements. It forms the basis of each person's psychic life (Marty, 1991, p. 13), and brings into existence the basic processes of free association, dreaming, and fantasy. Thus, the emphasis is placed both on the topographic (as revised within an expanded view of the functions of the preconscious mind) and on the energetic-economic viewpoints.

Green and the Objectalising Function

Green (1984) sees the function of representation as the fundamental activity of the human mind, operating between the two poles defined by the drive and by thought (*la pensée*). Very much in the spirit of the *Project*, Green (1973, p. 236) points out that it is through some energetic reduction, some filtering process of quantitative energies that the work of thought can take place. Thinking is stimulated by the absence, loss, or failure of the object of desire to respond. It gradually takes form and provides form to the psychic apparatus, as it establishes a heterogeneous system of representations (hallucination, fantasy, cognition proper), as opposed to perception or action. Fantasy is the imaginative elaboration of bodily functions, a model of internalized action, which acknowledges fixations and regressions, connects the subject and the object, taking account of the relations between the conscious and the unconscious (Green, 2000a, p. 190).

Moreover, the function of representation modifies the traces of what was perceived and experienced, as staged through fantasy, to new levels of meaning and mental elaboration. Thus, between the object of desire and its representation remains an insuperable gap, the result of the mentalizing function. Green sees Bion's (1962) psychic alpha function, the process of converting raw data into meaningful mental contents, which can then be used for thinking, as creating this distance itself. He also reminds us that Winnicott situates thinking or fantasying within the same intermediate area of experience, between oral eroticism and true object relationship, between primary creative activity and projection of what has already been introjected, all designated by the paradox of transitional objects and phenomena (Winnicott, 1951/1987, p. 230). This foundational paradox defines psychical activity "at once on the side of the subjective object (wholly created by us, according to the pleasure principle) and of the object perceived objectively (discovered, according to the reality principle)" (Green, 2000a, pp. 23–24).

In this context, he puts forward the concept of the *objectalizing function*, which encompasses all meaningful investments, and its antagonist, the *disobjectalizing function*, aimed at robbing the objects of their unique singularity, by murdering representation (one of the forms of unbinding). Deeply influenced by Winnicott, whose reformulations and expanded views of the field of objects he finds "considerable" (Green, 2000a, p. 24), Green reconsiders the relation between drive and object, which he sees as mediated by the objectalizing function. This function actuates the psychical itself, as it transforms drive activity and its cathexes into psychical relations, creating both the subject and the subject in relation to its unique object, producing functional objects that support life (love). Its key characteristic is meaningful investment (Green, 1999, p. 85), a concept reuniting, at once, the quantum factor and the qualitative experience. Further, symbolization facilitates the objectalizing function as it transforms psychical relations into objects that become part of the ego's kingdom.

The disobjectalizing process, by contrast, refers to a destructive capacity, powerful enough to wreck the phenomena of Eros, aiming at nothingness, whose activity calls upon a process of unbinding from the erotic, the objectal and even from the positive aspects of narcissism (Green, 2000a; p. 157), leading ultimately to an almost complete withdrawing of investment. It is found at the limits of what is represented and what is not, the joint result of an unconscious process and a fundamental destructiveness, directed predominantly at the subject's own psychic functioning. The consequences are a dangerous atrophy and eradication of the subject within the ego, as the intentional desiring agent seeking pleasure, of its object (as seen in the empty transferences), and of virtually any meaningful investment (including treatment). For Green, this negative process is primary and leads to secondary deficits in mentalization, with an associated active withdrawal from investment in representations.

His previously suggested negative hallucination process is generalized and becomes the "representation of the absence of representation" (Green, 1999, p. 197), a piece of reality being obliterated. The
subject is itself negatively hallucinated, creating a gap (*manque*), a
hole in the self representation, the image being covered by the hallucination of a vacuity. This may account for various clinical phenomena, seen in moments of unbearable excesses in affect, such
as catastrophic and unthinkable anxieties, fears of breakdown and
annihilation, feelings of futility and psychic death, sensations of
abyss and extreme void.

Various forms of rejection and distancing organize this destructive withdrawal and negativity. Green argues that unbinding tends to
prevail over binding or rebinding, as the subject attempts to deal with
unbearable pain, and as one moves on and further away from repression toward negation (*Verneinung*), splitting (*Verleugnung*) and foreclosure or radical rejection (*Verwerfung*). This operates in a manner
close to a schizoid rejection (disavowal) and disinvestment* associated
with and implied in the splitting activities. The strength (power) of
this disinvestment is measured by the intensity of the feelings of psychic death (negative hallucination of the ego). In the end, for Green,
remaining close to Freud on this point also, the very existence of the
psychic function itself, which implies the possibility for mentalization, is a tributary of the intrication of the two drive groups.

Comparative Examination

One major underlying conception of mentalization processes derives
from Freud's central axiomatics provided in the *Project* that the
origins of thought are found in the oldest drive impulses linked to
elementary bodily functions (Green, 1999, p. 117). Another major
approach stems from a complementary demonstration and deep
insight that the origins of the subject's thinking are to be traced to

---

* The term disinvestment (of the ego, the object, of the psyche itself) is preferred
to decathexis in the present context as decathexis could imply the presence of
a well developed and mentally elaborate unconscious sector of the mind, from
which representations a cathexis is withdrawn. This would completely contradict
Green's point of a negativity, of a desiccation of the objectalizing function and of
its associated representational and symbolic activity. Disinvestment is also used
by Green's (1999) translator, see p. ix.

the internalized mirroring and differentiating (marking) experiences with significant others (Fonagy & Target, 2002; Gergely & Watson, 1996). As Fonagy and Target (2000, p. 856) describe the infant's situation: "The representation of his feelings is increasingly associated with the modulation included in the parent's reflection of them.... The infant will map the mother's modulated reaction on to his own feelings, and slowly this binds his emotional and physiological reactions." Intersubjective and relational events, particularly those occurring in primary object relations, significantly modulate the drives, and as we must now admit, to a far greater extent than what was thought possible, and no doubt, to an extent that is comparable to the events occurring in the intrasubjective scene.

A comparative examination of the different traditions of mentalization now seems possible, with hopes to achieve some integrative understanding. We think this can be initiated by a discussion of three issues: the mentalization of affective structures into drives, the mentalization of the object as it relates to the agentive self, and a comparison of the nature of the two primitive modes of thinking (psychic equivalence and pretend modes) associated with poor mentalizing.

Mentalization of Affects into the Drives

Offering a new perspective on drive theory, Kernberg (1992b, 2001) conceives that affects, far from being "mere discharge processes", are complex intrapsychic organizing schemes. In his view they are the "component substructures of drives" (Kernberg, 1992b, p. 21), acting as "bridging structures between biological instincts and psychic drives" (Kernberg, 1992b, p. 5). Further, affects are intermittent instinctive formations, of biologically given psychophysiological patterns, activated through significant developmental experiences, in the context first of primary object relations that become integrated as primitive affective memory structures. By contrast, drives (libido, aggression) are the unique, unconsciously intentional, continuous, individualized sources of motivation. Drives constitute the supraordinate integration of the various affect states, their psychic aspect, assembled and elaborated: libido organizing the erotically centered states, and aggression arranging such states as rage, envy, disgust, anger, irritation and so forth.

Affective structures provide direction and meaning to early communication processes. In partial agreement with contemporary affect theorists (Tomkins, Izard, Ekman, Stern), Kernberg suggests that affects include: (a) a rewarding or aversive subjective experience; (b) specific facial patterns; (c) a cognitive component (of self and object representations); (d) various muscular (action) and neurovegetative (somatic) outputs (discharge patterns). However, from a psychoanalytic perspective, the central feature of each affect is anchored in the "subjective quality of felt appraisal" (Kernberg, 1992b, p. 5).

Primitive affects (i.e., sexual excitement, rage) appear early (first 2–3 years), while emotions or feelings are the derived, psychically more elaborate, complex combinations of the primitive affects. Whether primary or derived however, affects in and of themselves, do not qualify as the truly appropriate, efficient intrapsychic motivational systems. Calling upon Freud's dream-work model to explain the complex secondary combinations and transformations involved in creating the higher level motivational organization classically referred to as the drives, Kernberg (2001) suggests that drives result from the ongoing psychical alteration, through displacement and condensation, of primary differentiated affective experiences. Once consolidated (sufficiently elaborated and mentalized), the drives may use affects as their signal or representatives, in addition to using them as their building blocks. Activating a drive thus actualises a corresponding affect state, which includes a specific self representation relating to a specific object representation, usually expressed as a concrete fantasy or wish. Elaborated and assimilated as repressed unconscious fantasies, these gradually differentiated experiences establish the support for unconscious wish or desire (Kernberg, 2001, p. 611) and create stable unconscious relations to the parental objects (internalized object relations units), of either feared, desired, idealized, or persecuting relations.

Kernberg's revision of drive theory is partly tributary to the Freudian tradition of the bodily origins of thought. And his new proposal establishes more fruitful connections with recent knowledge concerning affects as sign systems (i.e., Tomkins, Izard, Ekman, see Olds, 2003), their differentiated predisposed structures and components, and their transformation into the drives. This is a clear advantage when compared with the more restricted Freudian conception of affect, whose horizon was limited by the qualitative (pleasure–unpleasure) versus quantitative (Q factor) polarity (see Green, 1973). Moreover, through the concept of internalized object relations, Kernberg takes into account the determining influence of significant affective experiences with the other, and of the internalized other on a gradually elaborated and evolving subjectivity.

His views on the mental elaboration of affects being transformed into primary affective experiences and eventually into drives, imply, without developing it, a model of mentalization whose properties are those described by Freud's dream model of the neurotic mind (condensation, displacement, symbolism, and repression). Kernberg (2001), also partly follows the Kleinian understanding that reunites the source of the drive, its object, and aim under the umbrella concept of unconscious fantasy. This activity of fantasy is one way to account for the representational form and structure given to primitive affective experiences, uniting affect and representation into an indissoluble composite. Beyond their differences, this seems globally compatible with Green's objectalizing function described earlier. Yet, other mentalization processes are also involved in the crucial elaboration of affects, self and object into drive structures. Such transformation processes are present in Kernberg's model, because they are required by his model, but unfortunately, they are not explicitly spelled out and articulated by Kernberg with the other aspects of his metapsychology. This would be the task of a complete integrative psychoanalytic theory of thinking (mentalization).

Mentalization of the Object and Agentive Self

Turning again to the French tradition, mentalization has also been thought to require subjectivation and subjective appropriation of one's encounters with the object (Roussillon, 2001, 2002). Subjectivation requires having been able to represent and symbolize the internal traces of the effects of the subject's self states and encounters with the other. The subject is to represent something about the experience of self. The modulating (or eventually, the disorganizing) effects of the child's encounters with the mother (and the mother's encounters or nonencounters with the child, as experienced by the child) are represented and symbolized, in such a manner that traces of one's own self states are available to the reflective subject. Appropriation implies something else, based on the difference between something simply happening within and something happening *for* oneself. Roussillon (2001) argues that appropriation requires that the subject must further represent that he/she is representing something about himself, and also that he must be able to internalize (practice and elaborate) this self-directed psychical activity, as well as its productions (Roussillon, 2002, p. 76). This implies the establishment of a system of metarepresentations, based on the previously established second-order capacities of self-representation. To mentalize implies to become able to perceive oneself as being the agentive source of auto-representation and auto-symbolization. By definition, the agentive self demonstrates some degree of autonomy, beyond all other constraints, including from the intersubjective and interpersonal fields.

An important potential point of divergence is found here, whether one places the ultimate emphasis on the intergenerational transmission, via the work of mirroring and appropriate differentiation (marking), accomplished by the real object and caregiver in assigning meaning to the infant's affective experience (Fonagy and colleagues), or whether, ultimately, the subject's auto-representational and auto-symbolic activity is assigned the initiative, is given the final word. In our view, it is not obvious that one should have to choose between the one view and the other, and why one could not imagine a continual interactive sequence between both modules, although we would venture that most psychoanalysts would seem to agree that one final determination resides in the organized structures of the unconscious subjective experience. Further, a psychoanalytic view would find it difficult to let go completely of the intuition of the agentive subject as demonstrating its agency by some contemporary psychical action that takes hold of its immediate situation, including bodily pressures, the self, the object, the IIF and its productions, seizing them and transforming them into a renewed form and expression, creatively adaptive to the present context (e.g., Kennedy, 2000).

Concrete Thinking and the Mode of Psychic Equivalence

Concrete thinking is an achievement of the reality ego, but this occurs at the expense of a robust connection with the unconscious life forces. Freud (1911, p. 223) has offered a useful depiction of one of its key features: "the reality-ego need does nothing but strive

for what is *useful* (italics added) and guard itself against damage."
In concrete thinking, the ego is turned toward what is functional,
external, and adaptive, the more so since the external field is the
crucial area from which to expect the blows, thus fulfilling its self-
conservative functions. Compare this with the formulation of the
situation of the child surrounded by threat or actual trauma: "his or
her focus needs to be maintained so closely on the outside world and
its physical and emotional dangers that there is little room for the
idea of a separate, internal world" (Fonagy & Target, 2002, p. 857).
And with this statement by Green (1999, p. 123): "...But the essential
thing...is simply a question of surviving." This detour toward what
is practical and useful, is an adaptive achievement. But in situations
of trauma, what seems useful (vital) is to shut down, withdraw from,
channels of communication, of object seeking and investment, with
the possibility of further knowing of the subject and of the object of
its desire, as would be provided by Green's objectalizing function or
Fonagy and Target's mentalizing function.

This understanding of concrete thinking ascribes some of the
same key features attributed by Fonagy, Target, and colleagues (Fonagy & Target, 2000, Fonagy et al., 2003, Target & Fonagy, 1996) to
the primitive modes of thinking: it is action oriented, factual, and
utilitarian thinking, with exclusion of abstract and symbolic links
(teleologic reasoning and psychic equivalence); the observation that
thoughts and feelings have the quality of being actual, that is, experienced as concretely real; fragmented and dissociated thoughts and
memories without recall, in a movement from the initially normal
pretend mode to it's pathological versions in dissociative thinking;
impoverishment in the temporal structure and reduced preconscious
autobiographical functioning (De M'Uzan; Fonagy et al., 2003,
p. 440); emptiness and noncontactful quality resulting from inau-
thentic self. Thus, in the psychic equivalence mode, the thought of
shame is not only a thought, it is identical with shame (again, reminiscent of de M'Uzan), and internal psychic reality is equated with
the external perceived equivalent; consequences of actions are not
predicted, and prior intentions are not attributed to the other; affective experiences and their associated thoughts are expressed and
dealt with through physical action (enactments), either by using
one's body or through concrete experiences with other people in
sometimes frantic attempts to find oneself (failures of adequate mirroring); violent acts are understood as desperate, concrete defensive

measures against "the onslaught of shame," experienced in this con-crete mode of equivalence as real (Fonagy et al., 2003, p. 445). As Fon-agy and Target (2000, p. 859) put it: "Not being able to feel themselves from within, they are forced to experience the self from without." When extreme and severe, this is experienced as a feeling of numb-ness or deadness, reminiscent of descriptions by Green (1999) of the consequences of the work of the negative. Thus, while the assumed motivational factors involved by each tradition differ, the descriptive features of concrete thinking and of the primitive modes of thinking (psychic equivalence, teleologic reasoning) are quite convergent, as well as inclusive of the acknowledged differences between the more barren and affectively dried-up psychosomatic concrete presentation and the more impulsive and intensely affectively charged concrete behavior of the borderline.

The Pretend Mode and Primitive Dissociation

Several authors, including Freud, have called upon one form or another of a protective and adaptive mechanism of mental rejec-tion (*Verwerfung*). It is clear that important distinctions need to be specified and maintained between the various proposed expla-nations of this basic feature of the human mind, according to the different metapsychologies under which each author operates. Yet some convergence seems possible and important to consider, as these processes imply the important feature of actively antago-nizing linking, and, in general, the establishment of associative connections, a key ingredient of all mentalization processes, be it of drive pressures, object pressures, or the subject itself. Fonagy and Target (1996, 2000) make use of a basic process of rejection and differentiation to account for the pretend mode of thinking, seen when patients establish an area of thinking separate from the rest of the ego and protected from reality, which they present as "the only way to sever the connection between internal states and an intolerable external reality" (Fonagy & Target, 2000, p. 857). In faulty attachment the normal pretend mode of psychic real-ity becomes distorted and overtakes the IIF, with the consequent various forms of dissociative thinking (and traumatic memory) and their associated loss of reality. Reminiscent of Green's (1999) use of Freud's notion of unbinding within the disobjectalizing function, Fonagy and Target (2000) claim that there are moments when nothing can be linked to anything, nothing has implications for anything else.

Primitive Layers of Thinking

The layer of primary mental representations, that "form the equivalent of reality within the psyche" (Luquet, 2002, p. 50) also seems close to Fonagy and Target's (1996) formulation of the equivalent mode of psychic functioning, with some added considerations: concerned mostly with concrete body experiences, they are highly condensed and charged with affect, and are as easily discharged (economic criterion); they become and remain unconscious (not preconscious) for the most part (the topographic aspect); they form the basis of primary action fantasy, the precursor of true object relations. Further, the passages from the teleologic (more primary and concrete thinking) to the truly symbolic and intentional stance are depicted in compatible and converging ways, and the transformations involved in the next layer of metaprimary thought (Luquet, see Bouchard & Lecours, 2004) likely simultaneously emerge in close proximity to the intentional mode of secondary mental representations (Fonagy & Target). The purpose of both modules, however, seems different. The metaprimary thought system is "turned inwards," for the most part, forming an "internal sensory apparatus" (Kaplan-Solms & Solms, 2000), involved in the continual task of elaborating and representing the ever-changing bodily situation and needs into primary fantasies (in Freudian thinking, the primarily infantile sexual needs, urges, and pressures). This is in contrast to the IIF module, involved in interpreting interpersonal and intersubjective transactions, including, eventually, the failed processing of malevolent intentions coming from the real significant attachment figure, the source of external trauma that creates important internal distortions, and a maintenance of the primitive, teleological modes. In our opinion, both modules are required and their complementary functions are inherent to the complex processes involved in mentalization.

Discussion

Our review of the field of mentalization points to four recurring themes. First, the theme of early trauma and neglect, particularly involving primary object relations, is omnipresent, and survival in the face of psychic pain and psychic death is seen more clearly by several authors (Fonagy, Green, de M'Uzan, Target, etc.) as the crucial motivational factor involved in mental operations that will result in poor mentalizing. Second, beyond the important differences in conceptions, most authors use a concept of mental rejection as a vital adaptive and defensive set of mechanisms used by the infant, and maintained by the traumatized adult, whether it is called foreclosure (Green, Lacan), primitive dissociation, splitting or denial (Freud, Green, Kernberg, Klein), or dissociative modes (Fonagy, Target & Gergely). These operations simultaneously favor unlinking, that is, disconnections and active withdrawals. In the end, a sequence from early interpersonal trauma, to unbearable psychic pain, to various forms of protective deactivation of self (disobjectalizing, foreclosure, dissociation and the like), to the establishment of a functional deficit in mentalization capacities is highlighted by most authors, across traditions. Third, all authors point to a persistence of primitive forms of thinking, described in terms that are similar, but variously labeled as concrete mental activity (Marty, de M'Uzan and others), deficits in the preconscious system (Marty), the mode of psychic equivalence (Fonagy & Target; Gergely and Watson), and the like. These primitive modes of psychic reality have in common the demonstration of a failure in the normally occurring movement between one level of thought and the next, between primary and secondary order representations (Fonagy & Target), primary and metaprimary thinking (Luquet), representation and metarepresentation (Roussillon). In other words, failures in the symbolic function are involved, which is shown to be deficient, and or defensively disinvested (Green, Fonagy, Target). Fourth, affect dysregulation is common to most descriptions, construed as an indication of the disorganizing impact of excessive quantities of endogenous stimulation (Freud, de M'Uzan, Green, Marty), as the result of the development of pathological distorted object relations invested with primitive affect (Kernerg), or more recently, as the direct consequence of defects and distortions within the IIF (Fonagy, Target), and the predominance of dissociative and psychic equivalence modes of thinking, in the face of early interpersonal trauma. Robbins (1996) has proposed a converging set of criteria to describe what he refers to as "primitive personalities."

Mentalization seems to involve processes concerned with a transformation of three interconnected spheres: the drives, the object, and the subject. The Freudian and French traditions since the *Project* are unique in focusing on the mental elaboration through binding of bodily pressures as a primary source of thought. The transformation of primary affective structures and experiences into the drives has importantly been taken up by Kernberg (2001) in his recent efforts toward a renewed formulation of drive theory. The processes involved constitute one specialized aspect of the mentalizing ego, engaged in the activity of investment (Green's objectalizing function, Fonagy and Target's mentalizing function). This function is able to transform its bodily pressures and situations, and connect these with the perceptions of the external world, including perceptions and elaborations of the object and its availability, with the aim of achieving pleasure. It is part of the required work and effort leading to the representational elaboration of the drives into unconscious desires, thus, also shaping the subject's experience of the object.

One may accept the claim that affects are not fully accessible to the child, but discovered through mirroring, appropriate differentiation (marking) and internalization (Gergely & Watson, 1996). Nevertheless, it seems also inescapable that complementarily, affective structures, insofar as they indicate the body's present situation, are inseparably oriented and orienting. Calling for mental elaboration, they determine the direction and quality of mentalization. The process of transformation of affects into the drives (Kernberg, 2001), in the context of internalized object relations constitutes a special part of the mental apparatus, dedicated to the mentalization of these bodily pressures. This is how the self is to develop robust links to the bodily/constitutional self.

Until recently, most Freudians have openly rejected the view that the specialized apparatus, responsible for the mentalization of the drives, is itself reciprocally and crucially determined by the quality of primary caregivers: the ultimate initiative was to be given to the drive. Now it seems that by contrast, and accepting a growing body of convergent evidence to this effect, the transformation process of bodily pressures, its organization in the form of affective structures that become further elaborated into drive derivatives observed in the analytic situation, is itself modulated. Consequently, the drives are themselves partly also the product of primary regulations with the object. And the unique elaborations within a given subject's unconscious, of drives and wishes, reflects these reciprocal determinations.

Mentalization of both the subject and the (internal) object, through the modulating quality of primary relations with the object, is now increasingly acknowledged as a crucial determinant of psychic reality. This is the special kind of mentalization which Fonagy, Target, and colleagues are deconstructing, with a particular focus on early trauma and its catastrophic consequences. De M'Uzan (1994, 2003), Green (1999), Marty (1976) would not disagree, although they might insist that the psychic apparatus itself, as a source and container of all mental elaboration, needs to be established, nurtured, and protected before any intersubjective or interpersonal experience may become elaborated. They make the related point that the subject and the internal object are themselves a product of this mental apparatus, in close connection with its associated affective and drive dispositions. This is the essence of Green's objectalizing function concept, that self, object, and drive are mutually interactive in an on-going mentalization process. But in the end, it should perhaps never be forgotten that Green's selective observational stance within the analytic situation, with its exclusive focus on the vicissitudes of the internal self, is quite contrasted to the combined psychoanalytic and developmental-naturalistic external observer stance that Fonagy and colleagues partly rely on, traces of which are also to be found in their formulations.

Since Freud's *Project*, we are reminded, particularly by our French colleagues, that corporeal excitations create inputs from below and from within, and it seems impossible to dismiss the key determination of the quantitative endogenous aspect to the origins and nature of mental elaboration. And we are reminded also that traumatized individuals, while trying to adapt to the intolerable external abuse, now internalized, still need to elaborate their now neurobiologically dyseregulated and often excessive "bodily pressures." The undifferentiated, unmentalized, biological substrate consequently becomes an additional source of aggression for the mental apparatus, faced with an "insignificant (i.e., meaningless) economic" (see Bergeron, 2004). Nevertheless, the French account of mentalization processes is also subject to a number of objections and criticisms. First, a purely economic view of trauma, taken in isolation, seems implausible, in the face of the psychic agony experienced by the helpless, impotent child unable to move his objects, resulting in a loss of meaning within the intersubjective field. The intensity of the unmentalized affective experience only makes sense as part of a complex affective system whose structure has been activated, and is of a subject in the context of a drive pressure and in relation to an object (Kernberg, 2001; Roussillon, 2001). In and of itself, quantity cannot be thought of as the uniquely, most significant determinant of the ensuing disorganization. Although for De M'Uzan (2003), quantity remains the ultimate key aspect, it is particularly under conditions where it creates an almost complete intolerance to an otherwise overwhelming confusion between the inside and outside spheres of experience. Yet in situations of trauma and neglect, unmentalized, disruptive shame for example, becomes intolerable partly because of its inherent intensity, with threats of flooding the mental apparatus. Further, these individuals are often seen to actively reject mentalizing possibilities offered, which indicates their need to function at a virtually mindless, or teleological level (see discussion).

Challenging the view that the self would automatically emerge from "the sensation of the mental activity of the self" (Fonagy et al., 2003, p. 413), Fonagy and Target demonstrate that key interpersonal factors including parental mirroring, exert their influence within primary object relations, unwittingly shaping our subjectivities and ultimately, our functional interpretive capacities. The developing infant's sense of agency is the result of a subjective consciousness that is forged by its internal community with others. What was thought to be a product of our deepest individual, if unconscious, powers is transmuted into another, heterogeneous, and even more primary, kind of determination. This is because the child enters into a field situation whose rules it is not for him to determine, but rather, whose rules he/she must learn to submit to, master and use on the way to becoming an agentive self. Theirs is at heart a model of the impact of relational trauma, described in terms of the partial/temporary or irreversible collapse of the IIF on attention and stress regulation. Their model of treatment is importantly concerned with providing a sensitive solution to a current problem, experienced as actual (Bateman & Fonagy, 2004). It is a model focused on the recognition of the psychic reality of trauma.

There is little ground to ignore or reject the crucial determination of past and contemporary "actual" influences (regulations and dysregulations) from mutual interactions with primary caretakers and transferential objects. As Green (1973, p. 19), following Winnicott, points out: "No discourse on affect can hold that does not bring in the affects of the mother." But it also seems the case that psychic excitations and regulations, "from above and from without", in addition to their crucial modulating functions, are represented and integrated within the endogenous affective experiences, in the form of internalized object relations, and become part of each person's unique version of the life and death drives. This process constitutes a second special part of the mental apparatus, dedicated to the mentalization of the object and of the vicissitudes of our affective experiences with it. The global result is always an amalgam, the interleaving of the intrapsychic and the intersubjective, the objectalizing and disobjectalizing. Kernberg is cautious and rightly critical of theories of interpersonal functioning that explain away unconscious mental structures "as replicas of aspects of actual past interactions" (Kernberg, 2001, p. 606). The representational function (which includes the IIF) in one sense creates and modifies the traces of what was perceived and experienced in actual past and present interactions. These outcomes become active once again when recruited and staged through fantasy, to new levels of meaning and mental elaboration. Because of this process, the more mental transformation is allowed to take place, the further the distance between the initially perceived other's mirrored experience, and the internal sense of what that experience is. And one can imagine a virtually endless cyclic process of mentalization between the various identified components of drives, self, and object, each module producing a result which is ideally taken up by the other modules, forming, in the better conditions (i.e., equilibrium between the life and death drives), the material for further elaboration from the next module within its specialized realm.

References

Bateman, A. & Fonagy, P. (2004). Psychotherapy for borderline personality disorder: Mentalization-based treatment. London : Oxford University Press.

Beebe, B. & Lachmann, F. M. (2002). *Infant research and adult treatment.* Hillsdale, NJ: Analytic Press.

Bergeron, E. (2004), L'élaboration du sens dans la théorie psychosomatique. Perspectives sur la mentalization. Unpublished doctoral dissertation, Université de Montréal.

Bion, W. (1962). A theory of thinking. *Internat. J. Psychoanal., 43,* 306–310.

Bouchard, M. A. & Lecours, S. (2004). Analysing forms of superego functioning as mentalizations. *Internat. J. Psychoanal., 85*, 879–896.

De M'Uzan, M. (1973), A case of masochistic perversion and an outline of a theory. *Internat. J. Psychoanal., 54*, 455–467.

De M'Uzan, M. (1994). *La bouche de l'inconscient.* (Trans. title: *The mouth of the unconscious*), Paris: Gallimard.

De M'Uzan, M. (2003). Slaves of quantity. *Psychoanal. Inq., 72*, 711–725. Initially published as Les esclaves de la quantité In: Nouvelle Revue de Psychanalyse (1984), *30*, 129–138.

Fonagy, P., Gergely, G., Jurist, E. & Target, M. (2002). *Affect regulation, mentalization and the development of the self.* New York: Other Press.

Fonagy & Target, M. (1996). Playing with reality: I. Theory of mind and the normal development of psychic reality. *Internat. J. Psychoanal., 77*, 217–233.

Fonagy & Target, M. (2000). Playing with reality: III. The persistence of dual psychic reality in borderline patients. *Internat. J. Psychoanal., 81*: 853–874.

Fonagy & Target, M. (2002). Early intervention and the development of self-regulation. *Psychoanal. Inq, 22*, 307–335.

Fonagy, Target, M., Gergely, G., Allen, J. G. & Bateman, A. W. (2003). The developmental roots of borderline personality disorder in early attachment relationships: A theory and some evidence. *Psychoanal. Inq., 23*, 412–459.

Fosshage, J. (2000) Interaction in psychoanalysis : A broadening horizon. *Psychoanal. Dial., 5*, 459–478.

Freud, S. (1895). Project for a scientific psychology. *Standard Edition, 1*, 295–397. London: Hogarth Press.

Freud. (1900). The interpretation of dreams. *Standard Edition, 4*, 1–338. London : Hogarth Press.

Freud. (1911). Formulations on the two principles of mental functioning. *Standard Edition, 12*, 218–226. London: Hogarth Press.

Freud. (1915). The unconscious. *Standard Edition, 14*: 166–215. London: Hogarth Press.

Freud. (1918). From the history of an infantile neurosis. *Standard Edition, 17*, 7–122. London: Hogarth Press.

Freud. (1920). Beyond the pleasure principle. *Standard Edition, 18*, 7–64. London: Hogarth Press.

Gergely, G. & Watson, J. (1996). The social biofeedback model of parental affect-mirroring. *Internat. J. Psychoanal., 77*, 1181–1212.

Green, A. (1973). *Le Discours Vivant.* Trans. title: (*The Fabric of Affect in the Psychoanalytic Discourse*). Routledge, New library of Psychoanalysis. Paris: Presses Universitaires de France.

Green, A. (1984). Le langage dans la psychanalyse. *Langages*. Paris: Les Belles Lettres. pp. 19–250.

Green, A. (1999). *The work of the negative*, trans. A. Weller. London: Free Association.

Green, A. (2000a). The Chains of Eros: The Sexual in Psychoanalysis. New York: Karnac.

Green, A. (2000b). The central phobic position: a new formulation on free association. *Internat. J. Psychoanal., 81*, 429–451.

Kaplan-Solms, K. & Solms, M. (2000). *Clinical studies in neuro-psychoanalysis :Introduction to a depth neuropsychology*. Madison, CT: International Universities Press.

Kennedy, R. (2000), Becoming a subject: Some theoretical and clinical issues. *Internat. J. Psychoanal.*, 81, 875–892.

Kernberg, O. F. (1992a). A theoretical frame for the study of sexual perversions. *Aggression in Personality Disorders and Perversion*. New Haven, CT: Yale University Press, pp. 263–276.

Kernberg, O. F. (1992b). New perspectives on drive theory. *Aggression in Personality Disorders and Perversion*. New Haven, CT: Yale University Press, pp. 3–20.

Kernberg. (2001). Object relations, affects and drives: Toward a new synthesis. *Psychoanal. Inq., 21*, 604–619.

Lecours, S. & Bouchard, M. A. (1997). Dimensions of mentalization: Outlining levels of mental elaboration. *Internat. J. Psychoanal., 78*, 855–875.

Luquet, P. (2002). *Les Niveaux de Pensée*. (Trans. title: *The levels of thought*), Paris: Presses Univ. France.

Luria, A. R. (1973). The working brain: An introduction to neuropsychology. New York: Basic Books.

Marty, P. (1968). A major process of somatization: The progressive disorganization. *Internat. J. Psychoanal., 49*, 246–249.

Marty, P. (1976). Les Mouvements Individuels de Vie et de Mort. Essai d'économie Psychosomatique. (Trans. title: *Individual movements of life and death*), Paris: Payot.

Marty, P. (1990). *La Psychosomatique de l'Adulte*. (Trans. title: *Adult Psychosomatics*) Paris: Presses Universitaires de France.

Marty, P. (1991). *Mentalisation et Psychosomatique*. (Trans. title: *Mentalization and Psychosomatics*) Paris : Synthélabo. Coll. Empêcheurs de tourner en rond.

Marty, P. & De M'Uzan, M. (1963). La pensée opératoire. (Trans. title: *Concrete and action bound thinking*), *Revue française de psychanalyse, 37*, 345–356. Republished in 1994 in Revue française de psychosomatique, 6, 197–207.

Olds, D. D. (2003). Affect as sign system. *Neuro-Psychoanalysis, 5*, 81–95.

Robbins, M. (1996). The mental organisation of primitive personalities and its treatment implications. *J. Amer. Psychoanal. Assn., 44,* 755–784.

Roussillon, R. (2001). *Le plaisir et la répétition.* (Trans. title: *Pleasure and repetition*), Paris: Dunod.

Roussillon, R. (2002), Le transitionnel et l'indéterminé. (Trans. title: *The transitional and the indeterminate*). In: B. Chouvier (Ed.). *Les processus psychiques de la médiation.* Paris: Dunod, pp. 61–80.

Simpson, R. B. (2003). Introduction to Michel de M'Uzan's "Slaves of quantity." *Psychoanal. Quart., 72,* 699–709.

Stolorow, R. (1997) Dynamic, dyadic, intersubjective systems: An evolving paradigm for psychoanalysis. *Psychoanal. Psychol., 14,* 337–346.

Target, M. & Fonagy, P. (1996). Playing with reality II: The development of psychic reality from a theoretical perspective. *Internat. J. Psychoanal., 77,* 459–479.

Winnicott, D. W. (1951/1987). Transitional objects and transitional phenomena. In: D. W. Winnicott. *Through Paediatrics to Psycho-Analysis.* London: Hogarth Press, pp. 229–242.

Part II

Research

4

On the Origins of Reflective Functioning*

Howard Steele and Miriam Steele

Background

It helps to be in the right place at the right time. For us, London was the right place, and 1986 was the right time to have begun a longitudinal joint research endeavor that led to our doctoral degrees in psychology, and indirectly, to the discovery of the central role mentalization plays in human development and mental health. Our direct aim in the longitudinal work we began was to investigate intergenerational patterns of attachment just as the scientific study of attachment was undergoing a dramatic paradigmatic shift (Main, Kaplan, & Cassidy, 1985). In London, we could go to the Tavistock Clinic and receive advice and support from John Bowlby in the final years of his most productive life (1986–1990), which was a valuable addition to

* The longitudinal research work reported here has been supported by a project research grant (R000233684) from the Economic and Social Research Council (ESRC in the UK), and three generous project grants from the Köhler Stiftung (Germany). Post-graduate fellowships to research students working on the study have been received from the ESRC, the Medical Research Council (MRC, UK), the British Council, the Social Sciences and Humanities Research Council (SSHRC, Canada); and the Overseas Studentship Awards (ORS) in the U.K. During the early stages of the work, small grant support was received from the Nuffield Foundation, the Child Psychotherapy Trust, the Central Research Fund of the University of London, and the Collaborative Research Fund of the Anna Freud Centre. During the initial years of the longitudinal work (in the late 1980s), valuable insight and encouragement was provided by John Bowlby and George Moran. Particular thanks are owed to the families who have participated in the London Parent Child Project, for far longer than they (or we) imagined.

the spirited research supervision available from Peter Fonagy at University College London. We were inspired by the way Fonagy combined empirical psychological research with clinical training at the British Psychoanalytic Society. Fonagy's thinking, and our own as a consequence, was influenced by the distinctive admixture of Kleinian, Freudian, and independent thinking that has long characterized discussions and debate in British psychoanalysis. These factors are critical aspects to the background of the reflective functioning (RF) concept, currently one of the most vibrant areas of discussion in clinical psychoanalysis and psychoanalytic thinking.

The initial development of the RF concept was thus influenced by the epistemic space associated with diverse psychoanalytic and developmental psychological viewpoints. Given our starting point 20 years ago, that of using a highly promising interview technique (the Adult Attachment Interview, George, Kaplan, & Main, 1985) to investigate links between expectant parents' memories of their childhood upon their imminent new parent-child relationships observed with a previously validated and widely used observational technique (the Strange Situation, Ainsworth, Blehar, Waters, & Wall, 1978), we were inevitably influenced by attachment theory and research—but much else beyond. With Peter Fonagy, we were attentive to the exciting new relational perspective emerging within psychoanalysis in the late 1980s (Greenberg & Mitchell, 1983), the range of distinctive British object-relations and independent psychoanalytic perspectives being widely discussed at psychoanalytic meetings (including the views of Bion, Bollas, Bowlby, Sandler, & Winnicott), and the novel set of discoveries and writings on theory of mind and intentionality in development psychology and philosophy of mind so current at that time (Baron-Cohen, 1989, 1991, 1993; Dennett, 1978; Harris, 1989). Later RF would be wedded to emerging findings in cognitive developmental neuroscience (e.g., Fonagy & Target, 2005) but this, as we show, was not the initial intention for the concept. Initially, we saw our efforts in terms of finding a way to successfully operationalize a number of familiar core concepts in psychodynamic writings, for example, psychological mindedness, self-observational capacities of the ego, insight, and reality testing—showing their relevance to understanding parental contributions to individual differences in infant-parent attachment (Fonagy, Steele, Steele, Moran, & Higgitt 1991).

The interest value of our observation that parental reflective functioning is associated with infant-parent attachment quality depends largely on the predictive power of the Ainsworth strange situation (Ainsworth, Blehar, Waters & Wall, 1978). It is nothing less than amazing that an observational technique designed in less than 30 minutes (Ainsworth & Marvin, 1995), administered over 20 minutes in a laboratory setting with parent, child and stranger, permits reliable and valid inferences as to the quality of the infant's experiences in their primary attachment relationships (Ainsworth, Blehar, Waters & Wall, 1978). Where Anna Freud (1965)—in step with her father's writings and all range of psychoanalytic theory—argued that the infant's primary object relationship (typically to mother) is the central and most important of all developmental lines, Mary Ainsworth and colleagues showed that this is so, demonstrating how to reliably measure this relationship at one year of age. Crucially, a vast body of empirical work has demonstrated the long-term significance of primary attachment relationships for subsequent mental health (Carlson, 1998), peer relationship quality and powers of concentration (Suess, Sroufe & Grossmann, 1992), levels of academic achievement (van Ijzendoorn, Dijkstra, & Bus, 1995), emotion understanding skills (Steele, Steele, Croft & Fonagy, 1999), functioning in romantic relationships in early adulthood (Roisman, Collins, Sroufe, and Egeland, et al., 2005), and overall sense of self or personhood (Sroufe, Egeland, Carlson & Collins, 2005). In the account of RF we provide later, we draw attention to a topic of much contemporary interest in psychoanalytic and developmental circles, namely the possibly distinctive contributions of mothers and fathers to their children's development, including their eventual capacity to reflect on how each of their parents influenced the persons they have become (Steele & Steele, 2005b)—a consideration vital to reflective functioning.

The RF concept, and its elaboration in the manual relevant to rating Adult Attachment Interviews (Fonagy, Target, Steele, & Steele, 1998), is anchored in careful study of how adults use, or fail to use, mental state language (beliefs and desires) when pressed to give an account of their developmental history. For the psychoanalytically-informed reader, our 1998 manual on RF (circa 100 pages) is rather like a translation of the literature on the ego and mechanisms of defense into mental state terms. For example, a low RF score is often assigned because the speaker demonstrates an impoverished ability to access the motivational roots of behavior in the self or others. When asked a question that ordinarily demands reflection— for example, "why do you think your parents behaved the way they did during your childhood?"—the speaker with very low RF skills is likely to respond "how should I know, ask them!" showing disavowal and isolation of affect. At the same time, such a response shows a lack of interest in exploring the internal world of one's parents, or—in other words—the source and content of one's introjects. Little surprise, then, that we would later show such speakers to have a pronounced restriction in the parenting domain of sensitively exploring their children's internal worlds. For speakers with evidently high RF skills, questions that demand reflection are embraced with interest and often joy. They typically show spontaneous readiness to contemplate the mental states that guided their parents' behavior toward them as a child, often doing so in a humorous and mindful way indicative of mature defense mechanisms. In the process they often allude to their grandparents' beliefs and behavior thus showing an intuitive understanding of intergenerational influences. At the same time, alongside a spirited curiosity about human motivation there is no insistent claim to knowing for sure what was in the parents' (or grandparents') minds—this we call an appreciation for the opaqueness of mental states. Freud's principle of overdetermination may be seen as a related concept and one that a high RF speaker would be naturally appreciative of.

The RF concept was not only influenced by Freudian and Anna Freudian theories. We were also trying to take account of Kleinian ideas regarding the nature of emotion and thought and the child's need for containment. Some of Bowlby's early (1956) writings reached in this direction as well, for example, when he spoke of the deep and inevitable feelings of hate, envy, and fear (normally matched and overcome by enduring feelings of joy, warmth and trust) that all children feel toward their parents. In the speaker with low RF skills, this range and intensity of human feelings is typically avoided (the hypo-RF stance), or presented in an emotionally aroused and often angry manner (the hyper-RF stance). By contrast, high RF speakers are freely disposed toward considering the diversity of positive and negative feelings that are both causes and consequences of behavior.

Other influences on the development of the RF concept, richly evident in the British psychoanalytic community, were the enigmatic writings of Donald Winnicott, and the creative way these ideas were being distilled in the late 1980s. As Adam Phillips put it in his biographical work that revealed as much as it described, "each of Winnicott's contributions to psychoanalytic theory came out of his deep visual sense of what mothers did for their infants…. When the infant looks at the mother's face he can see himself, how he feels reflected back in her expression. If she is preoccupied by something else, when he looks at her he will only see how *she* feels" (Phillips, 1988, p. 128). For Winnicott, the infant can only discover what he really feels by seeing it reflected back. If the infant is seen in a way that permits him to feel fully that he exists, in a way that validates him, he is free to go on looking. And, in RF terms, he is free to go on thinking and exploring the mental and emotional world of others, and go on thinking. These are only some of the psychoanalytic influences upon the development of the RF concept, but they perhaps offer an indication of the range of considerations upon the process of stumbling upon this idea compatible with contemporary developmental research on emotion, morality, and theory of mind, as well as the gathering force in psychoanalytic circles of relational ideas.

More specifically, the reflective functioning concept emerged out of attempts we made to refine our understanding of the rating and classification of the Adult Attachment Interview (AAI). The AAI (George, Kaplan, & Main, 1985), and the elaborate system—codified by Mary Main, Ruth Goldwyn and Erik Hesse—for rating and classifying adults' *language* when asked to describe and evaluate childhood attachment experiences, Notably, the AAI first appeared in the literature in the same year as Daniel Stern's landmark account of the multiple layers of the self arising out of interpersonal interactions, and representations based on these, over the first two years of life *before language* develops (Stern, 1985). The RF concept can be seen as one of the bridges connecting these two contributions. That is, between Main and colleague's account of parenting and Stern's account of the development of self in early childhood. The RF literature provides a model of how the healthy/reflective parent encourages in the infant an efficacious belief in the ability to initiate, and respond to, repair of miscues and ruptures in interactions. By contrast, the parent with longstanding attachment difficulties, and a correspondingly impoverished ability to reflect on these deficits in experience and character, will be at risk of frequent ruptures in communication between self/parent and baby that are *not* repaired, leaving parent and child exceedingly vulnerable to feelings of fragmentation, isolation, anger, and despair. Such a parent with low or hostile RF is likely to seriously skew the normal development of reflective functioning, and with it the course of self and personality development, in his or her child.

This is because the child will be compelled to use this natural mental ability in a strictly defensive manner to anticipate the feared and hostile mind of the caregiver—so as to know when to hide or run—in the service of survival.

Constructing the Reflective Functioning Scale

RF started to take shape in the weeks and months after our participation in the 1987 AAI Institute, convened at the Tavistock Clinic, London and taught by Mary Main with Erik Hesse. We set about applying the 150 page manual, which specifies a set of 9-point scales for rating probable past experience and current state of mind regarding attachment. Among the latter state of mind scales are three scales pertaining to the mental processes underling a speaker's language provided in response to the AAI. These three scales are (a) coherence of transcript; (b) coherence of mind; and (c) metacognition. To score coherence of transcript, one considers how well the interview agrees with Grice's maxims or rules of collaborative conversation, that is, *truth* or having evidence for what you claim, *economy* or saying neither too much nor too little, *relation* or staying on task, and *manner* or remaining conventionally polite. To score coherence of mind, one makes allowances for lack of schooling or sophisticated language and makes a judgment about the essential mind behind the speech—is it organized and stable? Finally, metacognition in the Berkeley manual, considers the extent to which the speaker monitors and, where necessary, corrects their speech in order to remain faithful to Grice's criteria. Not surprisingly, then, these three scales correlate highly with one another.

Yet, in reading the transcriptions of interviews we had collected from the expectant mothers and expectant fathers participating in the London Parent-Child Project, there were certain questions within the AAI protocol that seemed to call forth, in some speakers, a remarkable capacity to reflect on the motivational roots of behavior. We were particularly interested in two questions which appear late (typically 45–60 minutes into the interview) in the 15-question protocol comprising the AAI. These are questions that *demand* evaluation or examination of the motivations and influences guiding behavior in the self and others. Namely, *when you think about your childhood experiences, do you think they have an influence on who*

you are today (as an adult)? And, *when you think about your parents'*
behavior toward you when you were a child, why do you think they
behaved the way they did? We considered responses to these questions, and others across the AAI transcript as a whole, observing that
some speakers appeared to feel right at home with these questions,
distinguishing between their thinking as a child and later as an adult,
spontaneously describing behavior of the self or others in the family
that seemed to reflect hidden or unconscious motives, and using mental state terms (beliefs and desires) to account for effects of relationships upon relationships, across the lifespan and across generations.
To capture these observations, we found the most appropriate tool
was the existing metacognition scale (a 9-point index tapping modes
of monitoring one's own thought processes). We moved beyond this
precise definition given in the Berkeley manual so that the scale in
our hands would cover thinking about beliefs and desires in the self
and others, now, in the past and in the imagined future.

So, the metacognition scale we applied to the interviews we collected was centrally based on considering the speaker's awareness
of emotional and motivational processes underlying behavior in
the self and others. In addition, we paid close attention to linguistic evidence of the speaker being aware of the distinction between
conscious and unconscious processes, and to the developmental differences between child and adult thought processes. We paid attention to the quality of the speakers' understanding of intentionality, as
well as its depth in the sense of a conscious recognition of the role of
unconscious factors. We summarized the 9-point scale as follows:

Scores of 1–3: At the low end of the scale, there is the presence of
truisms and banal attributions which are unconvincingly metacognitive. There is scant evidence that the individual thinks either
about the motives which guided their parents' behavior toward
them, or about their own actions and responses.

Scores of 4–5: In the moderate range, there is either a general understanding of human motives but this is not applied to the subject's
own experiences, or (where there is a consideration of the motivations guiding child-parent interactions relevant to the self)
the conclusions drawn are inaccurate and/or do not distinguish
between child and adult thought processes.

Scores of 6–9: At the high end of the scale, there is organized and consistent understanding of the conscious (and unconscious) motivations

guiding one's own behavior (as a child and as an adult), and of the parent (then and now), and of the interdependence of these processes.

This was the skeletal structure of the scale that would later be extensively elaborated upon through the process of rating Attachment Interviews, and documented in a manual (Fonagy, Target, Steele, & Steele, 1998) as reflective functioning. We next briefly describe this metamorphosis from a one page modification of the metacognition scale to a distinctive theoretical contribution carrying the label RF— and one that has a valid psychometric base in the longitudinal data we have collected from the families participating in the London Parent-Child Project (Steele & Steele, 2005a).

In our widely cited paper (Fonagy, Steele, & Steele, 1991) on the ratings and classifications of primiparous mothers' AAIs and how these linked up with their infants' attachment to them one year later—there is no mention of either metacognition or reflective functioning. At the pre-publication stage we shared a copy of the accepted paper with Mary Main and Erik Hesse. They pointed out that the scores we were reporting for metacognition (RF in the making) were much higher than anyone else had observed (circa 6 for secure-autonomous mothers, 5 for insecure preoccupied mothers, and 4 for insecure-dismissing mothers). We were confronted with the enlargement we had made of their metacognition scale beyond their precise definition of metacognition as monitoring and correcting one's own speech. We corrected the manuscript in press by excising all reference to metacognition, and retreating to consider our metacognition results again.

We flirted with a number of terms for the metacognitive phenomenon we had observed before settling on the reflective self, and later— reflective functioning. First, we contemplated the *internal observer*. And, thus when Peter Fonagy titled the plenary address we gave to the London Regional Meeting of the World Association of Infant Mental Health in 1990, this read as "The role of the internal observer in the mother in promoting secure infant-mother attachment." At this point, we were guided most strongly perhaps by the literature on the self-observing function of the ego. Soon after, Peter carried word of an inspired talk he had heard given by the British Independent analyst, Christopher Bollas, where he had contrasted the prereflective (infant) and postreflective (adult) mind. This suggestion was compelling, and highly consistent with developmental and psychoanalytic assumptions, that is, that prior to the emergence of symbolic thought in the child (after 18 months of age), and every night in our dreams, we are governed by prereflective thought where, in Freudian terms, primary processes rule. Later, with and following the development of language, secondary processes begin to exert their influence and acquire control, at least of the conscious mind. This affords the possibility, indeed requires, reflection on the mind of the other, and on one's own emerging mind. The 1990 plenary address on the internal observer went to press with the title "The capacity for understanding mental states: The reflective self in parent and child and its significance for security of attachment" (Fonagy, Steele, Steele, Moran, & Higgitt, 1991). We did eventually stop referring to the reflective self as this was too often misunderstood as self-reflection which detracted from a central feature of our intention with the concept, that is, to underscore the fundamentally interpersonal nature of mind. And so, we settled on the concept of reflective functioning (RF). Before commenting on changes to the RF scale occasioned by our application of the scale to clinical, and especially forensic populations, we first summarize the evidence we have collected from the low-risk London Parent-Child Project concerning the discriminant, concurrent and predictive validity following our initial ratings of RF.

Reliability and Validity of the RF Concept: Summary of Findings from the London Parent-Child Project

Reliability and Correlations of Parents' Ratings

Our reliable ratings of reflective functioning in the Adult Attachment Interviews we collected from some 100 pregnant women and their partners (the expectant fathers) revealed that we were using most of, but not all, the points comprising the 9-point scale. Of immediate interest here is that there was no gender difference in the assignment of our scores. Men scored as highly as women on this dimension, though we did make it a condition of entry into the study that *both* expectant parents were required. Thus, we may have recruited in such a way as to maximize the possibility of finding thoughtful, reflective adults. Their reflective state of mind may have been facilitated by their older status (mid-30s on average), and life circumstance of awaiting parenthood. When we looked at whether the mothers' and fathers' RF scores were correlated with another, there was only a weak and non-significant link. Thus, we found no strong evidence of assortative mating on the basis of RF levels.

Is RF Distinct from Personality, Verbal Intelligence, and Educational Level Achieved (i.e., Factors We Would not Expect to Be Strongly Related to RF)?

A preliminary step in our research with the RF scores we obtained from the 96 mothers and 90 fathers in our longitudinal study was to establish the extent to which our ratings of RF were tied to personality characteristics (e.g., introversion or neuroticism) or aspects of verbal intelligence (IQ or education level achieved). We therefore administered, at the time of the one-year follow-up, standardized tests of personality (Eysenck, 1975) and verbal IQ (Raven, Court, & Raven, 1986)—neither suggested any significant overlap with RF scores assigned to the attachment interviews from the mothers or from the fathers. In other words, there were some highly introverted, neurotic, extroverted, or verbally clever personalities who scored low on RF, and others who scored high on RF—with variability in RF scores being unrelated to personality or intelligence. This being so, there was a modest correlation between RF scores assigned to attachment interviews from the fathers and their reported years in formal schooling, with higher scores for those with university experience. To the extent that RF skills empower one to believe in one's potential for achieving (academically), this makes sense. At the same time, it may be that inherent intellectual skills are partially responsible for making one predisposed toward reflective functioning. Later, under predictive validity we speculate further on this link in respect of mothers and fathers and their 11-year-old children.

Is RF Correlated with Other AAI Rating Scales and Classifications that We Would Expect It to Be Linked with (e.g., a Loving History with Own Parents, Coherence, Autonomy/Security)?

When we correlated RF ratings with the overall classification (insecure versus secure) of the Adult Attachment Interview, substantial and significant correlations were observed: For both the mothers and fathers their AAI security correlated highly with reflective functioning. When we compared our RF ratings with our reliable ratings of whether the pregnant women had been well loved by their own mothers, and own fathers, significant correlations of only a modest magnitude were observed. Substantially and significantly larger correlations were observed when we compared our ratings of RF with our ratings of coherence-the hallmark of an attachment interview that is ultimately rated as secure in the Main et al system. These correlations point to two different routes leading to high reflective functioning in adulthood. The first route applies to those adults who are highly reflective *because* they were well loved during childhood, the other route applies to those resilient adults who are highly reflective *despite not* being consistently or well loved during childhood and yet somewhere along the way they mastered the capacity to put themselves in the shoes of the other, and to see that the other may have different thoughts, feelings, and intentions than the self (see Fonagy, Steele, Steele, Target, & Higgitt, 1994). In sum, there was impressive and interpretable consistency in our ratings of the attachment interviews from the mothers and fathers in the London Parent-Child Project.

How Did RF Link Up with Infant-Parent Attachment?

When we computed the correlation between the observed quality of the infant-mother attachment (insecure versus secure), for the 96 infant-mother pairs observed at 12 months, with our ratings of mothers' RF skills a year before—we were astounded at the extent of overlap ($r=.58$, $p < .0001$). Of somewhat lesser magnitude was the correlation between infant-mother attachment security and classification of the mothers' AAIs (insecure versus secure) from one year before ($r=.47$, $p < .0001$). Extent of mothers' having been loved well (a past experience rating from the AAI rating scales) did not even correlate significantly with infant-mother attachment at 12 months ($r=.13$, N.S.), suggesting that some mothers with a history of deprivation nonetheless had securely attached infants. Coherence of mind, and coherence of transcript ratings, vital components of the AAI rating manual (Main, Goldwyn, & Hesse, 2002), of mothers' interviews correlated with infant-mother attachment significantly reflecting a conventional order of magnitude ($r=.37$, $p < .01$ and $r=.30$, $p < .01$ respectively).

When we computed the correlation between the observed quality of the infant–father attachment (insecure versus secure), for the 90 infant-father pairs observed at 18 months, with our ratings of fathers' RF skills in the interviews collected more than 1 and ½ years before—we were struck by a remarkable extent of association (r= .64, $p < .0001$). Looking pale in comparison were the correlations between infant-father attachment security with classification of fathers' AAI security (r= .37, $p < .01$). However, the correlation between coherence of mind in fathers' AAIs with infant-father attachment (r =.56, $p < .0001$) bears resemblance to the impressive observed RF/infant-father attachment association.

We have reported elsewhere (Steele, Steele, & Fonagy, 1996) how information from the mothers' AAIs was not useful in predicting the infant-father attachment, and nor was information from the fathers' AAIs useful in predicting the infant-mother attachment. These independent lines of influence across generations also hold with respect to the RF scores assigned to the interviews, and further underscore the relationship-specific nature of attachment during infancy. In other words, a baby forms a relationship with his or her father primarily because of the way that father interacts with his child, and because of the thoughts, feelings, and fantasies about close relationships that the father carries with him, out of his own childhood. This is at odds with the classical idea of the child's relationship with mother being the prototype of all later love relations. We have charted the largely distinct influences of mother and father upon child development over the years, and below we summarize these findings. First, we ask if parental RF predicted infant–parent attachment security more efficiently than the conventional AAI coherence ratings and classifications of security as distinct from insecurity.

Regression Results

Hierarchical linear regression results were computed with infant-mother attachment, and independently with infant-father attachment, as the dependent or outcome variable. In each regression equation we specified as independent variables the AAI classifications and AAI rating scales identified earlier with significant links to the infant-parent outcome (including RF in the last step) in order to observe the extent to which RF was making an independent contribution to the prediction of infant-parent attachment security, above and beyond the most powerful elements of the conventional scoring, namely coherence of transcript and mind (Main, Goldwyn, & Hesse, 2003). Hierarchic linear regression is useful in this context because it allows us to identify the extent to which predictor variables are independent or overlapping influences upon the outcome variable. It is useful to visualize the statistical technique as a ven diagram with two partially overlapping circles, for example, parental attachment and infant-parent attachment. The extent of overlap is a percentage amount given as the shared variance. The addition of each successive variable may map on to new territory or simply cover ground that is already shared by the existing circles. If the third (or further) variable contributes new or additional predictive power, then the *Fchange* statistic will be significant and the increase in variance (the square of the correlation) may be reckoned as meaningful, that is, worth paying attention to or pointing to something new in need of explanation. In the final model of a regression procedure, it is important to pay attention to the Beta weights as they reflect the independent contributions made by the variables in the final model to predicting the outcome. If there are a number of closely overlapping variables, only one of them may be present in the final model—the one that overlaps most with the outcome, that is, the one that makes the strongest contribution to the model. In terms of psychoanalytic metaphors, linear regression is akin to the situation of an analyst giving a referral for treatment to a potential patient. A number of colleagues able to provide treatment may be considered, but often one stands out as being outstanding for the particular task at hand, so it is with statistical procedures like regression. A number of variables may be helpful in predicting an outcome but, with the statistical technique of regression, we are able to identify the outstanding predictor—similar to but better than the rest.

First we specified infant-mother attachment (insecure vs. secure) as the outcome. At the first step we entered the AAI classification (insecure vs. secure) of the mother, $F (1,95) = 27.0$, $p < .0001$, with 22% of the variance in outcome accounted for. At the second step, we entered coherence of transcript, *Fchange* $(1,94) < 1$, N.S., with no additional variance accounted for. At the third step, we entered coherence of mind, *Fchange* $(1,93) = 2.3$, N.S., with a negligible further 2% of variance in outcome accounted for. At the fourth and final step, we entered reflective functioning, *Fchange* $(1,92) = 21.6$

$p < .0001$, with a further 14% of variance in outcome accounted for. Thus, cumulatively, the model explained 39% of the variance in infant-mother attachment security. Notably, the final model showing standardized beta weights, and observed significance values, reveals that the burden of prediction is being carried exclusively by AAI security of mother ($Beta=.31, p < .05$) and reflective functioning of the mother ($Beta=.56, p < .0001$). At this stage, because of overlapping variance with both the AAI classification and RF, the coherence scales do not make independent contributors to the model. In other words, above and beyond the frequently cited classification of mothers' attachment security, only the dimensional rating of reflective functioning made a significant and powerful contribution to the model predicting infant-mother attachment security.

Second, we specified infant-father attachment (insecure vs. secure) as the outcome. At the first step we entered father's highest level of education attained, $F (1,88) = 8.8 \ p < .005$, with 9% of variance in outcome accounted for. At the second step, we entered the AAI classification (insecure vs. secure) of fathers' interviews, $Fchange$ $(1,87) = 12.3 \ p < .001$, with an additional 11% of variance accounted for in outcome. At the third step, we entered coherence of mind, $Fchange (1,86) = 17.1 \ p < .0001$, with an additional 13% of variance in the infant-father outcome accounted for. At the fourth and final step, we entered RF of the father as observed in the AAI, $Fchange (1,86) =$ $15.5 \ p < .0001$, with a further 10% of variance in outcome accounted for. Cumulatively, the model accounted for 44% of the variance in infant-father attachment security. Notably, the final model showing standardized beta weights, and observed significance values, reveals that the burden of prediction is being carried exclusively by the rating of fathers' RF ($Beta=.73, p < .0001$). Because of extensive overlapping variance among these other variables in the model with RF and the uniquely high correlation of fathers' RF-levels with the observed quality of the infant-father attachment, only fathers' RF remains in the final model and it is in this sense that the full burden (or opportunity) of prediction falls on RF.

Parent's RF and Their Children's Theory of Mind Skills at Age 5

As we pondered the meaning of the previously mentioned results, a vital longitudinal hypothesis came to mind. If our ratings of RF were reliable and valid as we had shown in the early phases of the London Parent-Child Project, could we not more thoroughly examine the validity of our RF ratings? In particular, we expected that children's theory of mind skills might be advanced if their mothers (or their fathers?) had high reflective functioning skills. If the latter applied, such parents ought surely to have been more likely to engage their children in meaningful and stimulating discussions of how to guess accurately, and respond appropriately to, what is in the mind of the other. We further refined this prediction to not just *anything* that is in the mind of the other, but specifically to thoughts *and feelings* in the mind of the other. We put *feelings* in italics here to capture the excitement we felt at being among those who sought to push the theory of mind paradigm beyond the strictly cognitive domain, into the sphere of emotions. This is now a hot topic in the theory of mind literature (see Carpendale & Lewis, 2004). In 1994, however, the suggestion was new to argue that considering the emotions of others is a vital and necessary part of strategies for physical and social survival/success. We found a natural ally in the inspired work of Paul Harris, who shared with us an ingenious little puppet task he and his colleagues had developed for testing children's false belief understanding with respect to emotions. The task tests whether children can hold in mind the probable emotional state (surprise/anger) of a thirsty puppet elephant Ellie whose favorite cola drink has been poured out and replaced with milk by a mischievous puppet monkey. The act of mischief occurs *out of sight* of the elephant. Thus, a crucial part of the task is when children are asked "what does Ellie first feel" when she returns to her drink, *before* she takes a drink? To pass, they must say "thirsty" or "excited" or some other feeling that would credibly precede the act of drinking what you have been looking forward to drinking! A third of our sample of 87 five-year-olds failed this task by assuming that what they knew was somehow already known by Ellie—depicting her as angry *before* she took a drink. Correct emotion attribution and justification (e.g., she's excited 'cause she doesn't yet know there is milk in the can and not coke), we expected, would be associated with our earlier observations of the children's attachment and the AAI (especially our RF rating of it) obtained from the parents prior to the children's birth.

We found some modest support for our speculations about the possible influence of parents' RF upon children's overall success at the Harris puppet task assessing theory of mind in the domain of understanding the link between emotions and false beliefs. Specifically, 87 children's success at this task, observed at 5-years of age, was correlated significantly with infant-mother attachment at 12 months ($r=.27$, $p <.05$), with mothers' coherence of mind in the pregnancy AAI ($r=.27$, $p <.05$), with mothers' coherence of transcript in the pregnancy AAI ($r=.27$, $p <.05$), and with mothers' reflective functioning in the pregnancy AAI ($r=.30$, $p <.01$). Additionally, and not surprisingly, we observed a significant correlation between children's verbal IQ at age 5 and their success at accurately predicting and describing the deceived puppet elephant's feeling states ($r=.32$, $p <.005$).

We then considered the extent to which these correlates of children's understanding of false beliefs and emotions at age 5 should be regarded as overlapping or potentially independent predictors of the outcome. The most efficient regression model we identified involved entry of children's verbal IQ at the first step, $F (1,80) = 9.0$ $p < .005$, with 10% of variance in outcome accounted for. At the second step we entered the quality of the infant-mother attachment (insecure vs. secure) at 1 year of age, $Fchange (1,79) = 5.5$ $p < .05$, with a further 6% of variance in outcome accounted for. At the third and final step, we entered reflective functioning of the mother as observed in the pregnancy AAI, $F (1,78) = 4.3$ $p < .05$, with a further 4% of variance in outcome accounted for. Thus, cumulatively, the model including current cognitive skills of the child, the child's attachment to mother at 1 year of age, and the child's mother's reflective functioning skills *before* the child was born, was accounting for more than 20% of the variance in children's observed skills at accurately attributing to another, and verbally justifying their emotions, in a false-belief paradigm. The final model showing standardized beta weights, and observed significance values, reveals that the principal burden of prediction is being carried equally by the rating of mothers' RF ($Beta=.25$, $p < .05$), and by the child's verbal IQ, ($Beta=.25$, $p < .05$). Because of extensive overlapping variance between maternal RF and infant-mother attachment, the latter is no longer significant in the final model.

Interestingly, the parental contributions to the previously mentioned model all stem from the early (and ongoing) mother-child relationship—father appears to play no significant role in this story. We have written at some length about the possibly distinct influences of mothers and fathers upon their children's development (see Steele

& Steele, 2005a). In sum, our research experience with the London Parent-Child Project has supported the idea that the mother-child relationship is a domain where intimate discussions about emotion are most likely to occur, with consequent links observed between the early mother-child relationship and the child's understanding of emotion at age 5 (Steele, Steele, Woolgar, et al., 2003), at age 6 (Steele, Steele, Croft & Fonagy, 1999), and at age 11 (Steele, Steele, & Johansson, 2002). By contrast, the early father-child relationship appears to have long term influences upon their sons' ability to present a coherent account of self, family and friends at age 11 (Steele & Steele, 2005b), and upon their children's mental health at age 11 (Steele & Steele, 2005a). Below we present for the first time some evidence that this paternal effect upon the child's mental health, or rather upon the father's perception of the child's mental health, was also evident at the 5-year follow-up when we zoned in on the RF observed in the fathers' AAIs prior to the child's birth.

Parents' RF and Their Later Reports of Mental Health in Their Children at Age 5

When we conducted the 5-year follow-up of the Parent-Child Project we asked the mothers and fathers to complete the Child Behavior Checklist (Achenbach). There were complete records for 72 children. Here we report on those sub-scales of the CBCL which we found to be significantly related to the parents' reflective functioning observed more than 5 years previously in the AAI. There was no suggestion that maternal RF influenced her or her husband's estimate (across 8 dimensions) of behavior problems in their child. By contrast, Fathers' RF scores from the pregnancy AAI interview revealed three significant correlations with his own estimates of behavior problems in his child, and one significant correlation with his wife's estimates. In all cases, these are negative correlations, suggesting that as RF in the father went up, his estimate of behavior problems in his child went down. When fathers' RF skills were more in evidence prior to the birth of their first child, their estimation of behavior problems in that child were lower 5 years later in terms of withdrawn delinquent and aggressive behavior. That fathers' RF skills were linked not only to his own but also to mothers' ratings of withdrawn behavior problems suggests that fathers' lack of interest in thinking about their own childhood *before becoming parents,* and reflecting on their parents' behavior in a meaningful way, has somehow contributed to their children (*5 years later*) seeming uninterested in the social world, according to both parents' estimates. We also found an interesting difference in terms of whether the children were male or female and father's earlier assessed reflective functioning. Fathers with high reflective functioning scores saw their sons as less delinquent and less aggressive. These findings are particularly relevant to the role (see clinical and forensic implications noted later) of RF in facilitating the inhibition of aggressive and antisocial tendencies. Such tendencies we know are more prevalent in males as compared to females and in this context there may well be a special role that high RF fathers can play in ameliorating anti-social tendencies in their sons.

Can Parents' Reflective Functioning Predict Aspects of Development into Early Adolescence? Fathers' RF and Children's Mental Health and Self-Esteem at Age 11

This window upon the links between fathers' capacities for RF and their children's social and emotional well-being was further highlighted when we compared paternal RF (from the prebirth AAI context) with children's self-reported strengths and difficulties on a well-validated mental health screening device (Goodman, 1997). The screening tool has five subscales reflecting one strength (prosocial behavior) and four difficulties (hyperactivity, emotional symptoms, conduct problems, peer problems) and a total difficulties score. The total problems score derived from children's responses correlated significantly and negatively with fathers' RF. In other words, 11-year-olds' self-report of emotional, behavioral and peer problems was less likely if their fathers had shown high RF in the prebirth AAI nearly 12 years earlier. Fathers with higher RF skills prior to the birth of their first child appear to have long-lasting positive social influences for their children.

Further indications of the long reach of parents' RF in terms of influencing child outcomes were noted in our 11-year follow-up of the London Parent-Child Project. We were interested in examining the developmental trajectories from the prenatal parent assessments to different domains in the child's social and emotional development. One such area is that is often explored by developmental psychologists is self-esteem which we assessed relying on the widely used and previously validated Harter Scales (Harter, 1982). The questionnaire has 6 sub-scales to possibly distinct domains of self esteem (scholastic, social, athletic, appearance, behavior, and global) as well as an overall total self-esteem score. We obtained self-reports from 46 children at age 11. One is often left wondering with longitudinal research whether the participants who make themselves available for further research are in any way different from those who choose not to participate. Could it be that only the secure are agreeable to participate? Notably half the families were willing to participate after 11 years and we found no difference in terms of attachment variables, with a representative sample of insecure and secure profiles remaining. With respect to RF, the range of scores for the parents of these 46 children was much as we reported earlier for the full sample. Mothers' and Fathers' RF (from more than 11 years before) correlated positively and significantly with their children's self-reported scholastic self-esteem, so that mothers' with high scores in reflective functioning assessed before their children reached 11 years old with the higher self esteem scores. Reliable knowledge of the nature of mind, one's own mind in particular, and the mind of others, affords one an enduring sense of hope, control, resourcefulness in the face of distress (including the confidence you can rely on others for help), mastery (including the ready willingness to help others in distress), and often joy in relating to others and functioning in the world. The features of the parents' mind, to do with RF, linked to these outcomes would have presumably remained constant, so from these findings one cannot be sure whether these are the effects of early internalization by the child of the intentional stance presented by the parent(s). Equally likely is the fact that the parental mind which demonstrated high RF in pregnancy is the same mind that facilitated security in their infant children, and is also likely to remain reflective as the child enters early adolescence—a time when reflective capacities on the part of the parent are deemed very useful.

Concluding Results

Most recently, with a new, superb research team (including Drs. Alejandra Perez-Corres, and Francesca Segal) we have collected 49 Adult

Attachment Interviews from the young people at age 16 or 17. These interviews reveal a full range of RF responses. Most interesting in the context of understanding the origins of RF, higher RF responses are significantly related to proximity seeking toward mother upon reunion in the strange situation some 15 years earlier. Sophisticated psychological processes in midadolescence derive arguably, in part, from adaptive preverbal emotion-regulation strategies, and organized procedural memories including a sense of confidence in the availability of the mother when distressed. This we see as the optimal path toward RF in adulthood.

Clinical and Forensic Evidence: Further
Refinements of the RF Concept and Manual

The less optimal, much more troubled path toward high RF is observed in those individuals who have been *resilient* in the face of great distress. We looked at the question of resilience in the context of the London Parent-Child Project by examining levels of RF in those mothers who had, and had not, experienced severe deprivation during childhood. We computed deprivation scores from perusal of the AAI probable experience scales (covering love, rejection, neglect, and role reversal), and from a questionnaire (covering prolonged separations from— loss of, or physical/ psychological illness, or unemployment of—a parent, during childhood). We then computed an index of deprivation and divided our sample of mothers in the London Parent-Child Project into low-deprivation and high-deprivation groups. We cross-tabulated these groupings with low-RF and high-RF groups as well as infant-mother attachment (insecure vs. secure) groups. This allowed us to examine the number of infants who were securely attached to low-deprived mothers as a function of their RF-levels. Interestingly, RF-levels did not seem to matter greatly for these low-deprived mothers. Infants of these low-deprived mothers (n=70) appeared to have almost equal likelihood of being securely attached to their mothers, regardless of whether their mothers were low or high on RF. A strikingly different picture emerged for the 26 mothers who had suffered high-deprivation during childhood. For the majority with low RF (n=16), an expected outcome of deprivation, all but one of their infants was insecurely attached. For the minority with high RF (n=10), *all their infants were securely attached*. For the mothers, acquiring high RF—following the childhood deprivation she suffered—effectively removed the risk of insecure attachment to her infant (Fonagy, Steele, Steele, Higgitt & Target, 1994).

Against this background, it may be easy to agree that a central and natural aim of psychoanalytic work is the facilitation of reflective functioning in the patient. Correspondingly, the capacity to reflect on one's own internal world and to appreciate the perspective of another individual is a crucial question in the mind of the clinician when they are assessing a patient for treatability. Often there are limited resources with which to offer psychoanalytic services to those that seek it and could benefit from it. The question of how to assess whether an individual might make use of treatment is a critical one for the clinician, whether in public or private practice. A familiarity with the concept of reflective functioning might have a very important role to play in this challenging area of clinical practice. An example of an adolescent boy seen by Miriam Steele at the Anna Freud Centre, exemplifies a situation in which a capacity to reflect upon his painful situation was predictive of a good therapeutic outcome. Steven, at age 16 years suffered from intense bullying by his schoolmates. This included being locked in a locker at school for a full hour, and having a cigarette lighter held to his cheek. He was engaging in some self-harming behavior and was involved in a sado-masochistic relationship with his father with whom he battled on a daily basis. However, he was also able to comment at the diagnostic stage of potential treatment, "My father will never be satisfied … even if I was the type of boy my father thinks he'd be happy with, he still wouldn't be happy with me." Indeed, over the course of intensive psychotherapy that followed, Steven was able to explore and more fully appreciate his father's contribution to the pathological situation, distinct from his own reactions to, and contributing role in, the difficulties that greatly abated over the course of treatment.

Immense therapeutic challenges lie ahead when there are no indicators of RF present in the patient at the diagnostic stage of work. This is often the case with forensic samples where a history of abuse and violence is often a normative part of childhood (if not also ongoing) experience. It was after we rated AAIs from imprisoned offenders incarcerated for violent acts against others that an extension to the RF scale became obvious. It did not seem appropriate to code low RF or banal assertions when hostility was the central feature of questions demanding reflection. The nine-point RF scale became an 11-point scale with 0 being added when RF is disavowed or absent (e.g., when asked *why did your parents behave the way they did?* "I haven't got a clue?!") and a –1 assignment is made when there is outright hostility to a question demanding reflection (e.g., when asked *why did your parents behave the way they did?* "How the hell should I know; go ask them, you are the bloody psychiatrist." Exploration of how to treat such outbursts would take us beyond the scope of this chapter into the important literature on borderline pathology, where RF-informed mentalization treatments have documented validity and immense promise (Bateman & Fonagy, 2004; Bateman & Fonagy, 2006).

Wide-ranging evidence of RF, it should be noted, may also be found in narratives collected from parents when they are asked to speak about their infants or children *now* (see Slade, *AHD* special issue, Sept 2005, and this volume). This has enormous clinical usefulness, as parents of young children are more likely to see the relevance of discussing their views of their child, as opposed to their childhood. Both tasks are relevant to the psychoanalytic situation where adults (many of whom may not—at least not yet—be parents) are being helped toward more optimal emotional health and social functioning. In this context, RF may be an appropriate measure of outcome, and may potentially be rated in interviews concerning patients' experiences of the patient-analyst relationship. In these vital contexts where the promotion of mental health is the explicit aim, the elaborated version of the RF manual (Fonagy et al., 1998) may be shown to have its greatest relevance. It is in this 1998 publication where we describe on RF in terms of four vital distinct but related mental and emotional phenomena evident in speech: (a) awareness of the nature of mental states; (b) engagement in the effort to tease out mental states underlying behavior; (c) recognizing developmental aspects of mental states; and (d) awareness of mental states in relation to the present context.

Conclusion

With appropriate training, reflective functioning can be reliably rated in Adult Attachment Interviews obtained from adults in one generation. RF-ratings derived from this source have strong validity in terms of their documented links to a wide range of developmental outcomes in the next generation, including the probable quality of the children's attachments in infancy, their later reasoning in the domain of emotions and close relationships, core aspects of their self-esteem, and mental health through early adolescence and beyond. Given the range of evidence reported here, we are drawn inevitably to suggest: In order to help children grow from earliest childhood forward toward their full social and emotional potential, a central aim of intervention and prevention work must be to encourage reflective functioning in parents or parents-to-be. Our research, reviewed here, shows that reflective functioning regarding the *past* family context we come from has powerful and important influences on the *current* relational context in which we live.

References

Ainsworth, M. D. S., Blehar, M. C., Waters, E., & Wall, S. (1978). *Patterns of attachment: A psychological study of the strange situation.* Hillsdale, NJ: Erlbaum.

Ainsworth, M. D. S., & Marvin, R. S. (1995). On the shaping of attachment theory: An interview with Mary D. S. Ainsworth. In E. Waters, B. E. Vaughn, G. Posada, & K. Kondo-Ikemura (Eds.) Caregiving, cultural and cognitive perspectives on secure-base behavior and working models. *Monographs of the Society for Research in Child Development, 60,* (2–3, serial number 244), 3–21.

Baron-Cohen, S. (1989). The autistic child's theory of mind: A case of specific developmental delay. *Journal of Child Psychology and Psychiatry, 30,* 285–297.

Baron-Cohen, S. (1991). Do people with autism understand what causes emotion? *Child Development, 62,* 385–395.

Baron-Cohen, S. (1993). From attention-goal psychology to belief-desire psychology: The development of a theory of mind, and its dysfunction. In S. Baron-Cohen, H. Tager-Flusberg, & D. J. Cohen (Eds.), *Understanding other minds: Perspectives from autism* (pp. 59–82). Oxford: Oxford University Press.

Bateman, A. W. & Fonagy, P. (2004). Psychotherapy of Borderline Personality Disorder: mentalisation based treatment. Oxford: Oxford University Press.

Bateman, A. W. & Fonagy, P. (2006). Mentalization-based treatment for borderline personality disorder: A practical guide. Oxford: Oxford University Press.

Bowlby, J. (1956). Psychoanalysis and child care. In J. Bowlby (1979). *The making and breaking of affectional bonds.* London: Routledge.

Bowlby, J. (1969). *Attachment and loss, vol. I, attachment.* London: Hogarth Press and the Institute of Psycho-Analysis.

Bowlby, J. (1973). *Attachment and loss, vol. II, separation.* London: Hogarth Press.

Carlon, E.A. (1998). A prospective longitudinal study of attachment disorganization/disorientation. *Child Development, 69,* 1107–1128.

Carplendale, J. I. M., & Lewis, C. (2004). Constructing an understanding of mind: The development of children's social understanding within social interaction. *Behavioral and Brain Sciences, 27,* 79–151.

Dennett, D. C. (1978). *Brainstorms.* Cambridge, MA: MIT Press

Fonagy, P., Leigh, T., Steele, M., Steele, H., Kennedy, R., Mattoon, G., & Target, M. (1996). The relationship of attachment status, psychiatric classification, and response to psychotherapy. *Journal of Consulting and Clinical Psychology, 64,* 22–31.

Fonagy, P., Steele, H., Moran, G., Steele, M., & Higgitt, A. (1991). The capacity for understanding mental states: The reflective self in parent and child and its significance for security of attachment. *Infant Mental Health Journal, 13,* 200–217.

Fonagy, P., Steele, H., & Steele, M. (1991). Maternal representations of attachment during pregnancy predict the organization of infant-mother attachment at one year of age. *Child Development, 62,* 891–905.

Fonagy, P., Steele, H., & Steele, M., Higgitt, A., & Target, M. (1994). Theory and practice of resilience. *J of Child Psychol. & Psychiatry, 35,* 231–257.

Fonagy, P. & Target, M. (2005). Bridging the transmission gap: an end to an important mystery of attachment research? *Attachment & Human Development, 7,* 333–343.

Fonagy, P, Target, M, Steele, H, & Steele, M (1998). *Reflective-Functioning Manual, version 5, for application to Adult Attachment Interviews.* Unpublished manuscript. University College London.

Fonagy, P., Steele, M., Steele, H., Moran, G., & Higgitt, A. C. (1991). The capacity understanding mental states: The reflective self in parent and child and its significance for security of attachment. *Infant Mental Health Journal, 12,* 201–218.

George, C., Kaplan, N., & Main, M. (1985). *Adult Attachment Interview* (2nd ed.). Unpublished manuscript, University of California at Berkeley.

Goodman, R. (1997). The Strengths and Difficulties Questionnaire: a research note. *J of Child Psychol. and Psychiatry, 38,* 581–586.

Greenberg, J. R., & Mitchell, S. A. (1983). *Object relations in psychoanalytic theory.* Cambridge, Mass: Harvard University Press.

Harris, P. L. (1989). Children and emotion: The development of psychological understanding. Oxford: Basil Blackwell.

Harris, P. L., Johnson, C. N., Hutton, D., Andrews, G., & Cooke, T. (1989). Young children's Theory of Mind and emotion. *Cognition and Emotion, 3,* 379–400.

Harter, S. (1982). The perceived competence scale for children. *Child Development, 53,* 87–97.

Main, M., Goldwyn, R., & Hesse, E. (2003). *Adult attachment classification system.* Unpublished manuscript, University of California at Berkeley.

Main, M., Kaplan, N., & Cassidy, J. (1985). Security in infancy, childhood and adulthood: A move to the level of representation. In I. Bretherton & E. Waters (Eds.), *Growing Points of Attachment Theory and Research. Monographs of the Society for Research in Child Development, 50*(1–2, Serial No. 209).

Phillips, A. (1988). *Winnicott.* London: Fontana Press.

Raven, J. C., Court, J. H., & Raven, J. (1986). *Manual for Raven's progressive matrices and vocabulary scales.* London: H.K. Lewis & Co.

Renfrew, C. E. (1991). *The Bus Story: A Test of Continuous Speech* [2nd edition]. Oxford: C. E. Renfrew.

Roisman, G. I., Collins, A. W., Sroufe, A. L., & Egeland, B. (2005). Predictions of young adults' representations of and behavior in their current romantic relationship: Prospective tests of the prototype hypothesis. *Attachment & Human Development, 7,* 105–122.

Sroufe, L. A., Egeland, B., Carlson, E., & Collins, W. A. (2005). *The Development of the Person: The Minnesota Study of Risk and Adaptation from Birth to Adulthood.* New York: Guilford Publications.

Steele, H. & Steele, M. (2005a). Understanding and resolving emotional conflict: The view from 12 years of attachment research across generations and across childhood. In K. Grossmann & E. Waters (Eds.), *Attachmeent from Infancy to Adulthood: The major longitudinal studies* (pp. 137–164). New York: Guildford Press.

Steele, H., & Steele, M. (2005b). The construct of coherence as an indicator of attachment security in middle childhood: The Friends and Family Interview. In K. Kerns & R. Richardson (Eds.), *Attachment in middle childhood* (pp. 161–188). New York: Guilford Press.

Steele, H, Steele, M., Croft, C., & Fonagy, P. (1999). Infant-mother attachment at one-year predicts children's understanding of mixed-emotions at six years. *Social Development, 8,* 161–178.

Steele, H., Steele, M., & Fonagy, P. (1996). Associations among attachment classifications of mothers, fathers, and their infants: Evidence for a relationship-specific perspective. *Child Development, 67,* 541–555.

Steele, M., Steele, H., & Johansson, M. (2002). Maternal Predictors of children's social cognition: An Attachment Perspective. *Journal of Child Psychology and Psychiatry, 43* 89–98.

Steele, M., Steele, H., Woolgar, M., Yabsley, S., Johnson, D., Fonagy, P.,
    & Croft, C. (2003). An attachment perspective on children's emo-
    tion narratives: Links across generations. In R. Emde, D. Wolf, & D.
    Oppenheim (Eds). Revealing the Inner Worlds of Young Children
    (pp. 163–181). Oxford University Press.
Stern, D. N. (1985). *The Interpersonal World of the Infant: A View from Psy-
    choanalysis and Developmental Psychology*. New York: Basic Books.
Suess, G. J., Grossmann, K., & Sroufe, L. A. (1992). Effects of infant attach-
    ment to mother and father on quality of adaptation in preschool:
    From dyadic to individual organisation of self. *International Journal
    of Behavioral Development, 15*, 43–65.
van Ijzendoorn, MH, Dijkstra, J., & Bus, AG (1995). Attachment, intel-
    ligence and language: A meta-analysis. *Social Development, 4*(2),
    115–128.
Winnicott, D. W. (1971). *Playing and reality*. Harmondsworth, UK: Peli-
    can Books.

5

An Object Relations Treatment of Borderline Patients With Reflective Functioning as the Mechanism of Change*

*Frank E. Yeomans, John F. Clarkin,
Diana Diamond, and Kenneth N. Levy*

Introduction

Transference-focused psychotherapy (Clarkin, Yeomans, & Kernberg, 2006) is a form of psychodynamic psychotherapy specifically modified and structured for patients with borderline personality organization (BPO), a broad grouping of severe personality disorders that includes the more narrowly defined borderline personality disorder (BPD). Although there is growing evidence that TFP results in clinical improvement (Clarkin, Levy, Lenzenweger, & Kernberg, 2007) this paper considers aspects of how the treatment works. In psychotherapy research, it has become increasingly recognized that treatment development must involve empirical information not only on whether the treatment in question achieves its desired outcomes, but also on how that outcome is achieved through the specific interventions of the treatment package in question (Kazdin, 2001; Clarkin & Levy, 2006; Levy, Clarkin, Yeomans, Scott, Wasserman, & Kernberg, 2006; Gabbard & Westen, 2003). In this regard, the state

* This paper represents work from the Cornell Psychotherapy Research Project supported by a grant from the Borderline Personality Disorder Research Foundation. The Foundation and its founder, Dr. Marco Stoffel, are gratefully acknowledged.

of reflection on TFP is similar to that on other treatments for borderline personality disorder such as mentalization-based therapy (MBT; Bateman & Fonagy, 2004) and dialectical behavior therapy (DBT; Linehan, 1993).

Through clinical and research investigations we have established reflective functioning (RF) as one of the mechanisms of change in TFP. In this paper, we present a case illustration to demonstrate the specific techniques and tactics in TFP that promote RF, and place this case in the context of our general outcome data, including data demonstrating changes in RF over the course of one year of TFP. Like DBT and MBT, TFP is an entire treatment program, that is, it contains many elements in a year-long, or longer, intervention with borderline patients who bring both general and idiosyncratic issues to the treatment situation. Thus, although we emphasize transference interpretation as central to the therapy and therapeutic change, it is only one among many elements of the treatment (see Figure 5.1).

Our Working Model of Borderline Pathology

Our clinical research efforts in the development and evaluation of TFP have been guided by a model of borderline pathology based upon both psychoanalytic understandings of the structural organization

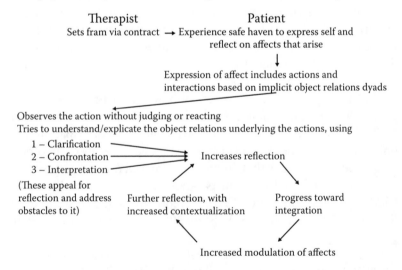

Figure 5.1   Proposed Mechanisms of Change in TFP

of personality (Kernberg, 1984, 2004), and the interaction between behavior and neurobiological aspects of the individual (Depue & Lenzenweger, 2005; Posner, Rothbart, Vizueta, Levy, Thomas, & Clarkin, 2002). The psychoanalytic view of borderline personality organization with the central concept of a split internal world and identity diffusion has been essential in understanding the psychological experience of the patient and guiding treatment (Yeomans, Clarkin, & Kernberg, 2002; Clarkin, Yeomans, & Kernberg, 2006). Our working model of BPD posits a dynamic interaction of temperament, especially a preponderance of negative affect over positive affect, low effortful control, and an absence of a coherent sense of self and others in the context of an insecure model of attachment. The borderline experience is characterized by an information processing system that is actively influenced by negative affect, faulty and ineffective conflict resolution, and insecure (primarily Anxious/Preoccupied and/or Disorganized/Unresolved) attachment organization (Fonagy et al., 1996; Bateman & Fonagy, 2004). Treating these features of borderline pathology requires specific therapeutic foci and intervention strategies. Interventions focused on the information processing system, especially in the social interpersonal sphere, will have the most impact on the patient in achieving the combined goals of symptom reduction and healthy involvements in relationships and work.

In the object relations model of borderline pathology, the patient's internal world is conceptualized as being made up of multiple sets of relationships dyads, comprised of a specific representation of the self and a specific representation of the other linked by a specific affect. In individuals with borderline personality organization, these relationship dyads consist of simplistic, polarized, and caricatured representations of self and others in contrast to the multifaceted and modulated sense of self and others that characterizes more mature individuals (Clarkin, Yeomans, & Kernberg, 2006). These one-dimensional representations of self and others are often in contradiction with one another and therefore underlie the identity diffusion and contribute significantly to the interpersonal difficulties of the borderline patient. The fragmented, diffused sense of self leaves the patient at risk for inaccurate, extreme perceptions accompanied by overwhelming affects in the experience of the moment, leading to misrepresentation of self and others, and to affect dysregulation—both of which are the focus of therapeutic intervention in

TFP. These split polarized representations are seen as the motivating force behind the patient's perceptions and constructions that lead to self-defeating and self-destructive relations with others. Treatment, therefore, must be structured in such a way as to control acting out and provide a frame within which the patient can experience, observe and reflect on his or her representations of self and others in a context that might allow modification and ultimately integration of the representational world.

Transference-Focused Psychotherapy

Recently, following the idea that from a scientific viewpoint, studies of psychotherapy outcome are incomplete if they do not address the specific mechanisms of change, we have investigated the specific mechanisms that promote change in TFP (Levy et al., 2006). TFP is based on the understanding that the object relations dyads that structure the internal world of the patient will emerge in the transference to the therapist. A fundamental mechanism of change is the facilitation of the reactivation of dissociated or projected internalized object relations under controlled circumstances. The therapist helps the patient elaborate his or her experience with the over-all goal of first observing and gaining awareness of the nature of the internal representations and then integrating them into a fuller, richer, and more nuanced identity. In order to achieve this goal, the therapist must create conditions that contain intense affects and acting out and enhance the possibility for reflection. The first step is to structure the treatment conditions in such a way as to avoid the disruption of the treatment and to create a frame that helps focus the patient's observations and reflection. This begins with discussion of a treatment contract to provide safety and stability in the therapeutic environment and containment for the reactivation of internalized relationship dyads. The dyadic intimacy of the treatment setting along with the unequal roles and relationships of patient and therapist lead quickly to the activation of the internal object relation patterns that underlie borderline pathology and that determine the patient's perception of self and others. As this occurs, the therapist tries to clarify cognitively what the patient perceives and its relation to what the patient feels. TFP emphasizes monitoring the three channels of communication between patient and therapist: verbal discourse, nonverbal communication and behavior, and the countertransference.

This model considers the role of mental transformation processes and does not assume that the reactivation in the present is an exact reproduction of what has actually happened in the past. The patient's responses to the therapist do not reproduce a specific experience or relationship from the past, but rather represent an internal construction, the ultimate origin of which cannot be identified precisely. Our focus is the current psychic reality and how it is structured, and this structure is the focus of modification in the treatment. The disorganization of the borderline patient involves not only fragmented internal representations of self and others with the predominance of primitive affects, but also the manner in which this fragmented structure defends against the anxiety that arises in the patient when opposing affects and representations approach one another. The protection of primitive ideal images of self and others from the rage associated with primitive aggressively-laden ones requires the maintenance of the fragmented internal state. This fragmentation functions as a defense against anxiety, but also prevents the patient from having full awareness of what is occurring in his or her internal world. This defensive structure distorts and erases awareness and thinking. Borderline patients manifest a fragmentation and disconnection of thinking by attacks on the linking of thoughts (Bion, 1967). At its extreme, powerful negative affects are expressed in action without cognitive awareness. A goal of therapy is to transform impulsive, automatic behaviors into an understanding of the internal relationships that gave rise to them.

The postulation of internalized relational scenarios that involve an image of self in interaction with another with concomitant expectations of interpersonal transactions is common to object relations dyads and to internal working models of attachment. By engaging the patient in identifying and observing these scenarios as they are experienced in the therapy setting, the therapist appeals to the patient's capacity to reflect on them as constructions rather than as veridical images of self and others, with the goal of increasing his or her cognitive capacity to represent affect. The therapist then helps the patient understand the anxieties that make it difficult to integrate primitive positive (libidinal) and negative (aggressive) affects. In cases where, for constitutional and/or historical reasons, the patient experiences high internal levels of aggression, movement toward integration of disparate affects with respect to the same fig-ure, including the therapist, may create anxiety because of fear that aggressive affects will destroy positive idealized representations. When paranoid anxieties predominate, the patient may fear that any expression/experience of libidinal affect may provoke an onslaught of mistreatment or persecution.

TFP fosters change by insuring that the reactivation of primitive object relations under the carefully constructed treatment frame does not lead to the vicious cycle of affective reactions that the patient usu-ally arouses in significant others. The therapist's stance of technical neutrality (not to be confused with coldness or indifference) assists both in the reactivation of the patient's characteristic object relations dyads and helps the patient to observe, to see, accept, and eventu-ally integrate parts of the self that previously were not consciously tolerated but were either enacted and/or projected, whether they be associated with aggressive or libidinal affects. By fostering reflection and containment through the identification of self object dyads and their linking affects, the repetitive re-enactment of such internal dyads is short-circuited, and there is a gradual cognitive structur-ing of what at first seems both rigid and chaotic. Through clarifica-tion, confrontation, and interpretation of the patient's self and object dyads in relation to the therapist and external figures, the patient is encouraged to expand his capacity to reflect on his understandings of self and others as an instrument in working toward an integrated identity. In trying to understand the process by which our patients develop the capacity to reflect on mental states of self and others in the service of integrating their internal worlds, we have reviewed the work of Fonagy and colleagues on mentalization.

Considerations of Mentalization and Reflective Functioning

Fonagy and colleagues have contributed to our understanding of the representational world of borderline patients (and personality pathology in general) by investigating, both developmentally and cross-sectionally, the development of the individual's capacity to understand and reflect on mental states of self and others. In this context, mentalization, which has been operationalized in the con-cept of reflective function (Fonagy, Steele, Steele, & Target, 1997), has been defined as an acquired capacity to envision and represent the mental states of self and others. Bateman and Fonagy (2004) use this concept as the basis for mentalization-based treatment (MBT) for borderline personality. Fonagy (Fonagy, Gergely, Jurist, & Target, 2002) posits the existence of an *internal interpretive mechanism* [IIM] or function that enables the individual to deal with interpersonal relations. It is hypothesized that this function is genetically defined and located in the medial prefrontal cortex (p. 132). In pathological conditions, such as severe personality disorders, this interpretive function is compromised, and the capacity for sustaining a clear distinction between self and other is defective. The functional ability to arrive at representations of the motivations of others uncontaminated by the motivations of the self (which may also not be clear to the individual) is severely compromised. In fact, the most complicated challenge in treating severely personality disordered individuals, according to these authors, involves strategies to approach the patient's externalizations of unbearable self-states. Our clinical vignette will demonstrate how TFP approaches the borderline patient's externalization of painful states and helps him or her to recognize them as part of him or herself, and to integrate them into more accurate and nuanced appreciations self and others.

Fonagy and colleagues (2002) conceptualize reflective functioning not as an invariant trait but rather as an evolving skill shaped by particular emotions, interactions with particular people and events. As such, an individual's reflective functioning will have uneven development and the individual will demonstrate variation in the use of the skill. RF is thus conceptualized as a particular skill tied to specific tasks and domains, and not as a general capacity. In the course of normal development, the individual tends to integrate the capacity for reflective functioning with other control systems. In contrast, in the development of the individual with personality pathology, unevenness in the use of reflective functioning across situations may be more marked, and may be a result of conscious or unconscious attempts to avoid reflecting on the mental states of others who have been experienced as abusive or neglectful. In such situations, the individual may shut down reflective capacities altogether or may adopt a hypermentalizing stance in which there is inordinate focus on the mental states of others and inadequate attention to the mental states of the self. These authors assume that experiencing abuse or maltreatment is associated with fractionation or splitting of reflective functioning across domains and tasks. It is especially in the context of conflicts in interpersonal relationships that the nonreflec-tive behavior may dominate in personality disordered individuals.

It is suggested by these authors that psychotherapy works precisely because it improves the functioning of the IIM. For any psycho-therapy to create this improvement, the treatment must be delivered in an interpersonal context that fosters an attachment relationship between patient and therapist, focuses on both cognition and affect, and proceeds with coherence and consistence. Although these general treatment strategies are accurately related to the goal of treatment, the therapeutic techniques to actually increase patient reflective functioning in the treatment sessions need further explication (see Bateman & Fonagy, 2004; Clarkin, Yeomans & Kernberg, 2006, for overlapping but somewhat different views of what is highlighted later). We agree with Bateman & Fonagy, 2004, as our case illustra-tion later suggests, that one of the most complicated challenges in treating severely personality disordered individuals involves the issue of how to approach the patient's externalizations of unbearable self-states. This may be why many therapies with a supportive, in contrast to an exploratory, emphasis accept the patient's externalization and attempt to help the patient cope better with problems, (e.g., by teach-ing coping skills) or to target symptoms (e.g., by medication) rather than to help the patient resolve conflicts between warring aspects of his psyche that, until recognized and integrated, prohibit successful life adjustment. Fonagy and colleagues (Bateman & Fonagy, 2004) indicate that the therapist should constantly encourage mentaliza-tion on the part of the patient, that is, the gradual clarification of what the patient is experiencing and what he thinks the therapist is experiencing, and how this motivates the therapist's actions—what we see as a first level of RF—with the idea that an improved ability to assess self states and the mental states of others will diffuse intense emotional reactions. We do not disagree with this position, but feel that more specific attention should be addressed to thematic and affective content in addition to focusing on the patient's processing of the interaction.

Bateman & Fonagy, 2004, are reluctant to go beyond this level of work with borderline patients in the early and middle stages of ther-apy because of their concern that the borderline patient's inability to mentalize curtails their capacity to work productively with interpre-tation. Thus, if they use interpretation, they delay it until a very late stage of therapy. They believe that borderline patients are not capable of symbolic representation. Because they see borderline patients as lacking this capacity, their focus is to use brief here-and-now statements that help the patient gain awareness of his current mental state and that of the therapist and thus understand the meaning and motivation in his own and the other's behavior. They describe the transference as the emergence of latent meanings and beliefs that are evoked by the therapeutic relationship and then are implicitly contrasted with the actual experience with the therapist. When a feeling is identified in the room, the patient is encouraged to consider who engendered that feeling, what their role may have been in engendering it, and how states of mind of self and other (the therapist) may differ. We agree with the overall strategy of the exploration of a mind by a mind within an interpersonal context. We differ in our understanding of the capacity of borderline patients to work with symbolic representation. We feel it is useful for the therapist to appeal to it and that it can be engaged to help the patient integrate split-off toxic material.

We believe that Bateman and Fonagy (2004) may underestimate the capacities of borderline patients and also misunderstand the interpretive approach in TFP, seeing it as an isolated technique that is applied regardless of the patient's individual characteristics or reflective capacities, rather than as part of an evolving process in which the groundwork for understanding and using interpretations is laid through prior focus on clarification and confrontation.

Interpretation in the here and now begins with an effort to understand an affect, or an action that may be geared to discharge an affect, in terms of the representations of self and other that lie beneath and motivate the affect/action. This often involves addressing attention to representations with characteristics that are unacceptable, particularly in terms of the affects and drives involved—whether they are aggressive or libidinal. Bringing these underlying representations to conscious awareness helps the patient clarify the motivation behind his feeling or action and allows for further elaboration of the accuracy of the representations. When successfully carried out, this increased understanding of self and other in the momentary experience helps the patient tolerate disavowed affect(s) without having to discharge it (them) in action.

In the clarification process, the patient is invited to expand his representation of present feeling states. The patient's feelings, toward the therapist or toward others, may be clearly articulated and noncontradictory at times, and at other times at variance with what the patient has communicated before, or at variance with overt behavior. Confrontation is the technique of addressing these variances. Confrontation is not a hostile challenge, but rather a matter of presenting the patient, who is often unaware of the discrepancy, with discrepancies in his articulation of feeling states, or discrepancies between articulated feelings and behavior. Clarification and confrontation constitute the level of the interpretation process that involves achieving a more accurate view of self and other in the moment. A second level of interpretation helps the patient become aware of how the understanding of a particular affect in relation to an object could be related to other, conflicting affects that exist within the individual. An example of this is: "It may be that you talk about dropping out of treatment after each session where we have experienced a positive contact because a part of you is convinced that my positive approach to you is geared to trick and ultimately hurt you. If this were true, it would make sense that you would want to leave, and explain that you seem to be more 'at home' in hostile relations." A later stage of interpretation might focus on the patient's split-off and projected identification with an aggressive part that makes it impossible to escape from relations that take on an aggressive tone and that, once understood, could be integrated, so that the awareness of the aggressive part both removes it as an obstacle to more successful libidinal fulfillment and allows for adaptive uses of aggressive affects, such as striving for higher achievement.

Fonagy describes mentalization as if it were a unitary function. In our view, mentalization can be conceptualized in two levels. Although we believe that changes in the cognitive sphere, and particularly in the individual's capacity to think about self and other in mental state terms are essential, our treatment is not focused on mentalization directly and exclusively as described by Bateman and Fonagy (2004), but rather on mentalization as it applies to the borderline patient's affectively charged internal representations of self and others. This model of internal dyads of the representation of self and others can be conceptualized at two levels of complexity and can be linked to RF. At the first level, the individual experiences his or her feelings in the moment of a specific interaction. The immediate experience involves a conception of self, a conception of the other, and an affect state related to these representations. The first level of RF is to understand this moment accurately. In borderline patients, this understanding can transform an action powered by an unarticulated and split-off affect into an understanding of self and other in the momentary experience so that the patient can tolerate and modify the affect without the need to discharge it in action.

Beyond achieving understanding of the mental state of self and other in the moment, at a second level of RF the individual is both aware of the representations of self and other involved in a momentary affective state and, furthermore, can place these representations into a general context of knowledge about self and other across time—an integrated view of self and other that has coalesced. At this level, the patient can contextualize momentary feelings toward another into the broad internal sense of experience of the relationship that has developed over time. In promoting the movement from identity diffusion to an integrated identity, TFP increases the patient's capacity to reflect at this higher level.

Empirical Research on Reflective Functioning

Improvement in the IIM can be assessed by the RF scale (Fonagy, 2002), according to these researchers. With funding from the Borderline Personality Disorder Research Research Foundation (O.F. Kernberg & J.F. Clarkin, PIs), we have conducted a randomized clinical trail (Clarkin, Levy, Lenzenweger, & Kernberg, 2004; Levy et al, 2006; Clarkin, Levy, Lenzenweger, & Kernberg, 2007) comparing three types of interventions in a one-year outpatient treatment study: TFP, dialectic behavioral therapy, and a psychodynamic supportive therapy. Additional funding from the American Psychoanalytic Association (PI: Kenneth Levy) enabled us to administer the AAI before and after the one-year intervention to the patients in all three treatments. Our data analysis suggests that in general the three treatments were effective to varying degrees in reducing symptoms and improving functioning from the beginning to the end of the treatment year. Patients in all three treatment groups showed significant positive change in depression, anxiety, global functioning, and social adjustment. Only TFP and DBT were significantly associated with improvement in suicidality. Only TFP and supportive psychodynamic therapy were associated with improvement in anger. TFP and supportive therapy were each associated with improvement in facets of impulsivity. Only TFP was significantly predictive of change in irritability and verbal and direct assault (Clarkin et al., 2007). Most relevant to the current article, we conceptualized reflective functioning as a mechanism of change in the treatment of borderline patients, and hypothesized that by the nature of the treatment, RF would improve in TFP but not in DBT or supportive psychotherapy. Results showed that the mean RF score of the patients who had been treated with TFP increased while the RF score of the patients in the other two treatments did not change significantly (Levy et al., 2006).

A first question in response to this finding is what the clinical relevance of increased reflective functioning may be. A second question is what these data suggest in terms of therapeutic techniques that help in the treatment of borderline patients. With regard to the first question, the increased ability to reflect on one's own and an other's mind should lead to less of the inaccurate attribution of negative intentions to others that is typical of patients with BPD. Consequently, benign or positive events will no longer be seen as malevolent and the patient will be able to avoid the downward spiral of misinterpretation and engendering of negative responses. We would predict that individuals with increased RF make better choices in work, social and love relations and are able to achieve not only stability but also fulfillment in their lives. The case example found later offers one example of this, but more importantly, we are engaged in a long term follow-up study of our cases with the hypothesis that patients whose RF increased are more able to maintain their symptomatic improvement and are also able to have fuller involvements in love and work relations.

With regard to relevance to therapeutic technique, the data suggest that interpretation has a role in increasing the patient's RF. Our study compared TFP, in which the interpretive process is considered a mechanism of change (see Figure 5.1), with DBT and a manualized supportive psychodynamic therapy that avoided the use of interpretation. Interestingly, DBT includes an emphasis on mindfulness, which shares certain characteristics with mentalization: the encouragement of the nonjudgmental awareness of the self in the here-and-now moment. The fact that our data do not show an increase in RF in the patients treated with DBT suggests that interpretations that expand the patient's awareness of split-off and projected parts of himself and help build the broader contextualized sense of self and other that we consider the second level of RF may be instrumental in achieving increased RF. The fact that the supportive psychodynamic treatment, which also did not lead to an increase in RF ratings, emphasized clarification of internal states without interpretation further supports the idea that interpretations have a role in increasing RF.

Clinical Illustration of Improvement in Reflective Functioning: The Case of Sara

Sara was a single, unemployed woman of color who started TFP at age 36 after many years in other treatments. Over the years, her condition had worsened to the point where she spent the prior 6 months isolated in her apartment, lying in bed with chronic suicidal ideation, watching television, gaining weight, and only rarely bathing. Sara was the middle daughter in an upper middle class family. She described her father as preoccupied with his career and his children's educational performance. She portrayed her mother as emotionally unstable and unable to consistently care for her children. The patient's education ended when the patient dropped out of college after one year. She then held a series of jobs in lawyers' offices but was repeatedly fired from these jobs because of difficulty getting along with others. She stopped working when news of her belligerent character kept her from being hired. The patient felt that her relations with others were negative because of the prejudice she felt everyone bore toward her racial group. Sara had no history of sexual relations except for one occasion when a man she had dated three times began to make love to her. She panicked, stopped the interaction before intercourse, and later brought formal rape charges against him.

Sara had a limited history of overt self-destructiveness. She cut herself superficially on occasion and talked frequently about her wish to kill herself. She had had three psychiatric hospitalizations. Her prior therapists most often diagnosed her with bipolar disorder. She had been on many medications, all of which were discontinued during the first year of TFP. In the research evaluation of this patient, she met IPDE criteria for not only borderline personality disorder, but also narcissistic personality and avoidant personality. She met SCID criteria for current dysthymia. On the IPO she scored very high on identity diffusion, high on primitive defenses, compromised reality testing, and aggression. Her AAI revealed an attachment classification of CC/E2/D2, which indicates that she showed contradictory and inconsistent strategies of representing her early attachment relationships, shifting chaotically between inchoate anger and dismissing devaluation. Her reflective functioning (RF) score prior to the initiation of treatment was minus one (–1), the lowest possible score, indicating that she actively repudiated any consideration of mental states of self and other.

She began therapy with an immediate demonstration of her defensive structure. Walking into the office for the first meeting, she was talking nonstop about someone who had looked at her on the subway, complaining angrily that the woman was looking critically and hostilely at her. Her therapist had to talk over her to remind her that this was a consultation session and that he could not address a specific problem with her yet because he did not yet have a sense of who she was, how to understand her problems or what treatment approach to recommend. His efforts to carry out a structural interview were limited by her ignoring his questions and talking over him in a pressured way. After three such consultation sessions, the therapist decided that the patient's presentation provided the information necessary to proceed with treatment even though the factual information derived from the interviews was limited. His diagnostic impression was borderline personality with narcissistic features. He discussed this and a corresponding treatment contract, explaining to the patient that the treatment would require agreement on certain conditions. One was that Sara would have to engage in a structured activity, in the form of either studies or some type of work, at least on a part time basis, in addition to attending therapy sessions. This treatment parameter was geared to help Sara reflect on the difficulties that arose in situations with others. Sara initially rejected the idea, saying that this was precisely where she had trouble. Her therapist suggested that therapy offered the possibility to reflect on her experience as she was having it in a way which could help her sort out the difficulties in these situations. Sara announced in the next session that she had obtained a part-time volunteer job, indicating a motivation and health-seeking side that had not been apparent in her earlier presentation.

Once the therapy began following the contracting phase, Sara filled every session by flooding her therapist with a pressured stream of discourse, and by interrupting him when he attempted to intervene. He perceived her relentless monologue and lack of tolerance for his interventions as an intense need to control every interaction as a means of attempting to diminish the anxiety she experienced in interactions with others. Sara's interactive style posed a particular challenge for psychodynamic therapy: in a setting where the basic rule is for the patient to associate freely, there was the risk that this patient would continue talking indefinitely with a controlling discourse without changing. Initially the most effective intervention was to tolerate the confusion and frustration that such a stance engendered in the therapist and to explore the countertransferential feelings that emerged. The initial period of tolerance and self exploration on the part of the therapist was followed by discussing the representations of self and other he observed in the interaction and experienced in the countertransference with the assumption that these underlying self and other representations would help explain her anxiety. The main dyad being enacted appeared to be one of a controlling dominant figure interacting with a subordinated, trapped figure.

In sessions, Sara described this dynamic in various areas of life: in the description of a father who rigidly controlled his children with critical comments while ignoring their feelings, and in the racial discrimination she perceived in school and that paralyzed her. Sara attributed her paralysis and anxiety to this perception of constant criticism and rejection from the world. She spoke mostly of these themes, often repeating that she could never succeed because of the animosity others held toward her. She regularly included her therapist with those who were responsible for her fate: "You *don't* know what I'm talking about! You're white. And you're not helping me. You're just like the rest."

Although the therapist acknowledged and empathized with the difficulties she endured because of her minority status, he attempted to help her to understand how her difficulties were also a reflection of her internal world, such that she repeatedly perceived the roles of oppressed versus critical oppressor and abandoned versus abandoner in a stereotyped and polarized manner that stunted her relationships and inhibited her development. The therapist noted elements of envy and hostility in Sara's descriptions of her interactions with others and also in the here-and-now interactions with him. Yet from Sara's point of view, these affects always originated in others.

The therapist's efforts to conceptualize the situation centered on three things. First, the fact that Sara was anxious and was flooding him with material, which he experienced as both an effort to control him and yet also a maladroit form of reaching out to him for help.

Second, the fact that every time he spoke up, she disregarded him and spoke over him, suggesting that narcissistic issues—the need to be in control and be powerful and right, and to devalue the other— were more apparent than dependency issues at this stage. Third, the fact that his experience in sessions was often of being mistreated, of being treated rudely, and with no consideration, just as Sara complained she was treated by others. Thus the relational dynamics were quickly present in the transferential arena. An aspect of TFP that is illustrated in this material, and in which we differ from MBT, is attention to working in the transference with the aggressive elements in the representational world. Some of the internal self-object dyads of borderline patients are generally infused with aggressive affects. Although the patient's conscious experience of the dyad is typically to identify the self as the victim of aggression and the other as the aggressor, the whole schema is internalized with, as we see it, an identification with the aggressor as well as the victim. Clinically, as described earlier, one sees repeated oscillation between the roles. The work of therapy includes encouraging awareness of both identifications so that the aggressive affects can be integrated into a more nuanced whole, with the goal of enhancing the patient's capacity to manage his or her aggressive strivings.

MBT rejects the notion of identification with the aggressor. The MBT therapist would not interpret the hostile or destructive element as part of the self. Rather, he or she would hold and contain the projection of the aggressive object with the assumption that as the patient is able to achieve better mentalization of self and other, the sense of the hostile or aggressive other who is persecuting the patient will dissolve. We are aware that the TFP strategy of guiding the patient to take back the projection may temporarily increase the patient's anxiety because it challenges his defensive system of segregating internal parts, but we feel this way of working dynamically with the material can help resolve splitting operations, with the patient taking back his projections and both modulating affects and enriching his internal world with a fuller range of affective coloring and drive mastery.

With Sara, the therapist pursued the strategy of focusing on her affect in the context of her style of interacting, her way of being, with him. In the fourth month of therapy, assuming that what he saw on the surface was defending against material that was split off or dissociated, he made the following intervention:

"You know, since you are speaking so quickly and often change topics, it's hard to focus on what you say. At this point there might be more important information being communicated in *how* you are saying it—how you are interacting with me. Have you had any thoughts about the way our interaction goes?" [appealing to the patient's reflective function]

Sara angrily replied: "I'm just doing what you told me to do—to say whatever's on my mind. What's your point?"

Therapist: "It's true that I said that, but then our job is to observe what happens then. In most sessions, your way of carrying out seems to be to talk almost nonstop and to talk over me when I speak up. This creates a situation where you seem in control and I am a captive audience. I think it would help to try to understand what feelings or fears may lead you to do that. It's as though you are holding me in the grip of your words. Do you have any thoughts about that?"

Sara: "Now you're proving what I always knew anyway—you're not really interested in what I have to say. Why should I expect anything different? You're white, and you're rich. You just sit here and use me as your guinea pig for your study. You probably say bad things about me behind my back, like everyone else."

The therapist realized that describing the dyad he saw as operant on the surface—that of the controller and the controlled—did not engage the patient's curiosity; however, he noted an alternate dyad revealed in the patient's last comment that might be more directly linked to the affect she was experiencing in the moment. Interventions are most likely to strike a chord if they address the immediate affect. This dyad was that of an indifferent, and critical, caretaker relating to a neglected, disliked child who is longing for caring. The therapist thought the affects related to this dyad—longing, fear of neglect, criticism, and abandonment—might explain the predominance of the controlling/controlled dyad.

Considering both the possible motivation of her controlling behavior and the sense of being neglected that came through the last comment, the therapist said: "We might have the answer to why you behave with me the way you do right here in your last comment. You may be convinced that I'm not interested in you, that I don't care, and that I have a negative opinion of you. You feel that you're always doomed to neglect. Someone who believes that might want to control the interaction for fear that if she weren't in control, she'd be mistreated by the other person or lose him altogether."

Sara replied, bursting into tears: "Of course I'd lose you. Even my parents weren't interested in me, so why should you be?"

Sara's direct expression of affect seemed a first breaking through of her chronic defensive system. Her therapist's making contact with her affect in spite of her defensive pushing him away momentarily broke through her conviction that he was indifferent, neglectful, and critical. His ability to empathize with a part of her which was split off and only obliquely visible suggested that she might be dealing with a different other. This experience confronted her with two possible others: the familiar indifferent, critical, rejecting other and a "new" other who was concerned enough to make the effort to see other aspects of her. In that moment, she seemed to experience a confused combination of connection and wariness, of trust and mistrust. The situation itself, catalyzed by the therapist's empathic comment, was a challenge to her belief system and thus an invitation to reflect—a confrontation in action. This situation marked a beginning of communicating in therapy with a sense of authenticity. Sara was now able to intermittently question her negative beliefs with regard to her therapist and these moments allowed her to consider the possibility of a new object relation—where the other party was not threatening and might even have positive intentions toward her—and thus to interact in a less defensive way.

The therapist pointed out that Sara did not generally allow herself the chance to find out if he was interested in her. By controlling the interaction to create a *semblance* of interest in her, she supported the belief that he was not really interested in her. In the process of this, she devalued him and experienced herself as devalued. He further suggested that while attempting to hold him in her grip, she was actually remaining distant from him, because her monopolizing the interaction did not allow him to be in the room as a full-bodied person. For the first time, there seemed to be a dialogue in the room. Sara became calmer and could acknowledge that she did not allow her therapist to exist in the room and that this was because of her fear that he would treat her badly or leave if she left him to his own devices. As the discussion continued, it became clear that this strategy left her alone in relation to others, a condition she traditionally blamed others for.

After this positive session, Sara returned to treatment with much the same style of interaction that she had presented from the beginning. Her therapist had to return again and again to the interpretation of her omnipotent control and the fear it represented. It was only after repeating this interpretation many times, in the context of the therapeutic relationship where Sara questioned her initial convictions, that she could sort out what feelings came from whom. She began to alternate between moments of complaining about how others treated her and noting how she treated others, including her therapist aggressively. She began to talk about her own racism toward whites, an indication of her beginning to take back the projection of an aggressive element.

In a session 2 months later, Sara initially presented with a similar defensive structure, but was able more quickly to reflect on the interaction and consider other perspectives. She began by angrily reporting suicidal ideation and that she had taken a minor overdose. As the therapist tried to understand the affect and the fantasized relationship motivating it, Sara said: "My wanting to kill myself has nothing to do with your going away." [The therapist was to be away the following week]. The therapist pointed out that Sara had made this connection herself and that it must be humiliating to care so much about him when she felt he did not care about her. At that point, Sara became tearful and hid her face in her hands. Her therapist pointed out that it was difficult for her to experience or reveal the longing that she felt, that she was more comfortable expressing rejection of him and anger to avoid the feeling of rejection and humiliation. Sara replied that before the session she had had a fantasy of humiliating him, and added: "I just feel like the tragedy of everything, of all of this, is that I have help available... You're actually working with me....I guess there's a longing in a way, cause I did come on time, I didn't really want to come, but I do long to come here, in a way, I guess I do."

Thus, we see two major interpretive thrusts: One—of her need to control the other as a means of controlling a critical, rejecting part of herself that she experienced as coming from others; and 2—of her difficulty acknowledging her longing for love and caring, that she hid because of her anticipation of rejection and humiliation. Both involved naming a part of the patient that she experienced as other and helping her see it as part of herself. MBT might see this type of intervention as threatening the stability of the self-system by encouraging awareness of a toxic element that the patient could not tolerate. Yet our clinical experience and research data show that patients can work with these interventions when they are done tactfully and lead to a broadening of the general context of the patient's knowledge of self and others across time.

The work focuses on clarifying what part of the experience comes from the other and what part from the self. Sara begins feeling rejected and humiliated by her therapist's planned absence, while presenting rejecting behavior and describing a fantasy of humiliating him. The exchange between them clarifies that what she has experienced as external is within her. This shift from a chronic defensive belligerent stance toward others can be understood in relation to Sara's having begun to take back and metabolize the negative affects she had consistently projected onto others. Her initial psychological structure was based on a primitive separation of positive and negative affects. Her baseline assumption that others would treat her badly and eventually leave both led to a chronic effort to control others that engendered negative affects, and also allowed her to experience and express her own negative/aggressive affects as though they were a justifiable, acceptable, and even good response to the mistreatment by others. Her therapist's approach was to ask her to reflect on this system as it played out between her and him. Did she notice that she was controlling of him in sessions? What view of him, and her, might lead to this chronic behavior? This line of inquiry and interpretation allowed movement beyond the chronic defensive position to the experience and discussion of positive affects that were concealed, and thus protected, by the assumptions of the defensive position.

Interpreting the patient's use of omnipotent control in the first year of therapy helped the patient observe and understand this behavior, free herself from it and enter more deeply into other themes that it had been defending against. With the help of her therapist, Sara began to reflect on the theme of being criticized and attacked by others, and how it might defend against longing for closeness. Interpretations at that point addressed Sara's projection of an internal critical part in her mind—a part that could be aimed at herself or at others. With the therapeutic dialogue more established, Sara could begin to see what her therapist had tried to point out at the beginning: that she was capable of treating others as she complained they treated her. She became more aware of an angry critical part of herself that she experienced as residing in others but that both resided in herself and was directed at herself.

In her external life, Sara's complaints of mistreatment decreased. She began to report less anxiety and more positive interactions in her work setting, where she was offered a paid position. With regard to her initially split-off libidinal strivings, Sara's discourse and behavior in therapy began to give evidence of positive, loving feelings. With regard to intimate and sexual relations as they evolved in the course of treatment, in the period of time when Sara was still under the influence of primitive defense mechanisms—omnipotent control and projective identification—she was attracted to a narcissistic, unavailable man into whom she had deposited her critical judgmental part. After these defenses began to give way to more mature ones, she became involved with and eventually married (after 3 years of therapy) a more appropriate man.

The evaluation of the AAI after a year of therapy revealed that this patient advanced from a reflective functioning score of minus one (–1) to a score of 6 by the end of the first year of therapy, which shows not only clear and coherent evidence that she understands the mental functioning of self and others, but also some marked and original formulations of mental states. A fuller discussion of her RF and attachment classification ratings and their relation to the clinical course will be available in a forthcoming paper (Kernberg, Diamond, Yeomans, Clarkin, & Levy, in preparation).

In summary, we share Fonagy's view that a most difficult aspect of therapy is helping the patient resolve the externalization of unbearable self-states. Our clinical vignette presents an approach to this challenge in which engaging the patient's reflective capacity and interpreting the function of maladaptive defenses go hand-in-hand. Clarification, confrontation, and interpretation of affects and attributions in the here-and-now enhance the patient's reflective capacity by helping the patient consider the externalized material and reflect on its source. Acknowledgment of some measure of this material opens the way for integration and mastery of what had previously seemed external and immutable. Mentalization, the ability to reflect on heretofore irreconcilable internal conflicts of self and other representations, may both contribute to the process of integration and be furthered by that process. As projections are accepted internally, they become part of a richer appreciation of self and others which in turn increases the capacity to reflect on internal states.

References

Bateman, A., & Fonagy, P. (2004). Psychotherapy for borderline personality disorder: Mentalization-based treatment. New York: Oxford University Press.

Bion, W. R. (1967). *Second thoughts*. Northvale, NJ: Aronson.

Clarkin, J. F., Levy, K. N., Lenzenweger, M. F., & Kernberg, O. F. (2004). The Personality disorders institute/borderline personality disorder research foundation randomized control trial for borderline personality disorder: Rationale, methods, and patient characteristics. *Journal of Personality Disorders, 18*(1), 52–72.

Clarkin, J. F., Yeomans, F., & Kernberg, O. F. (2006). *Psychotherapy for borderline personality: Focusing on object relations*. Washington, DC: American Psychiatric Publishing.

Clarkin, J. F., & Levy, K. N. (Eds.). (2006). Psychotherapy for patients with borderline personality disorder: Focusing on the mechanisms of change. *Journal of Clinical Psychology, 62*.

Clarkin, J. F., Levy, K. N., Lenzenweger, M. F., & Kernberg, O. F. (2007). Evaluating three treatments for borderline personality disorder: A multiwave study. *American Journal of Psychiatry, 164*, 922–928.

Depue, R. A. & Lenzenweger, M. F. (2005). A Neurobehavioral Dimensional Model of Personality Disturbance. In M. F. Lenzenweger & J. F. Clarkin (Eds.), *Major theories of personality disorder*. (2nd ed.). New York: Guilford.

Fonagy, P., Leigh, T., Steele, M., Steele, H., Kennedy, R., Mattoon, G., Target, M. & Gerber, A. (1996). The relation of attachment status, psychiatric classification and response to psychotherapy. *Journal of Consulting and Clinical Psychology, 64*, 22–31.

Fonagy, P., Steele, M., Steele, H. & Target, M. (1997). Reflective-Functioning Manual: Version 4.1. For Application to the Adult Attachment Interviews. Unpublished manuscript, University College London.

Fonagy, P., Gergely, G., Jurist, E. L., & Target, M. (2002). *Affect regulation, mentalization, and the development of the self*. New York: Other Press.

Gabbard, G. O. & Westen, D. (2003). Rethinking therapeutic action. *International Journal of Psychoanalysis, 84*, 823–841.

Kazdin, A. E. (2001). Bridging the enormous gaps of theory with therapy research and practice. *Journal of Clinical Child Psychology, 30*, 59–66.

Kernberg, O. F. (1984). *Severe personality disorders: Psychotherapeutic strategies*. New Haven, CT: Yale University Press.

Kernberg, O.F. (2004). Aggressivity, narcissism, and self-destructiveness in the therapeutic relationship: New developments in the psychopathology and psychotherapy of severe personality disorders. New Haven, CT: Yale University Press.

Kernberg, O. F., Diamond, D, Yeomans, F. E., Clarkin, J. F., & Levy, K. N. (in preparation). Mentalization and attachment in borderline patients in transference-focused psychotherapy. In E. Jurist & A. Slade (Eds.), *The Future of Psychoanalysis: Mentalization, Representation and Internalization*. New York: Other Press.

Levy, K. N., Clarkin, J. F., Yeomans, F. E., Scott, L. N., Wasserman, R. H., & Kernberg, O. F., (2006). The mechanisms of change in the treatment of borderline personality disorder with transference-focused psychotherapy. *Journal of Clinical Psychology, 62*(4), 481–502.

Levy, K. N., Meehan, K. B., Kelly, K. M., Reynoso, J. S., Weber, M., Clarkin, J. F., & Kernberg, O. F. (2006). Change in attachment patterns and reflective function in a randomized control trial of transference focused psychotherapy for borderline personality disorder. *Journal of Consulting and Clinical Psychology, 74*(6), 1027–1040.

Linehan, M. M. (1993). Cognitive-behavioral treatment of borderline personality disorder. New York: Guilford.

Posner, M. I., Rothbart M. K., Vizueta, N., Levy, K., Thomas, K. M., & Clarkin, J. (2002). Attentional mechanisms of borderline personality disorder. *Proceedings of the National Academy of Sciences, 99*, 16366–16370.

Yeomans, F. E., Clarkin, J. C., & Kernberg, O. F. (2002) *A Primer on Transference-Focused Psychotherapy for Borderline Patients*. Jason Aronson: Northvale, NJ.

Part III

Clinical

6

Reflective Functioning in
Panic Disorder Patients
Clinical Observations and Research Design*

*Marie G. Rudden, Barbara Milrod,
Andrew Aronson, and Mary Target*

Introduction

The Reflective Functioning scale was developed in the context of research that closely observed patterns of attachment and the impact of parental attachment styles on children's attachment status. Reflective functioning refers to the psychological capacities underlying mentalization (Fonagy, 1991), and the RF Scale offers a measure for assessing a person's capacity to conceptualize and understand mental states in himself and others. It was examined as a potential mediator through which parents, by anticipating and understanding their children's emotional reactions, might promote secure attachment. Parents' RF scores indeed showed a strong relationship to their infants' behavior in the Strange Situation test of attachment security (Fonagy, Steele, & Steele, 1991), with higher parental RF scores predicting greater security in their children.

The relationship of psychiatric classification to differing capacities for Reflective Function was also a focus of study during the development of the measure (Fonagy et al., 1996), and a significant

---
* This paper was supported by a grant from the American Psychoanalytic Association Fund for Psychoanalytic Research, by NIMH grant K23 MH 1849 01-05, and by a fund in the New York Community Trust established by De Witt Wallace.

relationship was discerned between RSF (the capacity for reflective self-functioning, a forerunner of the RF construct), the presence of physical and sexual abuse, and a diagnosis of borderline personality disorder. Low RSF and a history of abuse taken together were found to be predictive of the borderline personality disorder diagnosis. The relationship was thought to perhaps reflect a tendency of victims of childhood abuse to cope by

> refusing to conceive of the contents of their caregiver's mind and thus successfully avoid(ing) having to think about their caretakers' wish to harm them…this initially defensive disruption of the capacity to depict feelings and thoughts in themselves and in others becomes a characteristic response to all subsequent intimate relationships. The failure to understand mental states becomes a core symptom of their disturbance and accounts for many aspects of the clinical presentation of BPD. (Fonagy et al., 1996, p. 29)

As a dimension of examining mediators of change in our treatment, our research group chose to study Reflective Functioning in patients with panic disorder before and after Panic-focused Psychodynamic Psychotherapy (PFPP; Milrod, Busch, Cooper, & Shapiro, 1997). Patients with panic disorder have been seen to characteristically use not knowing as a way of defending against conflicted feeling states. (Busch, Shear, Cooper, Shapiro, & Leon, 1995; Milrod et al., 1997; Milrod, 1998). Certain identifications, internalized object representations, affects, or fantasies perceived as dangerous are disowned through compromise formations that express the inner dangers via physical anxiety symptoms, but disguise the nature of the threat through repression, externalization, and reaction formation. In these compromise formations, the patient is punished for his conflicted and disowned anger or for his desire for sexual expression or for autonomy by the experience of the anxiety itself. Such compromise formations often result in an inhibited capacity for patients with panic disorder to recognize that their psycho-physiological symptoms are related to internal mental states. This not knowing about conflicted areas of mental life is often mirrored in the agoraphobic symptoms that can accompany panic disorder. The specific symptoms of not feeling able to explore certain areas of a city, for example, or to leave a neighborhood, or to take a subway, may offer a symbolic expression of the inner danger being disavowed (Abraham, 1913; Deutsch, 1927; Kessler, 1996; Milrod, 2007).

In one of the cases in our open trial, for example, (Busch et al., 2001) a patient avoided subways because of panic states precipitated when the train would stop in a tunnel. During treatment, her fear of this situation was discovered to relate to her unconscious connection between feeling imprisoned in the stalled subway and suppressed feelings and fantasies about a punishment she had incurred in childhood, of being locked in the basement after being beaten. In this case, the patient had consciously adopted a position of having been unaffected by such punishments, but in treatment realized that she had felt quite frightened, humiliated, abandoned, and enraged—all feelings she had disowned because of the sense of great vulnerability they caused. In another case, a patient's terror at leaving her neighborhood was seen to mirror her fear of having thoughts and feelings that strayed from the very circumscribed ones that she thought would be acceptable to her physically and emotionally abusive mother: going "too far afield" was experienced as risking punishment.

The model of panic disorder used in Panic-Focused Psychodynamic Psychotherapy is conflict-based. We consider that biogenetic or temperamental diatheses in panic patients become interwoven with compelling unconscious conflicts to result in considerable anxiety about separations, real or anticipated, from important objects in the patient's life (Milrod, 1998; Milrod et al., 1997; Rudden et al., 2003). Many panic patients experience ambivalence and conflicted anger toward parents perceived as unprotective (of their propensity toward anxiety states) or neglectful. The sense of not being adequately protected or nurtured leaves the patient feeling needy, helpless, hurt, angry, and insecure about his ability to function when apart from the needed parent. The angry feelings come to be feared especially as potentially pushing the needed parent away even further, although the experience of the needy feelings makes the patient feel weak, ashamed, and vulnerable to attack.

Other patients describe their parents as over-stimulating or over-controlling figures who discouraged their autonomy and were thus experienced as suffocating. An angry or distancing reaction from the parent on the child's part, however, seemed to cause frightening retaliatory anger or a confusing reactive distance by the parent, leaving the child to feel overwhelmed, confused, and alone with his emotional reactions. This chronic pattern of relating with the parent can contribute to anxiety over expressions of autonomous function, including separations.

Anger about the anxiety-filled separation or expression of autonomy escalates a patient's anxiety,

> as the aggression is imagined to be so intense that it will alienate, over-
> whelm, or eliminate needed loved ones, or bring about frightening fan-
> tasied punishments or losses. Often, the fearfulness is experienced as
> shameful and infantile. Sometimes this stimulates counter-dependent
> fantasies or behaviors that may in themselves become additionally anxi-
> ety-provoking. (Rudden et al., 2003)

These preoedipally based dynamics may intensify fears about
oedipal-phase dangers. For example, competition with the same-
sex parent may escalate fears about disrupted attachments. Panic
attacks may represent a compromise solution, then, in which regression to a dependent state, emphasizing the patient's neediness and
fears, defends against aggressive, sexual, or competitive wishes and
feelings. At times, such regressions can stimulate longings that may
cause further anxiety, as in Rey's (1979) description of the claustro-
phobic-agoraphobic dilemma, or may be reacted to by a defensive
flight into counterdependent, aggressive behaviors. This, in turn,
however, can escalate anxiety over aggression (Busch et al., 1999).

Panic-focused Psychodynamic Psychotherapy focuses on identifying and understanding these conflicts with the patient, first
through a close exploration of the circumstances surrounding the
panic attacks, and later by an examination of other ways in which
these conflicts evidence themselves, such as in anxiety over separation within the transference. Through this treatment, what has been
not known by the patient about the kinds of conflict that create escalating anxiety becomes recognized and incorporated into his or her
vision of himself.

Our research group found the RF measure to be one of the few
constructs that are operationalized, reliable and valid that offer a way
of capturing the process through which our study patients begin to
know more about their inner lives. Although it is a measure that can
encompass many different kinds of unconscious compromises that
can result in knowing or not knowing about one's own or others'
mental states, and thus is nonspecific, it is nonetheless fully compatible with a conflict-based theoretical and therapeutic approach. We
were concerned; however, that Reflective Functioning in itself might
be too broad a measure for our purposes. Although some patients
with panic disorder evince a global kind of not knowing about their

inner lives (see e.g., Case A in Milrod, 1998), others are quite perceptive about their own mental states and those of others, with the exception of the inner conflicts that precipitate their symptoms. This aspect of the overall reflective functioning capacity is not surprising, in that it is a synthetic ego function that seems likely to be affected by unconscious conflict and compromises, as are other ego functions such as the capacity to tolerate affects. Thus, we decided not only to investigate RF itself, but also to adapt the concept to a more specific item, Panic-Specific RF (PSRF), that is geared directly to examining changes in the patient's perceptions of underlying mental states connected with his panic attacks.

We hypothesized that (a) an increasing ability to reflect on the sources of the anxiety experienced by patients with panic disorder, evidenced by an increase in Panic-Specific RF, would be provided through PFPP, and further hypothesized that (b) this enhancement in PSRF would correlate with symptomatic improvement, as evaluated on our primary measure, the Panic Symptom Severity Scale.

We also hypothesized that (c) General RF is not characteristically compromised in all panic disorder patients, and also that (d) Panic-Specific RF would be lower in this patient group at baseline compared to General RF.

The Panic-Focused Psychodynamic Psychotherapy Study

Panic-focused psychodynamic psychotherapy (PFPP) is a 24 session (twice-a-week sessions for 12 weeks) psychotherapy that uses an interpretive focus based on our understanding of common dynamics, defense-mechanisms and transference paradigms observed in patients with this illness (Milrod et al., 1997). Outcome for this treatment was originally tested via an open trial of 21 patients that demonstrated statistically significant, clinically meaningful improvements in panic disorder symptoms, overall anxiety, depression, and psychosocial function at termination, sustained at 6 month follow-up (Milrod et al., 2000, 2001).

PFPP was then studied (Milrod et al., 2007) in a randomized, placebo-controlled trial in comparison with a less active form of psychotherapy for panic disorder, Applied Relaxation Training (ART; Ost & Westling,1984). The comparison treatment also comprises a 24-session format, delivered twice weekly, in which progressive muscle relaxation training, discrimination training, generalization, relaxation by recall and cue-controlled relaxation training techniques were offered sequentially.

Patients gave informed, written consent and were evaluated diagnostically and symptomatically before, after and at 6 and 12 months post-treatment termination by clinical raters blinded to patient condition with a series of administered and self-report symptomatic measures including the Hamilton Anxiety Rating Scale (1959), Hamilton Rating Scale for Depression (1960), the Sheehan Disability Scale (1983) and the Panic Disorder Severity Scale (Shear et al., 1997), the primary dependent variable. Graduate psychoanalysts who underwent a 16-week training course in Panic-Focused Psychodynamic Psychotherapy served as the study therapists, and therapist adherence was monitored with adherence instruments using videotaped sessions.

The Reflective Functioning study, a separate part of the ongoing randomized controlled trial, examined patients' mentalizing capacities via rating a semistructured interview for RF described later. It also evaluated patients' abilities to envision inner mental states as connected to their panic symptoms through scoring Panic Specific RF on a new interview that we piloted. The interviews were administered at baseline and treatment termination by clinical raters blinded to patients' condition, to n=18 patients in the PFPP condition and to n=8 in ART. RF is rated according to the scoring manual provided by Fonagy, Target, Steele, and Steele (1998) and for Panic Specific RF by a new manual, which can be obtained from Dr. Rudden. Reliability was achieved between our first rater (MGR) and the Fonagy group (1998) and has also been achieved between the two raters for general RF and PSRF (MGR and BLM) in the current study. Dr. Rudden's ratings, which were analyzed in the quantitative testing of our hypotheses, were made blind to the patients' condition.

The RF Interview

Given a patient burden of over four hours for assessments in the PFPP study, it was impossible to administer the complete Adult Attachment Interview used by Fonagy and colleagues (1998) for scoring Reflective Functioning in this setting. Thus, we abbreviated and adapted the interview as follows to test for general reflective functioning.

TABLE 6.1   Interview for general reflective functioning (adapted from the Adult Attachment Interview (Main and Goldwyn, 1995)):

---

1. A.   Can you tell me about one of your parents? What is that parent like?

   B.   How do you think your parent came to be that way?

   (If the pt answers, "because of their parent(s)," ask whether they mean that their parent inherited that trait or disposition or style, or if it came about through some impact the grandparent had. Ask them if they can expand on that, if the answer is very brief.)

2. A.   Can you tell me about your relationship?

   B.   Can you tell me about a specific memory of that relationship or about that parent from childhood (ages 5–12)?

   C.   Do you have any thoughts about how the relationship came to be that way? (*Alternative forms of question: About how these conflicts and problems developed? About how it came to be such a good relationship?*)

   D.   Can you tell me how this relationship has changed over time? (*Ask why it has changed if they don't address this in their answer.*)

3. Can you tell me what impact this parent has had on your life?

4. Can you tell me why you chose to talk about this parent?

To test for Panic-Specific Reflective Function, we developed a second interview.

The interview for panic-specific RF is scored in a fashion similar to that for general RF, with ratings that range from –1, (negative RF, in which a patient thoroughly refuses to engage in reflection, or misattributes internal states in a paranoid or bizarre manner) through 1 (apparently lacking in RF, with no demonstrated ability to reflect on one's own or others' mental states), 3 (questionable RF, characterized by clichéd or concrete descriptions of mental states), 5 (an average ability to have a working knowledge of mental states), 7 (marked capacity to perceive mental states in oneself and others) to 9 (exceptional RF). Examples of the categories scored most often (those from 3 to 7) and sample interview responses that might correspond to those ratings for Panic-specific RF are as follows:

TABLE 6.2   Interview to Assess Panic-Specific Reflective Function

1. Why do you think you have panic attacks?
2. Do you ever notice that you get more panic episodes when you are upset about something?

   If yes:

   A. Ask what the patient might be upset about.
   B. Ask if the patient has any ideas about how being upset about these things might connect to his panic symptoms.
3. Do you notice any pattern at all as to when you might get your panic attacks?

3—Questionable or Low RF: Mostly biological meanings are attributed to the panic symptoms, along with unspecific and concrete psychological responses.

Q: Why do you think you have panic attacks?
A: My mother. They happen because of her. (When asked to elaborate on how these are related to mother, says: "I'm not sure—I guess maybe I inherited this from her. The gene pool. And also, just the way she was, her personality. You know, how she affects me.")

Q: Do you get them when you're more when upset about something?
A: No...um, I'm not really sure why I get them. I'd say the heat brings them on more.

Q: Do you notice any pattern at all?
A: Well, heat, but also going to unfamiliar places—I have worries about that. I get afraid when I am away from a place where I feel safe.

5—Ordinary RF (the modal rating): The interviewee mentions a combinations of stressors that can include but are not limited to biological factors, may mention simple or unspecified childhood influences on the development of the symptoms, and shows some working awareness that his symptoms are related to inner states.

Q: Why do you think you have panic attacks?
A: I used to think they were triggered by alcohol or something that made me feel guilty, like maybe cheating on my boyfriend. I think that was probably connected. But now, they seem to just come out of the blue—I can't figure it out any more.

Q: Do you get them more when you're upset? What about?

A: I noticed that they escalated when I went back to class and couldn't handle the stress of work plus school.

Q: How might this be connected to the attacks?

A: I over-think and over-worry everything. My mom was like that and I think it affected me, being around her and feeling all that anxiety.

7—Marked RF: Interviewee demonstrates a very specific awareness of inner emotional states as triggering the attacks, is able to connect the symptoms in a fairly complex and specific way to earlier experiences or to ongoing internal conflicts.

Q: Why do you think you have panic attacks?

A: I think it's because I bottle up a lot of feelings, especially my angry and hurt feelings, and I just can't verbalize them- I suck it all in. At some point, it just all comes out in feeling overwhelmed with anxiety.

Q: Do you have them more when you're upset? What about?

A: I get anxious and helpless sometimes about financial matters, but mostly I notice that I get panicky when I'm feeling a lack of control in personal relationships. I feel that others are going to leave me behind, or I may want to leave them.

Q: How do these things connect to the panic attacks?

A: I think that those feelings are connected to situations in my childhood when I felt pretty alone. My mom seemed always to be very busy with her job and with her friends and I felt very bad and angry about that. I think I'm afraid that I will be too needy or not taken care of again, and that turns into panic.

Qualitative Clinical Observations from the Study

A statistical analysis of our study results (Rudden et al, 2006), reveals that PSRF scores at treatment termination improved significantly more after PFPP than after ART. In this report, we describe the kinds of interview responses seen before and after therapy in the treatment group, and offer some perspectives on the change in Panic-Specific RF seen in one clinical case from the study. We trace interventions in that treatment that seemed to enhance reflective functioning about the panic symptoms, and discuss how this improvement in capacity seemed to connect with the symptomatic outcome.

Sample Interview Responses

One patient, A., demonstrates how even a fairly reflective person with above average RF can still have difficulty envisioning her panic symptoms as being related to mental states. In her intake interview, A. provided fairly nuanced answers and was rated 7 (marked) for general RF. When asked to describe her mother, for example, she spoke of her as:

> nosy, very involved, very much wanting to be in the loop, wanting to seem hip, young. She is actually a good person, but when I developed bulimia in adolescence, instead of seeing it as a problem or saying, "that's terrible," or trying to help me with it in some way, she said, "Oh, yeah, I did that too...."

> She gets jealous rather easily, for example when one of my sisters lost weight, she seemed rather competitive about it... She did the best she could—she had a lot of difficulties in childhood herself—but she still can cause my sister and I a lot of stress.

When asked about how her relationship came to feel, as she described it now, uncomfortable and distant, A. responded:

> When I went away to college, she had a lot of separation issues—she wasn't ready for the baby to leave home and grow up. I tried to establish my independence and had a serious relationship, but she didn't deal well with it at all....I guess it's because she was worried I'd get married and have a baby too young like her. But that's when the relationship just deteriorated. I don't share a lot with her, because I fear that she will either disapprove, or worry too much about me. Neither feels like a comfort to me.

In contrast with these fairly nuanced answers about her parent, A. was stymied by the questions about her panic attacks. Asked why she thought she had the panic attacks, A. said simply: "I don't know. I wish I did and then I could fix them. It's become physical, and I just don't get that." Asked if she had these attacks more when she was upset, her answer was: "Yes, if I'm upset about something. If I try to suppress being upset, it's bad."

When the interviewer asked how being upset might connect to her symptoms, A. said, "I don't understand the connection. Even if I don't seem to be thinking about something, I worry that my body will react or clue me in. But I don't know..." Finally, when queried as to whether she had noticed a pattern to her attacks, A. mused: "They usually happen during rush hours—in the evening or in the morning when I have to get to work. Sometimes when I'm tired."

This interview was rated as demonstrating less than an average RF, a rating of 4. The patient had some idea that her symptoms might connect to mental states, musing that when she suppressed an upset feeling, "it was bad." But her answers still seem vague and puzzled in contrast with her general interview, and the response about noticing a pattern to the attacks "rush hours, when I'm tired" is disconnected from her mental life. Thus, a patient who was able to make fairly easy and meaningful observations about aspects of her mother's motivations and about her own responses to these over time, was more vague and had generally less thoughtful or specific responses about the conflicts or kinds of upset feelings that might connect to her panic attacks.

Patient B. shows evidence of an increased capacity to reflect on her panic symptoms after her treatment with PFPP. Prior to treatment, B. was asked why she thought she had panic attacks, and responded: "I think I am high-strung. I get nervous a lot and people tell me to calm down about a lot of things." When the interviewer questioned whether B. was more often panicked when she was upset, and if so, what she might be upset about, B. reflected: "Some of them are triggered by being upset and crying, like if I felt inept or unqualified to do something. It's not just about when something is bad in my life, though, because my grandpa died two weeks ago and I haven't had them since." Asked how being upset about these things might contribute to the panic attacks, B.'s response was:" I see the attacks starting and I try to stop them. I think that on some given days, I just am more high strung." Finally, questioned whether there is a pattern as to when she gets her attacks, B. replied: "When I have to work, if I delay things, I will start freaking out about it."

This interview was rated a 5, or showing average RF, as it contained a mixture of answers, most having to do with some mental state. Some of descriptions were diffuse: "I am high-strung, on some days I am more high-strung," while others seemed more specific, without being particularly nuanced or complex: "Like if I felt inept or unqualified to do something," or "if I delay things, I will start freaking out about it."

After her treatment with PFPP, this patient, when asked about why she had panic attacks, responded: "I think I had them because of a lot of issues that happened when I was a child and growing up. And then September 11 had a lot to do with it, with bringing those things up for me again…"

Her interviewer followed the question by inquiring whether she got them more when she was upset, and B. answered that yes, she did. Sometimes "stupid things" stimulated her upset feelings, such as when her train got caught in a tunnel, but this connected to other things inside her, and she saw that the upset didn't "just come out of the blue." Questioned as to how being upset about things connected to the panic symptoms, she replied, "They happened because I was scared. It seemed before as if there was no rhyme or reason to it all, but in the bigger picture, I see a common thread of fear about certain things….deeper issues that have troubled me."

The latter interview was rated as a 6, which is between average and marked RF. B. seemed less vague than in the original interview and more aware of childhood experiences and inner fears that she connected now to her panic attacks. Had she elaborated more specifically about these and offered more details, she may well have been scored as having marked RF, or 7. But it did seem clear that B. now connected her experience of her attacks with much more specific inner experiences, including early experiences from childhood resurrected by the trauma of September 11, and that she could now identify and know about why, for example, a train stopping in a tunnel might be upsetting to her.

Case Study (C)

A married woman in her mid 30s, C. presented for treatment with increasingly frequent panic attacks in the weeks following the birth of her second child. She described her first panic attack as having occurred years before, during her first semester of college, when C. had matriculated at a school requiring several hours of air travel from her home. Her first panic attack occurred on the tarmac as she was about to fly home for her initial visit to see her mother since beginning college. C. understood the symptom simply as a new fear of flying.

Though initially her panic attacks were triggered by airplane travel and later were experienced within other enclosed environments, over the ensuing years her symptoms had become increasingly generalized. At the time of presentation, C. remarked "I can almost talk myself into panic anywhere."

C. was the only child of parents who divorced, after a tumultuous marriage, when she was 5-years-old. The patient had been witness to the physical abuse of her mother by her alcoholic, dysfunctional father during her early years. Despite her father's abusiveness, after the divorce and his departure C. idealized him and yearned for his further involvement with her, but this happened only rarely and unpredictably. Deeply disappointed, she felt rejected, failed and forsaken, and began to lie about him to her friends, describing him as an enterprising, successful businessman whose absence from her life resulted from his busy schedule, rather than from his own failings.

Mother too was idealized, though in many respects seemed to deserve her daughter's admiration. A working class laborer, mother struggled relentlessly to afford her daughter the advantages of which she herself had been deprived, and successfully gained her placement in a private school attended mainly by children of affluence and of a different race. Mother was seen as warm and loving, devoted to her daughter and claiming little for herself, but also came to be seen by C. as rather pitiful and tired, in contrast to the affluent parents of her friends. In her single-minded devotion to her daughter and her own self- neglect, mother likely contributed to her own early and sudden death from heart disease 10 years prior to the time of C.'s presentation for treatment.

C. felt deep gratitude for her mother's devotion, but also was somewhat aware of a guilty shame about her mother's impoverished appearance. She remarked early in her therapy, however that "my mother was a sweet, gorgeous woman, my best friend, my idol. We were super-close. Since her death, I have always searched for the feeling that I had with her. I am constantly looking for that feeling—of someone loving you that much—that way of being safe."

In her treatment, it became possible to clarify how C. struggled mightily with feelings of both guilt and fear in her conscious ambition to become a successful and independent adult woman, mother and wife. Although to succeed was to satisfy her mother's fervent wishes for her, it also involved for C. a crucial sense of forsaking the experience of warmth and closeness in their relationship. Success and independence had become linked in her mind to a selfish abandonment of her mother, as well as an embrace of the dangers of adult womanhood as exemplified by the physical abuse and rejection mother had suffered in her marriage. The onset of panic was understood within this paradigm: C. had experienced herself just at the threshold of success as she was about to visit home and report to her mother about her happiness at her elite college. Her underlying guilt and the fear that she was abandoning her mother and was thus now all alone, however, were not known consciously to her, and became expressed indirectly by the anxiety attack as she sat on the airplane, which also served to punish her for her enjoyment of college life.

C. learned in her treatment that her panic symptoms involved fantasies of both being forsaken and forsaking; of having no recourse: She felt that she could neither turn back to the delightful but insular closeness with her mother, nor move forward to a frightening future that involved the sense of abandoning her. This sense of being stuck, with no way out of her dilemma, came to be symbolized for her when she found herself in enclosed spaces and became suddenly frightened, feeling trapped. Through these understandings, C. was able to place in new perspective her childhood memories of "not wanting to grow up," her sucking her thumb and using "baby words" until she was 6 years old—her resisting a scary independence upon each new threshold.

Clarification of these themes, recognized with increasing definition and perspective, helped C. to feel less immobilized and stuck within the cycle of feeling forsaken, helpless, angry, guilty, and panic-stricken, and as she recognized the presence of these themes in her various experiences of panic, her anxiety symptoms remitted. C. became less prone to guilt and fear in her independent activities, and better able to affirm her substantial capacities. She took newfound pride in her role as "mother times two," realizing that her intensified panic symptoms with the second pregnancy expressed her guilt at surpassing mother by having something she never was able to—a second child. C. also began to take better physical care of herself, no longer guiltily bound in identification with her debilitated mother. She recognized that she could have matriculated to a college closer to home but had aspired to independence, and was able to take comfort in appreciating how her independent strivings were consonant with those that her mother had cherished for her.

Termination revived the familiar anxieties that so attended autonomy and progress, though by this time it had become possible to know about her anxiety and what it represented in this context. In the concluding sessions C. was able to tolerate sadness in ending the relationship with her therapist, and she was able to recognize and reflect on the associated sad memories of movement away from her mother with less guilt, a sense of prideful accomplishment and much less fear.

C.'s Interview Responses

Before treatment, C. showed marked Reflective Functioning, or a rating of 7 on her interview. Asked about one of her parents, she described her mother:

> My mother was my best friend. She died 10 years ago. She was a very cool woman, very sweet, very smart. She went through a lot in her childhood, she was not very acknowledged in her family. My grandmother wasn't into her, so she went through a lot of sadness as a kid, a lot of depression that followed her as an adult....She kept working on herself, though, battling her weight and depression, and often had a happy, optimistic outlook on life—things would get better...She tried to make me into the person that she wasn't....

When the interviewer questioned further about their relationship, C. described it thus:

> We kind of grew up together. It was just her and me since I was five. We were friends to each other, not a lot of discipline. My whole life, she was always the one I wanted to tell things to first. She created a great place for me to work out things with my dad. She made me feel safe and secure. My dad was an alcoholic who kind of disappeared from my life and she let me talk about that, maybe to a fault. I was probably too young to be talking about that so much, but she wanted me to have the opportunity she never had to talk and have feelings.

When asked to consider about how her relationship changed over time, C. noted:

> ...The hardest thing was that when I was 17 and went far away.....for college.....She wanted me to have the life experiences that I wanted. The physical move was difficult, but we became women friends, talking about different things....we got closer in a different way, which was cool.

The interview demonstrates an ability to offer fresh, heartfelt, and specific details about her mother, to show an awareness of the influence of her mother's family life on her personality development, an appreciation that her mother's mood states could be contradictory (both depressed and yet optimistic), and a capacity to entertain different points of view herself about the impact of her mother's behavior on her, as in when she appreciated mother's allowing her to talk about her anger toward her father, but acknowledged that this may have been "to a fault: I was probably too young to be talking about it" so much.

In her Panic-specific RF interview, C. still showed a fairly marked ability to think about her internal states, but this was not as highly developed as in the more general interview.

When C. was asked about why she thought she had panic attacks, she mused:

> I think there is something about control. I never thought I had control issues. But when I think about how it all started, that was a big mental state for me. I needed to be responsible for my life, leaving college, I don't know—maybe it has something to do with having to deal with something that I don't really want to do. A scary, lack of control thing.

When questioned about whether she noticed when she gets her panic attacks, C. observed:

> I feel that when my security is threatened in any big way, I become more anxious. Claustrophobic stuff—elevators, subways, cars. Those trigger things. I also am uncomfortable because I'm not being acknowledged in my life. I'm generally just not feeling cool—a low grade "something" is going on.

Finally asked how this might connect to her panic symptoms, C. stated:

> You know on one level, I feel that my marriage is not stable, so of course I would have free-floating anxiety, and there are other situations that don't feel secure. Then there are those instances that don't make any sense at all, when I am completely relaxed. Why is it so horrifying if I am going on a great vacation, to be in a certain kind of car, in a certain situation, or why does it matter if a certain kind of music is playing on the radio?... Or if I am happily pregnant, getting on the elevator to go to the doctor's, why is it different that there are four people taking up room instead of three?

This interview was rated a 6, greater than average but not quite demonstrating marked reflective capacity about her symptoms. Although C. was able to speculate on different mental states that might be related to her panic symptoms—a lack of feeling in control of her life as she graduated from college and perhaps didn't fully want to take on adult responsibility, a lack of security in her marriage, a sense of being unacknowledged now—she still struggles to see how these all connect to her symptoms. The idea of potentially having two minds about something—being ambivalent or conflicted about a vacation, or—given a sense of insecurity in her marriage—about her pregnancy, does not seem to occur to her as potentially contributing to her anxiety when she is in happy situations. Likewise, C. gets caught up with the details of what kind of car she is in, or of how many people are on the elevator, without thinking about what particular feelings—for example of being stuck, unable to move or to escape—might be prompted by that extra—crowded sensation in the car or on the elevator.

After termination, C.'s answers to these questions do become more articulated, and her answers are overall rated as 7, or as showing marked Panic-specific Reflective Functioning.

When she is asked about why she has panic attacks, she now replies:

> I think that I have them because as a kid, I sort of felt like I didn't have control over certain big things or big feelings. A lot of times, that left me feeling uncomfortable or scared. That developed into panic when I went to college. It was as if all that fear that had always been there jumped out and took on its own life, because I was alone, in a kind of scary place, and I wasn't sure what I was really doing with myself. I think that when I have a feeling that I have recourse, it makes me feel less helpless, and I don't need to panic.

Further, when queried about whether the panic episodes seem to connect with being upset, C. noted that

> I get more panic attacks if I've been drinking...when I drink I feel very raw and vulnerable. And on a plane or other places and times that I feel I don't have control over what is going on. In my marriage, maybe feeling I have so many plans and obligations related to being a mom. And when I can't tell my husband what is going on at any given moment—I can feel trapped.

Asked to consider further how being upset in these ways connected to the panic states, C. commented that "I really feel it's the lack of control— in pregnancies, my body feels out of my control, I get claustrophobic. And nursing—I feel just a sense of like a lack of personal space, I feel trapped."

In these answers, her reflections on her mental states are more elaborated, more specific. C. is able to see a connection between old feelings from her childhood with the emergence of her panic attacks during college. She is also able to know about the ambivalent feelings that may accompany otherwise pleasurable activities—nursing, pregnancy, and to say more specifically what in her marriage may contribute to making her feel more trapped—that is, the sense that she feels that she has many obligations in her family life, but can't always talk with her husband. Further, the idea of having recourse versus feeling trapped that she worked on in her treatment seems to have meant a good deal for her in filling in some of the blanks in her earlier responses. More is known by C. now about her inner life, its history, resonant feelings and areas of conflict, and these find their way into her sense of having recourse and thereby diminishing the need to panic.

C.'s general RF rating remained at a 7, or showing marked capacity for reflection. But in this interview, her observations about her mother, quite similar to the ones expressed earlier, still were drawn with added shadings that suggested her ability to now comprehend more about her own conflicting mental states. The biggest change was in her response to discussing how her relationship with her mother had changed over time. C.'s answer was now much more complex:

> When I went away to college, I felt very guilty about leaving her, I felt that I was leaving her behind. There was guilt about not bringing her with me and later, about not affording her a better life. I don't think it changed how we felt about each other, but it did change things.

The not knowing about her feelings of guilt and conflicted independence had changed during the treatment to a new capacity to speak about her guilt and about the idea that even though the two continued to care deeply about each other after she left, that C.'s move toward independence did change things. This knowing actually decreased her anxiety, however, as she had been able to observe her feelings of shame and guilt toward her mother and to realize that having these emotions had not changed the depth of feeling that each had for the other, and did not genuinely represent disloyalty or an abandonment on either side, as much as she had dreaded and feared this earlier.

Conclusion

In examining interview responses from two different patients before and after PFPP, and particularly from a case in which the treatment interventions are described, it is possible to see the ways in which the Panic-Specific Reflective Functioning and the general RF measures capture the process that has occurred in this psychoanalytic treatment of patients with panic disorder. Through the treatment, patients' tendency to not know about the conflicted inner states connecting with their internal experience of danger and the resulting panic attacks is seen to change, as reflected in their more complex articulated awareness of their inner mental states. Our hypotheses that patients with panic disorder will have a lower Panic Specific RF than general RF, that their general RF will not necessarily be impaired, and that patients' PSRF will increase with treatment in a way that corresponds with the diminishment in their panic symptoms, seem to be borne out by these examples, as they have been through a qualitative examination of the sample of 26 patients to date. It is of interest that none of the 8 interviewed patients in the ART group have been rated as demonstrating a higher RF or PSRF after their treatment so far. Upon completion of the clinical trial, the data will be analyzed quantitatively to determine whether or not these findings achieve significance and offer validation of our new measure.

References

Abraham, K. (1913). A constitutional basis of locomotor anxiety. In Abraham, K (Ed.), *Selected papers on psychoanalysis.* NY: Brunner/Mazel, reprinted by Hogarth Press, 1927 pp. 235–243.

Busch, F. N., Shear, M. K., Cooper, A. M., Shapiro, T. & Leon, A. C. (1995). An empirical study of defense mechanisms in panic disorder. *Journal of Nervous and Mental Diease, 183,* 299–303.

Busch, F. N., Milrod, B. L., Rudden, M., Shapiro, T., Singer, M., Aronson, A. & Roiphe, J. (1999). Oedipal dynamics in panic disorder. *Journal of American Psychoanalytic Association, 47,* 773–790.

Busch, F. N., Milrod, B. L., Rudden, M., Shapiro, T., Roiphe, J., Singer, M. & Aronson, A. (2001). How treating psychoanalysts respond to psychotherapy research constraints. *Journal of American Psychoanalytic Association, 49,* 961–984.

Deutsch, H. (1929). The genesis of agoraphobia. *International Journal of Psychoanalysis, 10,* 511–569.

Fonagy, P. (1991).Thinking about thinking: Some clinical and theoretical considerations in the treatment of a borderline patient. *International Journal of Psychoanalysis, 72*, 1–18.

Fonagy, P., Steele, H., Steele, M. (1991). Maternal representations of attachment during pregnancy predict the organization of infant-mother attachment at one year of age. *Child Development, 62*, 891–905.

Fonagy, P., Leigh, T., Steele, M., Steele, H., Kennedy, R., Mattoon, G., Target, M., & Gerber, A. (1996). The relation of attachment status, psychiatric classification, and response to psychotherapy. *Journal of Consulting and Clinical Psychology, 64*, 22–31.

Fonagy, P., Target, M., Steele, H. & Steele M.(1998). *Reflective-Functioning Manual, version 5 for Application to Adult Attachment Interviews.* (unpublished, available from authors).

Hamilton, M. (1959). The assessment of anxiety states by rating. *British Journal of Medical Psychology, 32*, 56–62.

Hamilton, M. (1960). A rating scale for depression. *Journal of Neurology, Neurosurgery and Psychiatry, 23*, 56–62.

Kessler, R. (1996). Panic Disorder and the retreat from meaning. *Journal of Clinical Psychoanaysis, 5*, 505–528.

Main, M., Goldwyn, R. (1995). Adult Attachment Classification System. In M. Main (Ed.), *Behaviour and the Development of Representational Models of Attachment: Five Methods of Assessment.*Cambridge, UK: Cambridge University Press.

Milrod, B., Busch, F. N., Cooper, A. M. & Shapiro, T. (1997). *Manual of panic-focused psychodynamic psychotherapy.* Washington, DC American Psychiatric Association Press.

Milrod, B. (1998). Pregnancy fantasies as an underlying dynamism in panic disorder. *Journal of American Psychoanalytic Association, 46*, 873–890.

Milrod, B., Busch, F. N., Leon, A., Shapiro, T., Aronson, A., Shear, M. K. et al. (2000). Open trial of psychodynamic psychotherapy for panic disorder: a pilot study. *American Journal of Psychiatry, 157*, 1878–1880.

Milrod, B., Busch, F. N., Leon, L, Aronson, A., Roiphe, J., Rudden, M. et al. (2001). A pilot open trial of brief psychodynamic psychotherapy for panic disorder. *Journal of Psychotherapy Practice and Research, 10*, 239–245.

Milrod, B., Leon, A., Busch, F. N., Rudden, M., Schwalberg, M., Clarkin, J., et al. (2007) A randomized, controlled clinical trial of psychoanalytic psychotherapy for panic disorder. *American Journal Psychiatry, 164*, 265–272.

Milrod, B. (2007). Emptiness in agoraphobia. *Journal of the American Psychoanalytic Association, 55*, 1007–1026.

Ost, L. G., & Westling, B. E. (1984). Applied relaxation versus cognitive behavior therapy in the treatment of panic disorder. *Behaviour Research and Therapy, 33,* 145–158.

Rey, J. H .(1979). Schizoid phenomena in the borderline. In LeBoit, J. & Caponi, A. (Eds.), *Advances in the psychotherapy of the Borderline Patient.* New York: Jason Aronson.

Rudden, M., Busch, F. N., Milrod, B., Singer, M., Aronson, A. ,Roiphe, J., et al. (2003). Panic disorder and depression: A psychodynamic exploration of comorbidity. *International Journal of Psychoanaysis, 84,* 997–1015.

Rudden, M., Milrod, B., Target, M., Ackerman, S., Graf, E. (2006) Reflective Functioning in Panic Disorder Patients: A Pilot Study. *Journal of the American Psychoanalytic Association, 54,* 1339–1343.

Shear, M. K., Brown, T. A., Barlow, D. H., Money, R., Sholomskas, D. E., Woods, et al. (1997). Multicenter Collaborative Panic Disorder Severity Scale. *American Journal of Psychiatry, 154,* 1571–1575.

Sheehan, D. V. (1983). The Sheehan Disability Scales. In D. V. Sheehan (Ed.), *The Anxiety Disease.* New York: Charles Scribner & Sons.

7

Working with Parents in Child Psychotherapy
*Engaging the Reflective Function**

Arietta Slade

Introduction

This paper is about working with the parents of children we treat in psychotherapy or psychoanalysis. It is organized around several basic premises. The first is that virtually all child therapists work—in some way or other—with the parents of the children they treat in psychotherapy. As I will describe later, this work takes many forms, such as separate meetings with parents as an ongoing part of the treatment, direct work with the parents *instead of* work with the child, or inclusion of parents in the therapy sessions themselves. These are but a few of the many permutations that are typically part and parcel of this work, all of which arise in some organic way out of the process of an ongoing treatment. There is certainly no single way

---

* This paper evolved from a presentation originally made to the Canadian Association for Psychoanalytic Child Therapists in association with the Toronto Child Psychoanalytic Program, on September 28, 2002. Revised versions were presented to psychoanalytic institutes in and around the New York metropolitan area, including the Institute for Psychoanalytic Training and Research, the Postgraduate Center for Mental Health, the Westchester Center for the Study of Psychoanalysis and Psychotherapy, and the William Alanson White Institute. I would like to thank the many colleagues who helped shape my thinking along the way, particularly Steve Tuber, Arnold Zinman, Phyllis Beren, Mary Target, and Peter Fonagy.

of approaching this work that will be universally helpful to children and families. As child clinicians, we often find our way as we go.

We find our way as we go because, for the most part, there has been little articulated theory of the nature and purpose of this critical aspect of child treatment within the psychoanalytic literature,* and little comprehensive examination—within either the clinical or theoretical literature—of the complex issues involved in this work. Often we are guided largely by our intuition in translating our clinical and developmental knowledge into parent work. Intuition is not necessarily a bad thing; in fact, as seasoned clinicians know, intuition can be key. But it would certainly help to have more theory and attention to practice in directing these intuitions.

Notable exceptions to the relative absence of attention to parent work within the context of ongoing child treatment are the writings of Diana Siskind (1987, 1997) and Kelly and Jack Novick (Novick & Novick, 2001, 2002; Novick & Novick (2002a, 2002b). A slightly different approach has been described by Saralea Chazen (2003) and Kate Oram (2000), who have written about working concomitantly and sometimes jointly with parents and children. Pat Pantone (2000) and Linda Jacobs and Carol Wachs (2002) suggest seeing parents as an alternative to working directly with children. In her wonderful book *Working with Parents* (1997), Siskind puts it simply and pungently: "When we review the literature on the therapist's work with the parents of child patients, it quickly becomes apparent that this is a neglected subject. It is surprising that this topic has failed to be represented as a complex and important treatment issue, one requiring a theoretical framework and careful discussion of its clinical application" (p. 4). Siskind wonders about "this shrinking away" from a difficult area of our work: "we write about everything that passes our consciousness" and yet, not this (p. 5). Indeed, it is very interesting to think about why this work has received so very little attention in the vast literature on child psychotherapy and psychoanalysis. My suspicion is that the failure of therapists to write about this complex topic is multidetermined: it is very messy, it is often fraught with countertransferential feelings and impulses, and—for many therapists—it hits very close to home. Most therapists are parents, too, and may or may not be able to consider these issues objectively.

---

* The same could be said for virtually all child therapy approaches. See Target, Slade, Cottrell, Fuggle, & Fonagy, in press.

One of the great ironies of the relative absence of attention to parent work in the literature is the fact that experienced therapists—almost without exception—acknowledge that creating a working alliance with parents is crucial to successful work with a child. The more disturbed the child or the family, the more this is the case. We can all think of instances in which we have lost or bungled a case as a result of somehow failing to establish a meaningful, collaborative, and compassionate relationship with parents. This was a lesson I learned again and again during my training, and during my early years in practice. Even now, after nearly 25 years in practice, I sometimes have to learn it all over again.

Experienced therapists are also the first to acknowledge that parent work is often very difficult; in fact, generally speaking, work with children is *easy* relative to the work with parents. Child work can be fun, it can be tedious, it can be exhausting or it can be exhilarating, but we know what to do. Perhaps it is more accurate to say that we know how to play. But because of its inherent complexity, parent work is continuously challenging.

Most parents bring children to therapy so that we can fix them. They may or may not have any interest in trying to figure out who the child is and what makes him tick, and they may or may not have an interest in thinking about their own emotional life as it pertains to the inner life of the child. When they do, of course, the work can be enormously productive and inherently rewarding. The effect on the child is palpable. But so often the parent and therapist have subtly competing agendas: although we may view parent sessions as intrinsic to helping provide a more sustaining holding environment for the child (which may in some cases mean that we are working very directly to curtail a parent's toxic behaviors and interactions), the parents may view these sessions as open season to criticize and complain about the child. In addition, work with parents is often fraught with transference and countertransference issues, all played out within the framework of a relatively amorphous and poorly defined treatment situation. For instance, making a transference interpretation to a parent who is feeling rivalrous and inadequate in the face of the child's developing relationship with the therapist will be possible only in the most evolved parent-therapist relationships; and yet, these dynamics often come to the fore early in a therapist's relationship with a family. Similarly, the therapist's feelings of identification with the child and competitiveness with the mother can derail a treatment in very short order.

As child therapists, we are faced with a number of crucial questions with respect to parent work: What is it that we do with parents? What are we aiming for in this work? How do we see ourselves and our role within the framework of this process? How do we imagine this complex web of relationships: child, therapist, parents, separate, but profoundly interconnected?

My efforts to think coherently about this very complex topic began in my work with Michael, a boy who first came to see me when he was three, now over ten years ago. I have written about this work elsewhere (Slade, 1999b), but let me briefly talk about my work with Michael's mother. I began by seeing Michael and his mother together in parent-child psychotherapy, an approach dictated by Michael's age and the nature of his difficulties. As our work progressed, I also began to see Michael's mother individually. The focus of these sessions was almost exclusively her relationship with Michael. For five years, I saw Michael once or twice weekly; I also saw his mother every other week. Slowly, Julie began to understand Michael and more importantly to understand her own complex dynamics as they pertained to her interaction with him. What began as a discussion of Michael's biological disruptions gradually evolved into a textured discussion of the intersection of their inner lives. As her work deepened, and particularly as she began to be able to put into words the many meanings Michael had for her, he began to flourish in all ways, most notably in the development of the symbolic function.

When I began to think about what had happened in my work with Julie, I was helped by my background in attachment theory and research. I had from the beginning thought of my work with Julie as aimed at helping Michael feel more secure in relation to her, and as strengthening the flexibility and integrity of their attachment relationship. But what I began to realize was that I had in part done this by *engaging her capacity for reflective functioning* in relation to Michael. Over the course of our work, she had developed the capacity to *mentalize* his experience. This was what I came to think had been central in our work; without thinking about it consciously, I had been helping her think reflectively about her child. The more I thought about this, the more I began to think that much of what we do with parents generally is to try and engage their reflective capacities. Ultimately, I found this subtle reframing of the aim and function of parent work both helpful and organizing.

In this paper, I outline what I mean by the notion that parent work involves the development of mentalizing capacities in parents. I begin with a brief history of psychoanalytic notions of parent work. I then describe how the last two decades' advances in psychoanalytic theory—and specifically attachment theory—demand a paradigm shift in the way we think about working with parents, and in how we see ourselves in relation to this work. I specifically emphasize Fonagy and Target's work on the development of the reflective function (see Fonagy, Gergely, Jurist, & Target, 2002 for a complete review). In the final sections of this paper, I outline the relevance of these constructs to what we actually do in parent work.

I want to emphasize that I do not think this is necessarily a new perspective with regard to parent work. Whether or not we are conscious of it, most psychoanalytically oriented child clinicians have been profoundly affected by the theoretical shifts I describe later. *Indeed, I am trying to describe what I believe many child therapists are already doing, but often intuitively and unconsciously. The unconscious* aspect of this is I believe, what needs to be remedied: articulated guiding constructs are critical to our finding our way through the complex maze of working with parents. Thus, it is my hope that by trying to make these processes more conscious, and by articulating basic principles and conceptualizations, we can actually begin to develop ways of thinking about parent work that are more clear, coherent, and conceptually grounded than what we have today. But first, I begin with a bit of history.

The History of Approaches to Working with Parents

Much of the neglect and confusion within psychoanalysis about parent work can be understood by examining the history of psychoanalytic theories of development and treatment. Child therapy and psychoanalysis were first described in the 1930s by Anna Freud (1966–1980) and Melanie Klein (1932). Consistent with their belief in the importance of addressing the intrapsychic conflicts of children as the means to promoting symptom relief, little attention was paid to the involvement of parents in the child's treatment. Mrs. Klein reportedly found any involvement with parents to be highly annoying and irrelevant (Karen, 1997). Bruno Bettelheim believed that taking children away from their parents was crucial to recovery (Bettelheim, 1950). And according to what is likely an apocryphal story, Dorothy Burlinghame was supposed to have suggested a set of guidelines for working with parents at the Anna Freud Center (Alice Colonna, personal communication, January, 2002). She purportedly suggested three routes to take in dealing with parents: (a) ignore them, (b) take the children away from them, and (c)—most difficult and least advisable—work with them. These ideas are obviously inconsistent with the *child guidance model* that was to emerge from the Anna Freud Center in the 50s; indeed, Anna Freud was well aware of the need to establish ongoing relationships with parents. However, there is nevertheless, even in more contemporary psychoanalytic thinking, an unwitting assumption about whether transforming work can really be done with parents as part of the child's psychotherapy.

The *child guidance model* refers to a loosely defined approach to parent work, in which the therapist meets with parents in order to gather information on circumstances in the child's everyday life, help caregivers understand their child's development, develop strategies to manage behavioral problems and contextualize their children's difficulties. But in this model—as it originally emerged—the work with parents was hardly an intrinsic part of the therapy. The therapeutic frame of the work with the child, the engagement with his interior life, was sacred. This thinking was embedded in an equally sacred notion, namely that the child could change while his environment did not, or that he could somehow change his environment as he progressed in treatment.

Not infrequently—as this model was so often simply not adequate—therapists would (and obviously still do) end up working in an analytic fashion with parents *alongside* the child's therapy; this transmutation of the child guidance model reflects therapists' need to bring the parent's conflicts to the fore as a means of helping the child. But here, too, there was relatively little theory to guide this kind of work, and it often became two almost parallel therapies. Oftentimes, when this failed, the parent was referred for individual psychotherapy of his or her own as an adjunct to the child's therapy. Although this is often an entirely appropriate and crucial recommendation, a parent's individual treatment cannot—for reasons that are described in the sections that follow—supplant parent work.*

The more traditional analytic view of the individual child, whose development could be largely described as a function of the tensions and conflicts that inherently accompany maturation, was to evolve dramatically over the course of the 1970s and 1980s. These changes occurred as the result of a confluence of factors: developments in the field of infant research (Stern, 1985; Tronick, 1998), advances in attachment theory and research (Bowlby, 1988, Ainsworth, Blehar, Waters, & Wall, 1978; Main, Kaplan, & Cassidy, 1985), and the development of self psychological, relational, and intersubjective perspectives within psychoanalytic theory and technique (Kohut, 1969; Mitchell, 1988; Winnicott, 1965).

These shifts in theory were to have an enormous impact on the way clinicians thought about the child and his development. Instead, contemporary psychoanalysts embraced the notion that the child's own sense of his mind and his self-experience are dyadically and triadically created, emerging directly from his experience of himself in relation to his primary caregivers. From this perspective, the child's internal world could no longer be viewed as distinct and separate from his ongoing experience in relationships.

Attachment theory played a significant part in moving latter day psychoanalytic theory toward this more relational perspective. While there are many ways to describe the implications of attachment theory for clinical work (see Slade, 1999a, 1999b, 2000, 2004a, 2004b), what I will focus on in the sections below are the ways that mentalization theory (Fonagy et al., 2002) provides a particularly useful framework for what should and often does happen in successful parent work.

From Fonagy's perspective, the parent's capacity to mentalize is intrinsically related to the child's sense of self and of her own mind. Thus, working to develop the parent's reflective functioning is hardly outside the purview of psychoanalytic child treatment. Indeed, this perspective would suggest that parent work may

---

* Likewise, family therapy is sometimes recommended in these circumstances (Asen, in press; Kerr & Bowen, 1988; White & Epston, 1990). Although this work is in principle different from parent work, it may—by virtue of its potential to disentangle the child from family projections and distortions—have similar positive effects on the child, and on the parent's capacity to see the child as having a mind of his own.

function as a central—rather than peripheral—agent of change in successful child treatment.

Reflective Functioning

The construct of reflective functioning (RF) was introduced over 10 years ago by a team of psychoanalytically oriented attachment researchers: Peter Fonagy, Miriam Steele, Howard Steele, and Mary Target (Fonagy, Steele, Steele, Leigh, Kennedy, Mattoon, & Target, 1995; Fonagy, Steele, Moran, Steele, & Higgitt, 1991; Fonagy & Target, 1996). Reflective functioning can be understood narrowly as the capacity to understand one's own and others' behavior in terms of underlying mental states and intentions, and more broadly as a crucial human capacity that is intrinsic to affect regulation and productive social relationships. In just over 10 years, Fonagy and his colleagues have developed an extraordinarily rich and complex body of theoretical, clinical, and research work that elaborates the central importance of mentalization (Fonagy et al., 2002) in promoting secure and healthy personal and relational adaptations across a range of contexts. The more that human beings are able to mentalize, or "envision mental states in the self or other," the more likely they are to engage in productive, intimate, and sustaining relationships, to feel connected to others at a subjective level, but also to feel autonomous and of separate minds (Fonagy et al., 2002).

Although all human beings are born with the capacity to develop the reflective function, *early relationships* create the opportunity for the child to learn about mental states, and determine the depth to which the social environment can ultimately be processed (Fonagy et al., 2002). A mother's capacity to hold in her own mind a *representation* of her child as having feelings, desires, and intentions *allows the child to discover his own internal experience via his mother's representation of it.* A mother's capacity to make meaning of the child's experience will make him meaningful to himself, and allow her to go beyond what is apparent, beyond the concrete, and to instead make sense of the child's behavior in light of mental states, of underlying, likely unobservable, changing, dynamic intentions, and emotion. This helps him begin to symbolize, contain, and regulate his internal experience, and to develop coherent and organized representations of self and other. This also helps the parent contain and regulate her own internal experience *as well as her behavior.*

In many instances (and we see this often in our consulting rooms) this process is derailed, often with dire consequences for the child:

> If the caregiver's capacity is lacking in this regard, the version of itself that the infant encounters is an individual conceived of as thinking in terms of physical reality rather than mental states. If the child finds no interpersonal alternative where he is conceived of as mentalizing, his potential in this regard will not be fulfilled. In cases of an abusive, hostile, or simply totally vacuous relationship with the caregiver, the infant may deliberately turn away from the mentalizing object because the contemplation of the object's mind is overwhelming, as it harbors frankly hostile or dangerously indifferent intentions toward the self. (Fonagy et al., 1995, p. 257)

Under such circumstances, the experience of holding the other in mind becomes fraught and terrifying for the child.

For purposes of exposition, I would like to make a distinction between reflective functioning—that is, the crucial *human* capacity central to the development and maintenance of a range of social relationships—and *parental reflective functioning* (Slade, 2005). The latter term refers to the mother (or other caregiver)'s capacity to reflect on the current mental state of the child and upon her own mental states as these pertain to her relationship with her child,[*] as opposed, for instance, to her capacity to reflect upon her childhood relationship with her own parents. These two different forms of reflective functioning are likely to be highly correlated. In our research, parental reflective capacities, as assessed via parental interviews (Slade, Belsky, Aber, & Phelps, 1999), are significantly correlated adult attachment classification, as measured by the Adult Attachment Interview (George, Kaplan, & Main, 1996). However, parental representations of the child appear to be more influential than attachment organization in terms of predicting positive outcomes—such as secure attachment—in the child (Slade, Grienenberger, Bernbach, Levy, & Locker, 2005). We have also found such parental capacities to be related to a range of crucial adaptations in the child, and to positive caregiving practices in mothers (Grienenberger, Slade, & Kelly, 2005). Parental reflective functioning is also predictive of the child's capacity to play and symbolize (Fonagy &

---

[*] Reflective functioning, in this context, is often mistakenly equated with empathy. See Fonagy et al., 2002, for a full discussion of this question.

Target, 1996; Slade, 1999b). Thus, it would appear that this crucial parental capacity plays a number of vital roles in promoting child socioemotional development.

Evaluating Parental Reflective Functioning

In the next section, I briefly outline how we describe individual differences in parental reflective functioning, in both research and clinical settings. I do so because I believe that knowing a little bit about the scale is especially helpful in thinking about what to listen for and address within the context of parent work itself.

In Fonagy and his colleagues' original scoring system (Fonagy, Target, Steele, & Steele, 1998), as well as our adaptation of this scale for use with parental interviews (Slade, Bernbach, Grienenberger, Levy, & Locker, 2004), parental reflective functioning is scored along a continuum from absent to high. The lowest levels of the scale are used to score those descriptions of the self or the child that are devoid of mental state language, that emphasize behavior, physical traits, or personality, but fail altogether to consider internal experience. For instance: "my child is bad, pig-headed, stubborn, nosy, energetic, active, playful." Or, when describing oneself as a parent: "I'm calm, patient, busy, too neurotic, and so on." It is important to note that although some of these descriptions are positively tinged, none emphasizes emotional or internal life. Fonagy refers to this level of discourse as indicative of the physical stance—that is, an interpersonal stance that makes meaning of the self or other in physical, behavioral, or external terms (Fonagy & Target, 1996).

In some instances, parental representations of the child and his experience are manifestly self-serving and even bizarre. For instance, here is a description offered by the parents of their five year old child during their first evaluation session with me: "There's something rather inhuman about him—there's an absence of warmth, human feeling, fellow feeling. He has deformed the family life and marriage. On a bad day, he's violent, ungovernable, and underemployed." "He is without that current that passes between parents and children...Never a moment where there's a bond...he's attached in a way that doesn't strike us as normal..." "He's an animal, a psychopath."

Aside from the obviously troubling quality of these descriptions, there is no suggestion in any of these comments of an interest in the child's mind.

The next level of the scale is characterized by descriptions that evince some recognition of mental states; although such statements can be banal and superficial, they receive a slightly higher score. There is some recognition of one's own or the child's feelings, thoughts, and intentions: "He's *sad*." "He *likes* bananas." "She *knows* I'm gonna' feed her." The description of mental states is in and of itself not an indication of reflective functioning, however. Nevertheless, it is a crucial building block in the development of a reflective stance, and for some parents accurately recognizing even the most basic mental states in themselves or in the child can be an enormous accomplishment.

The development of the reflective or intentional stance is marked by the capacity to see behavior *as a function* of underlying mental states or intentions. *The parent achieves this score once they manifest the capacity to link the child's or her own internal state to behavior or to other internal states.* "He threw a tantrum in the store (behavior) because he was tired and hungry (physical state), and I'd been dragging him around all day and he was sick of it (mental state)." "She didn't sleep all night because she'd been so frightened by how angry I'd gotten at her." When work with parents in child psychotherapy is going well, we begin to see such shifts from a behavioral to a reflective stance. For instance: "Oh, so maybe he's been running away from me when I pick him up at school because he doesn't want me to know how much he's missed me!" rather than "How can I get him to stop running away when I'm trying to get him in the car after school?"

The reflective stance refers to the capacity to understand the nature of mental states, as well as to appreciate their dynamic nature and interpersonal functions. Thus, for instance, a reflective individual understands that mental states, by their very nature, can be disguised, or opaque to the observer. They understand that mental states change over time. They understand the *dynamic* nature of mental states: my feelings can affect the way my child feels, and vice versa. In addition, with reflectiveness comes increased accuracy in the capacity to make sense of mental states. So many times parents misread intentions and motivations; often our work results in their becoming more accurate and sensitive readers of their children's feelings and desires. Finally, the capacity to maintain a reflective stance (or at least have that as a goal) can be inherently regulating for the parent, and helps them to contain and modulate their own intense feelings and fantasies.

For example, imagine the following: It is early evening, and a mother has just finished work. She stops to pick up her 3-year-old child up from daycare, where he has spent the whole day. She has nothing to prepare for dinner, and so stops at the supermarket to pick up a few things. Even as she pulls her car into the supermarket parking lot, her child is starting to fuss and whine.

Let us imagine Mother #1, who quickly recognizes (probably long before they even get to the supermarket) that her child is hungry, tired, and just wants to get home, and *that his fussy behavior is indicative of these underlying affects and desires.* He has missed her, and is not happy about having to run an errand, one which will only further distract his already harassed and distracted mother. Because she recognizes the *meaning and intention of her child's "mis"behavior,* she will probably start trying to regulate his distress long before it escalates. She will verbally acknowledge that he doesn't want to go to the store, and that he just wants to go home and eat dinner, and that he has had a long day and misses her. She will give him something to eat as soon as he starts asking for food (rather than worrying about his spoiling his dinner. He is hungry *now.*) She will recognize right away that this will have to be a very short shopping trip. If he starts to tantrum despite all these efforts to anticipate his dysregulation, she will stop and try to settle him down by comforting him physically, giving voice to his feelings, trying to in whatever ways she can balance his needs with the reality of her mission. This does not mean that she will abandon her own goals, but that she will attend to the regulation of his needs along with her own.

Contrast this with Mother #2, who feels angry as soon as she picks up on her child's displeasure about the shopping trip, and so does little to anticipate or regulate his building distress. Thus, by the time he starts to fuss, she is already agitated, and denies all of his (increasingly annoying) requests for food, demands to get out of the cart, and so on. She is determined to get all the things she needs, and as she moves methodically through the aisles, his distress escalates. Within moments, the child is in a full tantrum, arching his whole body back, poised for a complete meltdown. In complete frustration, she mutters (or yells) "You're doing this on purpose. You're trying to drive me crazy. You never let me do what I need to do." Her grip is too tight and her jaw clenched when she lifts him out of the cart when they are ready to leave. By the time they get to the car, both mother and child are completely exhausted, dysregulated, and distinctly out of sync.

Obviously, Mother #1 was from the start able to reflect on her child's current mental state and adjusted her behavior and expectations in accord with that mental state. Mother #2 found the dysjunction between their distinct desires and intentions intolerable, and had great difficulty holding her child's (equally legitimate and understandable) intentions in mind. As she overrode her child's mental state, his distress escalated, as did hers. Finally, in her anger, she handles him roughly and misattributes malevolent intent to him. Thus, not only does she behave insensitively (because she is not using his mental states to guide her behavior), but she also obliterates his self experience by projecting her own feelings and desires onto his. Much of what we do in our work with parents, I believe, is try to help parents behave *and think* more like Mother #1 and less like Mother # 2, by helping them mentalize or reflect upon the meaning and intention of their child's behavior.

The highest points on the scale are used to describe parents who are capable of making sophisticated, complex, and sometimes surprising links between their own and their child's internal experience. For instance, here is a highly reflective mother describing an interaction with her toddler:

> Sometimes she gets *frustrated and angry* (child mental state) in ways that I'm *not sure I understand* (understands the opacity of her child's mental state). She points to one thing and I hand it to her, but it turns out *that's not really what she wanted* (child mental state). It *feels very confusing to me* (mother mental state) when *I'm not sure how she's feeling* (mother's mental state affected by child's), especially when she's upset (child behavior). Sometimes *she'll want to do something* (child mental state) and I won't let her because it's dangerous, and *so she'll get angry* (transaction between mental states). I may try to pick her up and she obviously *didn't want to be picked up because she's in the middle of being angry* (appreciation of the process of child's mental state) and I interrupted her. In those moments it's *me who has the need to pick her up and make her feel better*, so I'll put her back down (distinguishes own needs from those of child).

We do not usually hear talk like this from parents in our consulting rooms, at least in the early phases of treatment; when we do, it is likely that we are dealing with a relatively flexible and healthy family system, one that permits more complex and dynamic work. I recently had the experience of meeting a mother who—within minutes of our first session at the start of an evaluation of her 5-year-old son—described the child's current behavior *in light* of traumatic events he had experienced in his early childhood. It was instantly clear to me that this mother saw her child *as a psychological being,* despite the fact that her child's behavior was enormously troubling and infuriating to her, and that she felt guilty for her own part in her child's unhappiness. As I have gotten to know this mother, I have been impressed again and again with how eager she is to understand her child, and how readily she is able to adapt her behavior and expectations in line with these insights. Sadly, it is more often the case that mothers and fathers find it very difficult to enter their child's experience as a means of understanding them. Instead, they resort to primitive means of blocking out or distorting their child's internal life, resulting in distress and dysjunction all around (see Coates, 2004).

Working with Parents

The trend within psychoanalysis toward a more relational, interpersonal, and intersubjective view of child development necessarily changes the way we think about parent work. In particular, it implies that a significant aspect of what we do is help create the context for the emergence of healthy, sustaining attachment relationships. We do this by facilitating the parent's engagement with the child's true self (Winnicott, 1965), and by helping the parent become more sensitive, more of a secure base, more able to regulate and contain the child. In my view, such developments in the parent are often directly linked to the therapist's success in helping the parent to reflect upon the child's mental states.

Thus, when I work with a parent, I am trying to create a context in which he or she can slowly shift from a physical to a reflective or mentalizing stance. That is, *I hold the child in mind for the parent as a mentalizing being,* as a person whose feelings and behaviors are inextricably interrelated, and whose feelings and behaviors are inextricably intertwined with theirs as a parent. Most importantly, I see the child's behavior as *meaningful.* Hopefully the parent will come to internalize this view of the child, which will in turn allow them to hold this in mind for the child. The child can then begin to experience himself as a meaningful, connected, and feeling person, who then can begin to symbolize, rather than act. Although this may sound simple as a schematic, it is actually a very complex process. So—in an effort to try to formulate it—I describe in the sections below what I think are some of its component parts.

The Creation of a Playspace

All work with parents begins with the creation of an environment of reflectiveness; that is, we create a context for symbolization and meaning making on the part of the parent. As we know from Winnicott (1971), helping the parent feel safe enough to mentalize, to envision, name, and play with mental states, depends upon the creation of a playspace (see too Fonagy & Target, 1996, 1998, Slade, 1994). This is an odd term to use in thinking about parent work, which sometimes feels like a war zone, but it is actually a helpful word to keep in mind.

Creating this playspace begins with our inviting the parent to participate in the treatment. This means that from the beginning, we frame the therapeutic process to parents in such as way that they see their sessions with us as *intrinsic* to the treatment as are individual sessions with the child. This often means that we have to confront our own desires to keep the child all to ourselves, and challenge our implicit rescue fantasies, both of which inherently disparage the parent. These sessions need to be regularly scheduled, and frequent enough to move beyond reporting and catching up. Involving parents in this way raises a number of complex issues regarding confidentiality and boundaries. Although it is of course crucial to preserve the safety of the child's relationship with the therapist, such exigencies cannot be used as a justification for avoiding work with parents.

Understandably, many parents come to treatment with the fantasy that the therapist, as the expert, is going to either tell them what to do, or point out their abject failures in parenting. Upending this expectation of both advice and judgment is crucial, because under the best of circumstances the parent and therapist are collaborators in discovering who the child is and what he thinks and feels. In very real ways, parents know the child better than we ever will; it is our job to bring that knowledge and understanding into their relationship with the child. Most parents want help in improving their relationship with the child. They have come to us often because they feel lost, helpless, worried, and guilty, or because they are overwhelmed by feelings for the child that they cannot manage or articulate. If we can keep this in mind in inviting them to participate in the treatment, they can see us as helpful and facilitating, not judgmental.

In my experience, it is often difficult for less experienced therapists to incorporate parent work into child treatment in an ongoing way. This is often because they can be intimidated by parents, unsure of what to do, or just overwhelmed by keeping track of all the pieces of the work. It may also have to do with the fact that they are often not yet parents themselves, and so are more identified with the children, and less certain about how to establish a connection with the parents (Pantone, 2000). Many therapists (and not just beginning ones) struggle with countertransferential feelings in these situations, such that they inadvertently side with the child as victim of parental distortions and cruelty. Although aspects of this identification with the child are crucial to his finding safety in the therapeutic relationship, the therapist's relationship with and empathy for the child should not preclude attempting to establish a working relationship with the parent.

Holding the Parent in Mind

Creating an environment in which the parent can begin to hold the child in mind depends upon our capacity to first—and perhaps for a very long time—hold the parent in mind. Parents who are unable to reflect upon their children's internal experience have often had disrupted and traumatizing early relationships themselves, and our capacity to bear these parental distortions within the countertransference depends upon our remembering this. We must first be able to hear and tolerate the *parent's* experience of the child; creating an empathic bond that evolves from an understanding of the parent's intersubjective experience of parenting is critical to the formation of his or her capacity to recognize the child as separate and having a mind of his own.

Parents' feelings about the child make sense to *them* in a profound way. Parents often come to treatment feeling very badly about their children (and themselves as parents) and we need to sit with these awful feelings and understand them. We don't try to talk them out of these feelings (he's not bad, he's just curious), we listen to and try to understand them. We hold the parent's experience *for* them, however intolerable or distorted it may seem to us. For many parents, the experience of being held in mind by *anyone* is extremely rare. Thus, our willingness to hold and represent the parent's experience of parenting *this particular child* creates an empathic bond that is critical to the development of the parent's capacity to mentalize.

The parent's willingness to hold the child in mind is often the *end* rather than the beginning of the process. As my colleague Steve Tuber put it (personal communication, November 2002), it can be an act of generosity for a parent to contemplate the child's mind, and they must be supported and heard in order to take this leap. This means that we must listen to what it is like for them in hot or difficult moments with the child. It will also involve our learning—at some point, or at multiple points—their *own* story, so that the meaning of their own failures in holding and empathy become a crucial part of the dialogue, and of our own understanding.

Model the Reflective Stance

Both creating a playspace and keeping the parent in mind are first steps in establishing a solid working alliance with parents. Most essential to the work, however, are the ways in which we use our meetings with parents to *model the reflective stance*. We struggle to penetrate the opacity and complexity of the child's experience, and we try to symbolize it. We play with it, we wonder about it, we search for the right metaphors to make the child sensible to the parent. And we iterate—again and again—the essential aspects of reflective awareness. We talk about feelings, we link them to behavior, again and again, continuously underscoring the links between behavior and mental states ("Maybe he's up in the middle of the night because he was so afraid when you were away.") We talk about the transient nature of feelings: they will change (and become more tolerable) over time. We note the relations between a parent's mental state and those of her child. ("So maybe your daughter is so angry and hurtful to you because she has been frightened by your sadness and depression.") We try to be accurate in our descriptions of mental states ("So enraged doesn't really capture what you were feeling; you were frightened and helpless and so frustrated.") We understand what we don't know about another's internal experience. And we model curiosity and openness to discovering it—there are no easy answers, there is only a process of discovery.

One of the things we hope to accomplish by re-presenting the child to the parent in a reflective way is to mobilize their appreciation and recognition of the child's mental experience. Providing metaphors for the child's experience is one way that we bring the child alive for the parent, galvanizing both the attachment system as well as more sensitive caregiving. Let me provide a brief example. I was working with the parents of 6-year-old Luke. Their marriage was disintegrating in brutal and—for Luke—terrifying ways. I was trying to communicate to the parents how their increasing acrimony was shattering his basic sense of integrity, leaving him open to intense and frightening internal experiences and fantasies. In the effort to avoid each other, both parents were taking off for days at a time without notice; such random and unexplained comings and goings were quite disorienting for Luke. I hoped to articulate Luke's experience in a way that would override their hatred for each other and mobilize their concern.

I searched for a metaphor that would aptly communicate how important it was for them to create a predictable and organized world for him, and how intolerable their overt hostility was for him. In order to do this, I used a vivid and emotionally charged metaphor that I hoped would crystallize for them just how much pain he felt at the great uncertainty, rage, and chaos in his life. As he himself said, when I mentioned that his parents' comings and goings were so hard to understand, he looked at me and said "It's MORE than I can understand."

In my meeting with the parents, I told them about an interview I'd seen on TV in which a firefighter had described his experience of trying to orient himself in the immediate aftermath of September 11th. He was among those desperately struggling to free a small group of firefighters buried in the rubble that had once been the base of a central stairwell. He radioed to the trapped men for help in locating them; he wanted landmarks, orienting points. His trapped comrade radioed out: "We're right at the corner of West Street and Franklin. That corner, right there." The firefighter wept in recounting the story: "I knew that neighborhood like the back of my hand. I *know* where West and Franklin is. It wasn't there. It was gone." The basic landmarks that would lead him in this desperate situation had completely disintegrated. "It's like that for Luke," I said. "Everything that he knows is gone. And you have to give him the anchors, to create the order out of a universe that for him has exploded completely." It was my hope that—by using such a vivid metaphor to describe the depth of Luke's disorientation—I might be able to evoke their desire to nurture and protect him.

It is very common and natural for parents to ask for advice during the course of their work with us. Within the framework of a reflective model, advice always derives from understanding. In effect, I tell parents: "What you do with your child, or what I suggest you do with your child, depends entirely upon how we understand the emotional context of a particular situation. What I am helping you do is develop a way of thinking about and understanding your child; *what to do* will flow easily from that." Sally Provence, a wise and gifted child analyst, put it this way: "Don't just do something. Stand there and pay attention. Your child is trying to tell you something."

We are always trying to help parents wonder what that *something* is. For most parents, curiosity about their child's experience, and recognition that such experiences are separate from their own, emerges slowly, and often comes in moments of suddenly wondering: "Gee, I wonder why he did that? Oh, so maybe *that's* how she was feeling." Because it leads to understanding, the simple act of imagining the child's experience—even briefly—can be momentous and transforming of a parent's representation of the child. And it is only after the parent is engaged in wondering that developmental guidance and knowledge takes on real meaning and vitality.

Marie came to me in complete and abject despair. She felt as if she had really begun to hate her 3-year-old daughter, Leslie, who she described as intensely aggressive, provocative, and hyperactive, traits that were especially pronounced in *their* relationship. I met several times with Marie to try to get a sense of what was going on, wondering to myself what might have gone so quickly wrong in this dyad. When I finally met Leslie, I was indeed impressed with her energy, intensity, and willfulness. But both Marie and I were surprised when Leslie refused to let her mother leave the room. She clung to Marie and whimpered; her mother, of course, did not leave, and Leslie proceeded to play out a range of fears, notably abandonment. This child—who wished to be so big and scary, and who was in fact often so very frightening to her mother—turned out to be very frightened herself. The mother looked quite astonished, and did not for a second miss the implications of her daughter's play.

I scheduled an appointment with the mother for the following week. As I returned to my desk, however, I happened to glance out my office window. I saw the following scene unfold in the parking lot: Marie had buckled Leslie in her car seat, but—having forgotten something in the waiting room—pulled up to the office door, thinking Leslie was safe in her car seat. While Marie got out of the car and walked to the office door, Leslie quickly darted out of her car seat and jumped out of the car. By the time Marie got back in her seat, Leslie was standing directly *in front* of the car, a large SUV. Just as Marie engaged the engine, she saw her (small) daughter, directly in the car's path. She immediately jammed on the brakes and flew out of the car. In a terrified fury, she screamed and roughly yanked her daughter to the side and practically threw her into her car seat. The terrified mother was also terrifying.

When the mother returned the following week, we had two different things to talk about: how frightened her daughter was, and how frightening she could be in her anger. Marie, who had largely seen herself as a victim of Leslie's torments, could begin to appreciate her role in frightening her daughter and in provoking her acting out. What was most striking, however, was the change in her affect as we talked. She softened, she relaxed, and she began to see her child more sympathetically and more psychologically. She began to wonder what went on in her mind. Leslie was no longer a demon to her, but a frightened child.

Working at a Level the Parent Can Manage

It is crucial to work at a level the parent can manage. Some parents never use mental state words to describe their children, or their descriptions of their children's emotional life are full of distortions and misattributions. A parent's capacity to reflect upon the child's mental experience often begins with the simple understanding of their child's particular way of physically regulating himself; that is, while they cannot talk about mental states, they may be able to talk about physical states. This aspect of the child's internal experience can be approached with some neutrality, and can often be very helpful to parents, who may find it difficult to recognize even physical states, or levels and trajectories of arousal in their children. Thus, for instance, a parent experiences her child as being wild and out of con-

trol, without any sense of the triggers and patterns of his dysregulation. Developing a basic understanding of regulatory processes can
be a starting point in developing a reflective stance in the parent (see
Slade, 1999b).

With parents who have a very hard time imagining their child's
internal experience, it can often be helpful to focus very specifically
on "hot" or what Pine (1985) would call "affectively supercharged
moments" in the interaction. This approach derives in part from
mother–infant interaction and attachment research, and particularly
from Main's emphasis on the value of accessing episodic memories
(Main et al., 1985). Both of these approaches rely upon the observation or recounting of actual lived experiences. As happened in my
discussions with Marie, there is enormous value in getting into the
nitty-gritty of what actually happened between parent and child;
slowly trying to understand the "hot spots" often leads to the affect,
the dysregulation, and ultimately paves the way to greater understanding of the transaction between and interdigitation of child and
parent mental states.

Flexibility

There is no single format for conducting parent sessions. Rather, *reasoned* flexibility is key. This is not a monolithic or simple approach,
but rather a way of *thinking about and framing* the work. Sometimes
we may decide to bring a parent into the child's session (with the
child's permission, of course). Sometimes we will want to alternate
dyadic and individual sessions. Sometimes we will meet alternately
with parent and child, or have regular, concomitant sessions with the
parent. Sometimes the moments of transition in the waiting room
become critical moments of translation and reformulation. Many of
the decisions about which of these approaches is suitable in a given
clinical situation, will rest upon the developmental stage of the child,
the issues they are dealing with, and an assessment of the parents'
capacities. But because we are—among other things—trying to create shifts within the relationship, these variations remain dynamic
ways to accomplish such work. In his book, *The Motherhood Constellation*, Stern (1994) notes that once you introduce parents into the
psychotherapeutic situation, the work can seem messy, impure and
chaotic. But when theoretically guided, carefully thought out, and

respectful both of the child's boundaries and needs, as well as the parent's need for support and understanding, this work is not messy, but developmentally appropriate.

There are of course times when it is nearly impossible to do any productive work with parents at all. I have had experiences in which I realized that bringing the parent into a session with the child was toxic to the child, and that—no matter what my intentions—I could not protect the child. I have worked with parents whose narcissism and fundamental detachment from the child (whether manifest in entanglement or disengagement) meant that I couldn't engage them in even the most basic wondering. The story is set, the die is cast; my attempting to shake or challenge this story would disrupt my relationship with the child and threaten the treatment. In these cases, I do what I can with the child and hope that they can grow up and away very soon. I hope that the parents will catch my reflective stance, and I look for little windows to get through to them. Sometimes this seems like so little, but I try to keep in mind the understanding and pleasure that can come out of a single moment of true reflectiveness.

What Reflective Parent Work Is Not

Before closing, I think it is important to briefly consider what this type of parent work is *not*. It is not individual therapy for the parent. One of the most common occurrences in working with very disrupted families and disrupted relationships is that the therapist refers the parent for her or his own separate individual therapy. Although this may sometimes be very necessary, and can actually help a parent separate her experience from that of her child, it cannot replace the parent's work with the child's therapist. To do so obscures critical opportunities to work *on the relationship* and specifically to address the parent's capacity to come to know the child *through the therapist's eyes, and his or her particular vision of the child*. Individual therapy is usually about the parent, and not the relationship. Although individual treatment may be helpful, what the parent *also* needs is to find a way to understand the child, and the child's individual therapist is in a unique position to facilitate this discovery. We are not conducting an individual psychotherapy with the parent; we are trying to directly intervene in facilitating the parent–child relationship, using our understanding of the child as the lynchpin.

Parent work is also not *primarily* about understanding the parent's conflicts in relation to the child (Novick & Novick, 2001, 2002; Novick & Novick, 2002a, 2002b). Although such understanding may well, and perhaps always should, emerge from the parent's struggle to understand her child, such insights are *secondary* to the processes described here. Similarly, while a couple's dynamics may become an issue when working with a mother and father together, one is generally trying to use one parent's understanding of the child to inform the other's, rather than focus upon discrepancies in their views, and the conflicts that are the result of these discrepancies. Although a couple's conflicts will of course be an issue in certain circumstances, they can hopefully be addressed in such a way that the child's mind—as it exists in dynamic relation to the minds of his parents—can remain the focus of the work.

Parent work is not the same as family therapy. Family therapy is inherently about understanding and thus changing family systems. Although family systems are certainly affected by reflective parent work, it is the *particular relationship that a child therapist has with a child and with his mind* that is central to change in this model. The parent develops a different understanding not only of the child's affects and intentions, but also of his development, as it underlies and indeed motivates certain desires and beliefs. Such are the unique contributions of this sort of approach. From a technical and theoretical point of view, its closest cousin is infant–parent psychotherapy (Fraiberg, 1980; Lieberman, Silverman, & Pawl, 1999). In fact, the reflective model I described here can be applied to many aspects of clinical work with infants and their parents. As an example, interdisciplinary teams at the Yale Child Study Center have been applying these same principles in developing mother-infant reflective parenting programs for both high and low-risk families (Slade, 2006; Slade, Sadler, deDios-Kenn, Webb, Ezepchick, & Mayes, 2005; Slade, Sadler, & Mayes, 2005; see too Grienenberger et al., 2004).

There are multiple ways to extend this model to work with adults. Fonagy and his colleagues (Allen & Fonagy, 2006; Bateman & Fonagy, 2004; Fonagy & Target, 2005) have introduced a range of mentalization based therapies for use with children and adults. And, although there may be certain circumstances in which we meet the families of our adult patients with similar goals in mind, the model I described here seems most suitable to work with children and their parents, largely because of the continuing impact disruptions in parental mentalization have upon the child's capacity to grow and develop autonomously. Given the permeability of their boundaries, children and adolescents are especially vulnerable to their parents' minds and intentions.

Conclusion

In a paper, Sheldon Bach (2001) described the child's experience of being held in mind by a parent in a most poetic way:

> A person's specific memories and experiences are like individual beads that can achieve continuity and gestalt form only when they are strung together to become a necklace. The string on which they are assembled is the child's *continuous existence in the mind of the parents*, which provides the continuity on which the beads of experiences are strung together and become the *necklace of a connected life*. We know, for example, that many people whose parents were actively involved with them, but took a primarily negative view of things, tend to string their experiences on a negative filament, so that each new event is assembled and viewed from its negative aspect—just as was the parents' habit. But the most difficult therapeutic issues arise in those cases in which the parent was emotionally absent or uninvolved, for then the string of continuity on which to assemble experience is missing, and the child is left clutching a handful of beads or memories that form no discernible pattern. This feels similar to the momentary experience many of us have had when a necklace or bracelet suddenly breaks, and what had been a coherent pattern or gestalt a moment before becomes a confusion of separate elements, rolling every which way on the floor. (p. 748)

When we work with parents, we are helping them gather the pearls that they have dropped or perhaps not even seen, and to once again or even for the first time string them together in a single, coherent, strand. This gift to the child is *the necklace of a connected life*.

References

Ainsworth, M. D. S., Blehar, M. C., Waters, E., & Wall, S. (1978). *Patterns of attachment: Psychological study of the strange situation*. Hillsdale, NJ: Erlbaum.

Allen J. & Fonagy, P. (2006). *Handbook of Mentalization-Based Treatments*. John Wiley & Co: Chichester, UK.

Asen, E. (in press). Multi-contextual multiple family therapy. In L. Mayes, P. Fonagy, & M.Target. (Eds.), *Developmental science and psychoanalysis: Integration and innovation*. London: Karnac Books.

Bach, S. (2001). On being forgotten and on forgetting one's self. *Psychoanalytic Quarterly, LXX*, 739–756.

Bateman, A. & Fonagy, P. (2006). *Handbook of Mentalization-Based Treatments*. John Wiley & Co: Chichester, UK.

Bettelheim, B. (1950). Love is not enough: The treatment of emotionally disturbed children. New York: Free Press.

Bowlby, J. (1988). A secure base: Parent-child attachment and healthy human development. New York: Basic Books.

Chazen, S. (2003). *Simultaneous treatment of parent and child*. London: Jessica Kingsley Publishers.

Coates, S. W. (2004). After September 11, 2001: The parent's reflective capacity as mediator and moderator. Paper presented at the annual meeting of Division 39, The American Psychological Association, Miami, FL, March 19, 2004.

Fonagy, P. (2001). *Attachment theory and psychoanalysis*. New York: Other Press.

Fonagy, P., Gergely, G., Jurist, E., & Target, M. (2002). *Affect regulation, mentalization, and the development of the self*. New York: Other Press.

Fonagy, P., Steele, M., Moran, G., Steele, H., & Higgitt, A. (1991). The capacity for understanding mental states: The reflective self in parent and child and its significance for security of attachment. *Infant Mental Health Journal, 13*, 200–217.

Fonagy, P., Steele, M., Steele, H., Leigh, T., Kennedy, R., Mattoon, G., & Target, M. (1995). Attachment, the reflective self, and borderline states: The predictive specificity of the adult attachment interview and pathological emotional development. In *Attachment theory: Social, developmental and clinical perspectives*, In S. Goldberg, R. Muir, & J. Kerr (Eds.), Hillsdale, NJ: Analytic Press, pp. 223–279.

Fonagy, P., & Target, M. (1996). Playing with reality: I. Theory of mind and the normal development of psychic reality. *International Journal of Psychoanalysis, 77*, 217–233.

Fonagy, P., & Target, M. (1998). Mentalization and the changing aims of child psychoanalysis. *Psychoanalytic Dialogues, 8*, 87–114.

Fonagy, Target, M., Steele, H., & Steele, M. (1998). *Reflective functioning scoring manual*. Unpublished manual, University College London.

Fraiberg, S. (1980). *Clinical studies in infant mental health*. New York: Harper Row.

Freud, A. (1965). *Normality and pathology in childhood: Assessments of development*. Madison, CT: International Universities Press.

Freud, A. (1966–1980). *The writings of Anna Freud, Volumes I–VIII*. New York: International Universities Press.

George, C., Kaplan, N., & Main, M. (1996; 3rd edition). *The Berkeley Adult Attachment Interview.* Unpublished protocol, Department of Psychology, University of California, Berkeley.

Grienenberger, J., Popek, P., Stein, S., Solow, J., Morrow, M., Levine, N., et al. (2004). *The Wright Institute Reflective Parenting Program Workshop Training Manual.* Unpublished manual, The Wright Institute, Los Angeles, CA.

Grienenberger, J., Slade, A. & Kelly, K. (2005). Maternal reflective functioning and the caregiving relationship: The link between mental states and mother-infant affective communication. *Attachment and Human Development, 7,* 299–311 .

Jacobs, L. & Wachs, C. (2002). Parent therapy: A relational alternative to working with children. New York: Jason Aronson.

Karen, R. (1998). Becoming attached: First relationships and how they impact our capacity to love. New York: Oxford University Press.

Kerr, M. & Bowen, M. (1988). *Family evaluation.* New York: Norton.

Klein, M. (1932). *The psycho-analysis of children.* London: Hogarth Press.

Kohut, H. (1969). *The analysis of the self.* Madison, CT: International Universities Press.

Lieberman, A.F., Silverman, R., & Pawl, J. (1999). Infant-parent psychotherapy: Core concepts and current approaches. In C. H. Zeanah (Ed.), *Handbook of infant mental health,* pp. 472–485. New York: Guilford Press.

Main, M., Kaplan, N., & Cassidy, J. (1985). Security in infancy, childhood and adulthood: A move to the level of representation. *Monographs of the Society for Research in Child Development* (1–2 Serial, No. 209), 50: 66–107.

Mitchell, S. (1988) *Relational concepts in psychoanalysis.* Harvard University Press: Cambridge, MA.

Novick, J., & Novick, K.K. (2001). Parent work in analysis: Children, adolescents, and adults. Part I: The evaluation phase. *Journal of Infant, Child, and Adolescent Psychotherapy, 1,* 55–77.

Novick, J., & Novick, K. K. (2002). Parent work in analysis: Children, adolescents, and adults. Part III: The middle and pretermination phases of treatment. *Journal of Infant, Child, and Adolescent Psychotherapy, 2,* 17–41.

Novick, K. K., & Novick, J. (2002a). Parent work in analysis: Children, adolescents, and adults. Part II: Recommendation, beginning, and middle phases of treatment. *Journal of Infant, Child, and Adolescent Psychotherapy, 2,* 1–27.

Novick, K. K., & Novick, J. (2002b). Parent work in analysis: Children, adolescents, and adults. Part IV: Termination and post-termination phases. *Journal of Infant, Child, and Adolescent Psychotherapy, 2,* 43–55.

Oram, K. (2000). A transitional space: Involving parents in the play therapy of their children. *Journal of Infant, Child, and Adolescent Psychotherapy, 1,* 79–98.

Pantone, P. (2000). Treating the parental relationship as the identified parent in child psychotherapy. *Journal of Infant, Child, and Adolescent Psychotherapy, 1,* 19–38.

Pine, F. (1985). *Developmental theory and clinical process.* New Haven, CT: Yale University Press.

Siskind, D. (1987). *The child patient and the therapeutic process: A psychoanalytic, developmental and object relations approach.* Northvale, NJ: Aronson.

Siskind, D. (1997). Working with parents: Establishing the essential alliance in child psychotherapy and consultation. New York: Jason Aronson.

Slade, A. (1994). Making meaning and making believe: Their role in the clinical process. In *Children at play: Clinical and Developmental approaches to meaning and representation,* In A. Slade & D. Wolf. (Eds.), New York: Oxford University Press, 81–107.

Slade, A. (1999a). Attachment theory and research: Implications for the theory and practice of individual psychotherapy with adults. In *The handbook of attachment theory and research,* In J. Cassidy & P. R. Shaver (Eds.), New York: Guilford, pp. 575–594.

Slade, A. (1999b). Representation, symbolization and affect regulation in the concomitant treatment of a mother and child: Attachment theory and child psychotherapy. *Psychoanalytic Inquiry, 19,* 797–830.

Slade, A. (2000). The development and organization of attachment: Implications for psychoanalysis. *Journal of the American Psychoanalytic Association, 48,* 1147–1174.

Slade, A. (2004a). The move from categories to phenomena: Attachment processes and clinical evaluation. *Infant Mental Health Journal, 25,* 1–15.

Slade, A. (2004b). Two therapies: Attachment organization and the clinical process. *Attachment issues in psychopathology and intervention,* In L. Atkinson & S. Goldberg. (Eds.), Hillsdale, NJ: Erlbaum Press, 181–206.

Slade, A. (2005). Parental reflective functioning: An introduction. *Attachment and Human Development, 7,* 269–281.

Slade, A. (2006). Reflective parenting programs: Theory and development. *Psychoanalytic Inquiry, 26,* 640–657.

Slade, A., Belsky, J., Aber, J. L., & Phelps, J. (1999). Maternal Representations of their relationship with their toddlers: Links to adult attachment and observed mothering. *Developmental Psychology, 35,* 611–619.

Slade, A., Bernbach, E., Grienenberger, J., Levy, D., & Locker, A. (2002). *Addendum to reflective functioning scoring manual: For use with the parent development interview.* Unpublished Manuscript. The City College and Graduate Center, City University of New York.

Slade, A., Grienenberger, J., Bernbach, E., Levy, D. W., & Locker, A. (2005). Maternal reflective functioning and attachment. *Attachment and Human Development, 7,* 283–292.

Slade, A., Sadler, L., de Dios-Kenn, C., Webb, D., Ezepchick, J., & Mayes. L. (2005). Minding the Baby: A reflective Parenting Program. *Psychoanalytic Study of the Child, 60,* 74–100.

Slade, A., Sadler, L., & Mayes, L. C. (2005). Maternal Reflective Functioning: Enhancing Parental Reflective Functioning in a Nursing/Mental Health Home Visiting Program. In *Enhancing Early Attachments: Theory, Research, Intervention, and Policy,* L. Berlin, Y. Ziv, L. Amaya-Jackson, & Mark Greenberg, Eds., pp. 152–177. New York: Guilford Publications.

Stern, D. N. (1985). *The interpersonal world of the infant.* New York: Basic Books.

Stern, D. N. (1994). *The motherhood constellation.* New York:

Target, M., Slade, A., Cottrell, D., Fuggle, P. & Fonagy, P. (2005). Psychosocial therapies of children. *Concise Oxford textbook of psychotherapy,* In G. Gabbard, J. Beck, & J. Holmes (Eds.), pp. 341–352. Oxford, UK: Oxford University Press.

Tronick, E. (1998). Dyadically expanded states of consciousness and the process of therapeutic change. *Infant Mental Health Journal, 19,* 290–299.

White, M. & Epston, D. (1990). *Narrative means to therapeutic ends.* New York: Norton.

Winnicott, D. W. (1965). *Maturational processes and the facilitating environment.* New York: International Universities Press.

Winnicott, D. W. (1971). *Playing and reality.* London: Tavistock Publications.

8

Discussion

Diana Diamond and Otto Kernberg

This groundbreaking collection of papers shows the evolution of the concept of mentalization into a major force within psychoanalysis, providing a guiding framework for theory, research, and clinical practice. In developing the concept of mentalization, Fonagy and his colleagues have generated a research-based developmental theory, a theory of psychopathology linked to this developmental theory, and a theory and technique of treatment—all of which have been evaluated in systematic research. Contributing to this research is the development of the Reflective Function Scale (Fonagy et al., 1998), a quantitative index of mentalization in the context of attachment relationships, which has been used to investigate the mechanisms of change in psychodynamic treatment (Diamond, Stovall-McClough, Clarkin, & Levy, 2003; Levy, Clarkin, Yeomans, Scott, Wasserman, & Kernberg, 2006a; Rudden, Milrod, Aronson, &Target, this issue; Yeomans, Clarkin, Diamond, & Levy, this issue) as well as to assess the process by which trauma is transgenerationally transmitted (Fonagy, this issue; Slade, this issue). The papers in this volume reflect the magnitude of these contributions while further extending their utility for psychoanalytically oriented clinicians (a) by delineating how mentalization and RF evolved from core psychodynamic concepts, developments in philosophy (theory of mind) and cognitive science; and (b) by presenting research and case material which illuminate the concept's clinical utility as well as its relationship to modern conflict theory, attachment and ego psychology. In this discussion we address some of the overarching issues and controversies that have emerged from these investigations.

Fonagy's chapter "The Mentalization Approach to Social Development," presents a model of early development that emphasizes the caregiver's capacity to mirror the infant's affective experience in a marked and contingent manner which in turn enables the infant to experience him or herself as an intentional being. Such marked and congruent mirroring enables the infant to construct second order representations of primary affect states, setting the foundation for both affect containment and regulation, and the capacity to think in mental state terms about the thoughts, feelings, and beliefs of self and other. In this paper Fonagy not only provides an excellent summary of his previous formulations, but also pushes the concept of mentalization into new theoretical territory by reconsidering the role of affect in the development of mentalization, by reexamining the relationship between mentalization and attachment, by grounding mentalization in neurobiology, and by linking personality disorders to specific failures in affect mirroring.

Fonagy expands the concept of mentalization into the affective realm, examining the ways in which comprehension of intentional mental states encompasses the understanding of feelings, and the representations which underlie them, an area which Steele and Steele (this issue), Jurist and others have also explored. Invoking Jurist's (2005) concept of mentalized affectivity, a process by which one simultaneously experiences and reflects on feelings, Fonagy hypothesizes that mentalization results from the interaction of an affectively based Interpersonal Interpretive Function (IIF-A) and a cognitively oriented Interpersonal Interpretive Function (IIF-C). The latter is linked to a frontal cortical system that invokes declarative representations, although the former is regulated by a mirror neuron system in which visual apprehension of the affects of others immediately activates a set of visual-motor neurons and circuitry that trigger comparable emotions in the observer.

Because his focus is on articulating the immediate interpersonal environment and affective processes that are at the basis of mentalizing capacities, Fonagy pays less attention to the building up of the complex world of object relations or the ego structures that will inevitably modulate affect activation. He specifically neglects the gradual accrual of divergent sets of self and object representations in the internal world under the influence of early, contradictory affective experiences. Similarly, little attention is paid to splitting mechanisms and the self and object representations with which they are linked, or to the normal function of the gradual integration of affectively charged object relations. Yet Jurist himself has stated that mentalized affectivity refers not only to processes of affect regulation and understanding, but also to the "exploration of how our affective experience is mediated by the representational world" (Jurist, 2005, p. 429). Although Fonagy sees mentalization as emerging in the context of the building up of attachment relationships, he does not discuss the ways in which attachment itself represents the terminus of the building up of the internal world of object relations.

However, Fonagy does offer a more precise delineation of the relationship between mentalization and attachment, and addresses certain controversies that have emerged about their interconnection. Fonagy and colleagues have presented extensive research evidence to support the idea that mentalization emerges and flourishes in the context of secure attachment relationships, although it is curtailed or even grossly stunted in situations of attachment insecurity and/ or early attachment trauma (Allen, 2003; Fonagy, Gergely, Jurist & Target, 2002). These formulations have been challenged by recent FMRI studies (Bartels & Zeki, 2000, 2002), which have identified the neuronal structures and circuitry that are activated in maternal and romantic love. Their investigations showed that although the sexual and attachment systems involve both overlapping sets of areas (specifically the oxytocin and vasopressin sensitive circuitry), as well as areas that are specific to each, both the sexual/romantic and parent child attachment systems suppressed activity in regions associated with negative emotions, social and moral judgments—all aspects of mentalizing. These studies suggest that strong affectional bonds or attachments, whether in parent child or adult romantic relationships inhibit not only negative emotions, but also the neuronal networks involved in making social judgments about that person.

Fonagy acknowledges that these findings, which appear to contradict his original formulations, actually render the relationship between attachment and mentalization more complex. Attachment, a behavioral system that gets activated in times of danger, threat, and loss, will take priority over all other behavioral systems in the interests of ensuring survival. In danger situations, social judgments or reasoning about the trustworthiness of the attachment figure must necessarily be diminished as the attachment behaviors that ensure survival take priority. However, in situations of attachment security, the attachment system is deactivated, and therefore the mentalization system can flourish. In this view attachment is a behavioral system which once anchored is deactivated, so that other aspects of development and other systems may take precedence. First one needs a secure attachment to be able to mentalize, but the attachment system itself is an alarm system that signals danger, threat or loss under certain circumstances, and that alarm system activates defensive functions and reduces the capacity to mentalize.

As mentioned previously, Fonagy has refined our understanding of attachment by shifting the emphasis from attachment as a behavioral system that functions to ensure survival, to attachment as an Interpersonal Interpretive Mechanism (IIM); that is, a constellation of psychological functions and processes that serve the evolutionally functions of attachment, by allowing one to understand and interpret the affects, behavior and intentions of others. It is not clear, however, whether the secure attachment relationship is the precondition for the development of the IIM or whether the IIM is an overarching concept that subsumes attachment. In the latter case, there are a set of factors that must go into the IIM that have to do with the neurobiological components of attention, attentional control, neurobiological reactions to stress that Fonagy considers in his paper. However, in our view these contradictory formulations of attachment as a behavioral proximity seeking system that potentially reduces the functioning of other systems including mentalization in situations of extreme stress, danger, or unavailability of attachment figures, and attachment as an Interpersonal Interpretive Mechanism rooted in a secure affectional bond that fosters mentalization creates ambiguity.

Fonagy and colleagues have extended these formulations about the deactivation of mentalization in the context of insecure attachment relationships to the treatment situation, particularly for patients with borderline and other severe personality disorders, the majority of whom have been found to have insecure attachment (Diamond et al., 2003, Fonagy et al., 1995; Levy et al., 2006b). Fonagy stipulates that the activation of the attachment system in psychodynamic therapy, involves a concomitant shutting down of the mentalization system, which limits the individual's capacity to comprehend and use interpretation and other forms of symbolic thought. We address these issues in more depth later.

Finally, Fonagy attempts to expand the understanding of the neurobiological underpinnings of mentalization. In Fonagy's view, mentalization is a complex function involving multiple brain areas including a node involving perceptual processes of social stimuli or social detection; a node involving brain structures (the amygdala, hypothalamus, etc.) that generate and regulate affects, and a node involving cognitive regulation including mentalizing, effortful control, social and moral judgments and so forth. These formulations identify the neurobiological underpinnings of mentalization as a set of functions that are tied to particular neuronal structures, and to the dynamic processes among them. However, it is a long stretch from the firing of neurons or the activation of brain structures that may be involved in reflective capacities to the generation of complex psychological functions that encompass mentalization, and the translation rules from one sphere to the other are not yet clear. In our view, the concept of reflective function or mentalization is difficult to define and locate empirically because like concepts of identity, or self and other, it encompasses sets of interrelated circuitry, or complex sets of overlapping neuronal maps that may generate RF.

Gerhard Roth (2001), for example, provides a model of self and identity from a neurobiological point of view that also has implications for our understanding of the neural mechanisms involved in mentalization. In Roth's view I and self are *"unmittelbar gegeben,"* a composite structure that represents the synthesis of different states that are generated by the brain and which develop in tandem with the brain. Roth sees protypical self representations as developing through the evolution of a number of interrelated sets of mental maps in several areas: the integration of sensoric maps in the techtum colliculum superiore/inferiore; the identity of perception developed through sensorimotor feedback in the cortex; body identity, action identity and limbic system emotional identity, the latter involving the development of autobiographic or declarative memory in the cortico-hippocampal system, which inevitably involves the activation of memories of the self in relation to others. In this model, the consolidation of identity (which is believed to be related to the development of the ability to mentalize) is a complex and continuous function of a number of brain mechanisms and circuits that cannot be necessarily located in any one or even mulitiple structures. As Roth stipulates "the brain creates us, and it hides from us" (2003).

Gergely and Unoka's chapter, "The Development of the Unreflective Self," further expands the developmental model to offer a more complex view of how the attachment figure's capacity to mirror the child's affective expressions enables the child to construct a representational system. Heretofore, Gergely and Unoka's focus on transforming primary to secondary representations through marked and contingent mirroring interactions with primary attachment figures has emphasized the interpersonal aspects, to the neglect of the complex stages of the development of concept of self and other and the building up of the internal world of object relations. In this paper, they offer a more fine grained analysis of how these mirroring transactions are internalized as cognitive-affective schemas. Primary representations are seen as devolving from procedural visceral emotional sensations and experiences for which the child is hard-wired. The innate repertoire of affective responses and the capacity to read them in others serves the dual functions of survival and also of communication with primary attachment figures. In Gergely's view, second order representations develop through interactions with primary attachment figures that are marked and that allow the infant opportunities for contingency detection.

Gergely and Unoka identify two sets of contingencies that contribute to the development of representational schemas: (a) self to other schemas in which the infant forms a representation of his or her own affect as it is responded to by the other; and (b) other to self schemas in which the infant forms a representation of the characteristic affective responses of the other aroused in interactions that are not necessarily contingent on the infant's emotional signals or displays. The self to other models encompass the causal properties of his or her own affective displays and the responses of the attachment figure to them, while the other to self models represent the "predictable consequences for the self of the attachment figure's emotional states and emotionally significant behaviors" (Gergely & Unoka, this volume, p. 64). The important point here is that the infant forms a representation not only of his or her own affect as it is responded to by the other, but of the other's states of emotional arousal and of the specific events that might trigger those states, including, but not limited to, the infant's own affective displays or states of affective arousal. In situations where the affective responses of the other are negative or overwhelming regardless of the infant's emotional displays, the infant may inhibit or adjust his or her own emotional displays and modify his or her states of arousal accordingly.

These other to self and self to other schemas may be seen as the forerunners of internalized object relations consisting of representations of self in interaction with others, joined by a linking affect. The stipulation that other to self as well as self to other schemas contribute to the building up of both primary and secondary representations constitutes the acknowledgment that the mirroring transactions, whether marked or unmarked, contingent or noncontingent, lead to the formation of a world of internalized objects, as well as to the capacity for mentalization. Thus, in this paper, Gergely and Unoka have begun to link the process of the formation of second order representations and the processes of mentalization and affect regulation that it entails, to psychoanalytic concepts of internalization (Blatt, 2002; Behrends and Blatt, 1985; Kernberg, 2004).

Gergley and Unoka apply this expanded developmental model to the theory and treatment of severe psychopathology, and present a case in depth to show its clinical utility. This is a compelling and clearly successful treatment of a severely disturbed patient. They hypothesize that for this patient, whose psychotic mother reacted with undifferentiated and disintegrating rage to the full array of the patient's emotional displays, self to other and other to self emotional schemas include representations of a victimized self in relation to a traumatizing other. This view of a traumatizing other that will react in undifferentiated rageful ways to any emotional displays forms in Gergely and Unoka's view the "representational content" of the other to self emotional schema. However, Gergely and Unoka talk about this structure not as a split off internal object, but as a "causal illusion" which involves the representation of emotional states of others as external causes that induce disintegration or fragmentation in the self. Gergely and Unoka differentiate such a causal illusion from projective identification by noting that the former does not serve the function of defensive operations, and does not involve the externalization onto others of intolerable impulses or affects, with concomitant distortions of internal and external reality. Rather, this causal illusion is more akin to an "abnormal perceptual illusion" in that the individual's own physiological emotional reactions are subsumed by the "*activated mental representation of the likely external causal consequences* of the primary emotion response" which are experienced as "an actual reality 'out there' in the present, while the activated

internal arousal state remains largely outside of consciousness."
(Gergely & Unoka, this volume, p. 84). It should be noted that such a
mentalization based approach, which eschews transference interpretation and focuses on the identification and clarification of affective
states in a patient, such as Gergely and Unoka's, who presents as psychically dead and devoid of emotional reactions, has been shown in
several outcome and follow-up studies to be efficacious in the treatment of borderline patients (Bateman & Fonagy, 1999, 2001).

However, in our view Gergely and Unoka's formulations of the
case fail to truly incorporate their unique developmental contributions, which postulate an internal world, composed of self to other
and other to self representations. What is missing from this case formulation is the patient's identification with the bad or alien internal object, notable in the two dreams presented. Gergely's concept
of the *causal illusion* appears to be consistent with Fonagy's notion
of the alien self, or alien fragments in the self-structure that derive
from poorly marked and incongruent mirroring. The alien self (Fonagy, this issue) constitutes a threatening, dissociated part of the self
based on overwhelming negative affective experiences with attachment figures which have been internalized in the course of development, but that must be continually projected onto others in order to
insure the stability of the self. In the course of treatment the patient
projects this alien or bad object onto the therapist, whom he then
experiences as a persecutory object. In our view, the alien self is not a
singular representation, but rather encompasses a specific fantasized
interaction; the pathological self representation must include the
traumatic relationship between intolerable self and object representations which have mutually complementary functions that tend to
get reversed or exchanged. In our view, it is this notion of an object
representation as part of the alien self that is missing from Fonagy
and Gergely's formulations. Whether the patient sees the therapist as
an alien self or alien object who is then experienced as disorganizing, attacking, and traumatizing like mother, or whether he behaves
as the alien self as was the case in the dream material, self and object
are in a complementary role which must be clarified and then interpreted in the interests of integration and modulation.

According to Gergely and Unoka, in severely disturbed patients
who have experienced trauma, such an interpretive approach may
actually stimulate states of arousal (in both the prefrontal and posterior cortical and subcortical systems) such that the individual shuts

down mentalization in the face of increased activation of attachment via the transference. In such cases, Gergely and Unoka suggest that interpretation ranges from useless to harmful. Gergely and Unoka conclude by saying that he is unclear about which interventions led to improvements in mentalization and self agency for the patient. Ultimately it is important to remember that progress in treatment is the result of both interpretive mechanisms and interpersonal aspects of the therapy, with different patients responding differentially to therapeutic interventions.

There is some evidence from neurobiological investigations that points to the importance of interpretation for the resolution of trauma. Le Doux (1996, 2002), for example, has stipulated that there has to be cognitive processing of traumatic memories in order for those memories to be accessed, modified and expressed in the verbal realm. Even if traumatic memories are encoded in the amygdala and limbic system, and thus in implicit memory, they can only be accessed through the prefrontal cortex, for example, through language and interpretation. The work of Le Doux and others thus suggests that the activation of affect through the cognitive filter of psychotherapy permits modification and elaboration of traumatic memories. Although there is some evidence that addressing trauma prematurely or too early in the treatment may worsen symptoms, the investigations of Stovall-McClough and Cloitre (2003) who apply a short term exposure therapy model to treatment of traumatized patients in which they are encouraged to focus on constructing a coherent narrative of their traumatic experiences indicate the efficacy of verbal expression and exploration for the resolution of trauma.

This debate about the nature of thought and representation involved in mentalization is continued in the work of Bouchard and Lecours. In their chapter, p. 103, "Contemporary Approaches to Mentalization in the Light of Freud's Project," Bouchard and Lecours present an intrapsychic view of mentalization that derives from Freud's *Project for a Scientific Psychology*. The term "Mentalization" has been used in French psychoanalytic thought to refer to the intrapsychic process by which drives penetrate the mind in the form of affect states that seek relations to objects, and in the process augment the development of symbolic thinking. In the French view, mentalization is conceptualized as a process that transforms drive excitation into affect states and symbolized mental contents by interpolating a gradually more complex activity of thought between instinctual demands and the action that would satisfy them. Bouchard and Lecours contrast this intrapsychic view of mentalization with the developmental intersubjective view of mentalization put forth by Fonagy and colleagues, which privilege marked and contingent mirroring transactions with the attachment figure in the development of mentalization.

Bouchard and Lecours do an excellent job of contrasting the two conceptualizations of mentalization however. In our view, they make an artificial division between mentalization as an interpersonal and intrapsychic phenomena. This bifurcation between the intrapsychic and the interpersonal may result from downplaying the inevitable role of the object in patterning the drives. In addition, they appear to graft the concept of mentalization onto Freud's Project. Mentalization, in Bouchard and Lecours' work appears synonymous with the development of ego functions—the capacity to control and modulate affect and impulses. Bouchard and Lecours contrast mentalization with primitive modes of thought that derive from the drives, but do not offer a precise formulation of such modes of thought, other than stating that they are devoid of links to symbolization and abstraction.

One danger is that the concept of mentalization is excessively stretched by trying to include both the Freudian concept which focuses on an internal sensory apparatus that is continually elaborating and representing bodily needs and experiences into primitive fantasies involving infantile sexual wishes and desires, and the intersubjective concept which centers on mirroring transactions between parent and infant through which primary representations are transformed into secondary representations. Bouchard and Lecours ultimately turn to Kernberg's affect theory which offers a theory of transformation of primary affective structures into drives in the context of internalized object relations. By delineating the complex stages in which the development of the concept of the self and others evolves out of primary affective experiences, Kernberg's theory integrates the interpersonal and the intrapsychic aspects of mentalization.

Like the paper by Bouchard, the paper by Steele and Steele, "On the Initial Development and Validation of the Reflective Functioning Concept," contributes to our understanding of the historical evolution of mentalization as it is operationalized in the Reflective Function Scale. The authors discuss how the formulation of the scale was inspired by ego psychological concepts of psychological mindedness, self observational capacities of the ego, insight, and reality testing, and also the concepts of coherence and metacognition as they were operationalized in the subscales of the Adult Attachment Interview (George, Kaplan, Main, 1998). The paper fills a major gap in the literature by presenting data on the reliability and validity of the RF concept, its independence from other factors such as IQ, level of education (except weakly for father's) along with its predictive validity. Steele and Steele also describe how they amplified the RF scale in a negative direction with the addition of a –1 rating to encompass hostile/ angry verbal and behavioral responses to RF questions found in forensic and other severely disturbed populations.

The research findings reported by Steele and Steele also illuminate the differential contributions of mothers and fathers to the child's personality development during different developmental stages. As such they broaden the concepts of attachment and mentalization beyond the near exclusive focus on the mother-child relationship to encompass father-child and also triadic mother-father-child influences. Steele and Steele presents an overview of research findings in which *both* mother's and father's capacity for mentalization (as measured by the RF scale applied to their AAI's before the birth of the child) has been linked to a wide range of personality and developmental factors in the next generation including quality of parent-child attachment at one year, reasoning in the domain of attachment and close relationships, and fundamental aspects of psychological functioning and development, including self esteem and identity through early adolescence and beyond. Although attachment security in the first year of life was predicted primarily by the security of mother's attachment and level of RF, the father's RF was significantly related to a number of interpersonal and personality factors in the child in middle childhood and adolescence. These included the son's ability to give coherent descriptions of self and significant others at age 11, and also the father's perspective on other aspects of the child's overall psychological functioning, such as the degree of social withdrawal and externalizing or delinquent behaviors. These findings coincided with child's own self report ratings, including his self reported self esteem, contributing to their validity.

That the father's RF seems to have a long term influence on the son's ability to give a coherent account of himself and others at age 11 provides one of the first empirical links between RF and concepts of identity formulation and consolidation. We have hypothesized that the development of the reflective capacity and the consolidation of identity go hand in hand because a consolidated identity involves the development of a coherent and differentiated representation of self and others against which momentary and transient mental states can be evaluated (Kernberg, Diamond, Yeomans, Clarkin, & Levy, in press).

These findings on the relationship between parents,' particularly father's, RF and the child's self esteem, ability to evaluate the self, and the consolidation of identity in middle childhood and adolescence also suggest some relationship between parental RF and oedipal outcomes. For example, the father's RF predicts negatively any aggressive or antisocial, or delinquent tendencies in the son. The identification with the same sex parent that is heir to the Oedipus complex anchors superego structures in the child; hence negative correlation between paternal RF and father's perception of externalizing and/or antisocial tendencies in the son, which bespeaks adequate superego development, would be predicted.

Although both maternal and paternal RF differentially predicted aspects of the child's development, mother's AAI ratings of attachment did not predict infant-father attachment, nor did father's AAI ratings of attachment predict infant-mother attachment. These findings suggest that attachment is relationship specific, with representations or internal working models of mother and father developing separately, rather than as one overarching working model of attachment.

The findings reported by Steele and Steele also speak to the complex relationship between attachment and reflective function. They report the intriguing finding that high reflective function in mothers predicted security of attachment in their infants only when mothers showed a history of deprivation. On the other hand, the majority of mothers who suffered deprivation in childhood and who had low RF scores were found to have infants who were insecurely attached, while for mothers with no history of deprivation, the mother's RF scores were irrelevant to the child's attachment status. These findings suggest that RF can act as a mediating factor, and speak to the importance of improvements in RF for intervention and prevention work, particularly in high risk families, where there is a history of neglect or deprivation.

These findings on the extent to which RF in parents predicts a number of aspects of mental health in the child, including self esteem, identity, affect management and regulation, and delinquency, bring us back to the some of the original questions that Steele and Steele started with: that is, what exactly is RF measuring? While these aspects of the child's psychological functioning are clearly correlates of RF, we might hypothesize that RF is an umbrella concept that provides a global index of psychological health and pathology, ego functioning and object relations, along with a measure of attachment related mentalization. It is also possible that low RF is a marker of character pathology in the parents which would predict not only insecure attachment, but also identity diffusion, poor self esteem and externalizing behaviors in the children. Thus, as was originally intended according to Steele and Steele (Chapter 4, this volume), RF offers a wider ranging measure of ego functioning, affect regulation and even psychopathology, as well as providing an index primarily to functioning in the cognitive sphere.

The investigations of Yeomans et al reported in their chapter, "An Object Relations Treatment of Borderline Patients With Reflective Functioning as a Mechanism of Change," illustrate the utility of the expanded RF scale to assess the capacity for mentalization in borderline patients and the way it changes in a randomized clinical trail of 90 borderline patients in three manualized treatments: Transference Focused Psychotherapy (TFP), Dialectic Behavior Therapy (DBT) and Supportive Psychodynamic Therapy (SPT). The study constitutes one of the first such randomized clinical trails with severely disturbed clinical population in which the RF rating scale has been used as an outcome measure. The preliminary data analyses indicate that all three treatments are equally effective in reducing symptoms and improving social functioning, but only the patients in TFP improved significantly in their mean RF scores after one year of treatment. These findings are particularly interesting because the primary goal of TFP is not primarily to target deficits in mentalization, but to foster the patient's capacity to understand and integrate the split polarized internal world of self and object representations that underlie the chaotic affect states and to resolve identity diffusion that characterize borderline patients.

These empirical findings suggest that the interpretative process that is unique to TFP may play a role in improving mentalization as measured by the RF scale. However, further investigation of other factors that might differentiate the clinical process in the TFP group from the DBT or STP groups, and that might contribute to improvements in RF are needed in order to definitively link increases in RF with interpretation.

That RF improved in the TFP group speaks to some of the controversies that have emerged between proponents of dynamic interpretive approaches and more supportive approaches in understanding
the mechanisms of change in treatment. Yeomans and colleagues (this
issue) have found that the RF measure, and the concept of mentalization on which it is based, augments their integrative object relations
model of borderline pathology. In their model, borderline disorders
are conceptualized as resulting from a confluence of temperamental
factors including low effortful control, the preponderance of negative over positive affect in the context of insecure internal working
models of attachment and associated deficits in mentalization. However, they also offer a critique and amplification of the concept of
mentalization based on both empirical and clinical investigations of
change. Yeomans and colleagues differ from Fonagy, Gergely, and
colleagues both in their understanding of how to approach these
deficits in mentalization in treatment, and in the nature of the internal world that underlies them. Both groups stipulate that among the
most important and challenging tasks of treating borderline patients
is how to approach the patients' externalization of unbearable self
states, to help the patient recognize these as an aspect of self, and
to reintegrate these in more tolerable, nuanced and accurate form.
Hence in the extended cases presented by both Gergely and Unoka,
and Yeomans and colleagues, the first stage of treatment involved
identification and clarification of the patient's mental states with a
focus on what the patient imagines is in the therapist's mind, with
the idea that the increased ability to identify and tolerate the mental
states of self and others is the first step in the containment of intense
and painful affects.

However, the object relations model in TFP stipulates that even
in the most primitive affect state there is always an object relation
even if self and object are not well-differentiated. Therefore repeated
clarification of what patient is experiencing and what he or she imagines the therapist is experiencing will lead to identification of the
representations of self and others involved in the affective experience. Further clarification of the self and object representations
along with the linking affects presents a cognitive schema for what
the patient is feeling, and helps to contain and modulate the affect.
The subsequent phases in TFP involve the identification of characteristic internal relational scenarios of self, object and linking affects
as they are activated in the here and now of the transference with the

idea that re-expereincing and observing these scenarios will enable the patient to reflect on them as mental states, rather than as veridical experiences. Based on their clinical model and empirical investigations, Yeomans and colleagues conceptualize mentalization as a multistaged process that involves (a) the capacity to identify the mental states of self and other or the specific self object affect constellation as it is experienced in an immediate interaction; and (b) to link mental states experienced in the moment to a diverse array of mental states, past and present, resulting in increased integration, depth and modulation in the representational world.

Yeomans and colleagues illustrate their expanded view of mentalization with an extended case example of a borderline patient who moved from a –1 to 6 on the RF scale, as rated from the AAI, after one year, indicating the clinical utility of expanding the scale in a negative direction to encompass those who like this patient, responded to the RF demand questions of the AAI with overt hostility and aggression at both the behavioral and verbal level.

One controversy that emerges from these papers is whether borderline patients can only tolerate or benefit from interpretation relatively late in the treatment. According to Fonagy, Gergely and colleagues, interpretive approaches are potentially retraumatizing to borderline patients because they lack the capacity for mentalization that would enable them to understand their affective experiences as mental states. In their view, borderline patients are mired in the psychic equivalence of mode of psychological functioning in which internal and external reality are poorly differentiated. Alternatively, interpretations of self and object dyads may create a pretend world for the patient, in which he or she may play with more complex formulations but without any connection to or change in functioning outside the treatment sphere. Because borderline patients lack symbolic function, along with a developed capacity for mentalization, the concrete nature of their thought does not allow for the maintenance of the symbolic or *as if* quality of the transference, necessary for patients to benefit from its interpretation. Instead transference interpretation may generate anxiety and hostility in borderline patients, who need in the early phases of treatment help in identifying inner experience, rather than interpreting its meaning. In these patients, there has been a collapse of capacity for mentalization because contemplation of the minds of others entails a confrontation with the threatening or fearsome intentions of primary attachment figures that have been internalized as an alien self. The task of the therapist is to hold rather than interpret the projection of the alien self, until the patient develops the capacity for mentalization which renders the alien self less terrifying and able to be reintegrated in somewhat ameliorated and tolerable form.

Yeomans and colleagues agree that with borderline patients the interpretation of unconscious material must be held in abeyance until mentalization is restored and identity is consolidated; but they also believe that the interpretation of consciously held but contradictory or polarized identifications, the result of primitive defensive operations such as splitting, improves mentalization. In TFP there is a step wise progression through various types of interpretation, including (a) identifying role reversals between self and object poles of the object relational dyads as they occur in the transference, (b) confronting splitting of idealized from persecutory aspects of self in to different dyads, and then (c) offering a hypothesis about why splitting occurs and gradually linking these primitive defensive operations to unconscious wishes, fears and motivations. This progression is not linear, but rather is a function of individual patient characteristics, the dynamics of the particular patient therapist dyad, and the dynamic issues under exploration, as indicated in the case presented. These formulations are buttressed by recent study by Høglend and colleagues (2006) which investigated the value of interpretation by comparing in a randomized controlled trail the efficacy of supportive (noninterpretive) dynamic therapy and expressive (interpretative) therapy in 90 patients, half of whom met Axis II criteria for personality disorders. Interestingly, although they found no overall differences in outcomes between the two treatment groups, they did find that patients with deficits in object relations (60% of whom had personality disorders) improved more from dynamic therapy with transference interpretation.

The interpretative approach in TFP is based on the idea that the symbolic function is not totally deficient in borderline patients, who have adequate reality testing under most circumstances, and who are able to symbolize except under conditions of intense affect. For example, when a borderline patient asked about early traumatic experiences, he or she experiences the act of being asked as a retraumatization. In other words borderline patients cannot differentiate the representation of an experience from an original traumatic experience, a proclivity which is evident in the high rates of lack of resolution of trauma noted on the AAI's of these patients (Fonagy et al., 1996, Patrick et al., 1994). All concrete experiences that activate a certain affect state may automatically bring the entire chain of affects in its wake; however, in affectively neutral situations borderline patients retain the capacity to differentiate a concrete fact from the general meaning of the act, in contrast to psychotic individuals.

These formulations are buttressed by the research of Blatt and Auerbach (2001) who compared the developmental level of representations of self and significant others in borderline and schizophrenic inpatients. Quantitative and qualitative analyses indicated that while the self and other descriptions of borderline patients were infused with negative affects that were cognitively disorganizing to a certain extent, they "were able to experience themselves as volitional, coherent and bounded entities, even if their self images were high reactive to their affect states" (p. 131). Further, borderline patient's self descriptions indicated that they were able to maintain the distinction between objective and subjective forms of self awareness, even though "they have difficulty integrating these two perspectives on the self into a cohesive and stable identity" (p. 148). By contrast, the self descriptions of schizophrenic patients showed little capacity to recognize the internal or subjective sources of their self concept, instead relying on external experiences, including their perceptions of how others perceive them, which are often delusional in nature, to arrive at self awareness. Further, in contrast to borderline patients who maintained boundaries between self and other, internal and external, schizophrenic patients showed a considerable confusion about the source of their volitions and about self other boundaries. As Blatt points out, these findings pose a challenge to the idea that borderline patients function in the psychic equivalence mode in which representations are undifferentiated and the boundary between internal and external permeable (Blatt, 2002; Blatt & Auerbach, 2001).

Kernberg (2004) has hypothesized that what appears to be a loss of the capacity for symbolic thinking in borderline patients may represent the reversion to symmetrical thinking as defined by Matte Blanco (1975, 1988). According to Matte Blanco's theory of bi-logical functioning, the dynamic unconscious operates according to a primitive logic, which involves treating all asymmetric relations as if they were symmetrical, or the converse of any relation as though it were identical with the relation. In this view, the fusional experience that accompanies primitive affects such as rage or sexual excitement becomes generalized, so that under the dominance of primitive hatred everyone, and even the entire world, is transiently experienced as hostile, destructive, or invasive. Thus, if the patient is enraged at the therapist, so the therapist is thought to be enraged at the patient; there is a cognitive component of this belief as well as an affective component, which is expressed through projective identification. The mental apparatus thus functions as a bi-logical system alternating between symmetric and asymmetric thinking, the balance of which will shift according to varying developmental levels, levels of affect activation, degree of regression, and level of personality organization.

Yeomans and colleagues stipulate that transference interpretation and countertransference analysis are highly effective vehicles through which to help the patient reinstate symbolic capacity and the balance between asymmetrical and symmetrical thought. First the therapist helps the patient to observe what he or she is feeling, identifies what the patient imagines the therapist is feeling, and, most importantly, tolerates the partial symmetrization of his or her own experience or, in other terms, tolerates or contains the projective identification in the transference and countertransference. Then, the therapist connects the patients' contradictory views of self and of the therapist under different circumstances, interpreting splitting mechanisms in this context. In our view the interpretation of splitting and other primitive defenses improves cognition because such defensive operations involve affective dyscontrol and polarized states that impair cognitive functions including symbolization.

Like the research of Yeomans and colleagues, the empirical and clinical investigations of Rudden, Milrod, and Target expand and refine the RF construct in a direction that makes it more relevant to investigations of change in clinical groups, in this case panic disordered patients. In contrast to patients with severe personality disorders who have pervasive deficits in their capacity to envision mental states of self and others, Rudden and colleagues hypothesize that patients with panic disorder may shut down their otherwise well developed or at least ordinary reflective capacity only or primarily to avoid contemplation of anxiety laden conflicts that might fuel their symptoms. With panic disordered patients, the repudiation of RF may not be a result of pervasive inability to contemplate the mental states of significant others, but of compromise formations in which anxiety or panic symptoms substitute for the aggressive or sexual impulses, or for conflicted identifications or object relations that must be disowned.

In order to refine the RF measure as a more precise measure of RF in this group and the way it changes over the course of treatment, they developed a measure of Panic Specific RF (PSRF) designed to assess the patient's understanding of the mental states underlying panic attacks. Accordingly they hypothesized that panic specific RF would be lower in this patient group at the beginning of treatment than would the overall RF. The authors, and others in their panic study group, also developed a panic focused psychodynamic psychotherapy (PFPP; Milrod et al., 1997), a 12 week twice weekly manualized treatment, which focuses on improving PSRF first by identifying and exploring the dynamic conflicts, such as those involving separation and or competitive oedipal strivings, that appear to contribute to panic attacks, and second on the manifestations of such conflicts in the transference.

The authors present both quantitative and qualitative preliminary findings. In a randomized clinical trial PFPP was compared to applied relaxation training; preliminary results suggest that that PFPP raises the specific PSRF, but not overall RF, while neither PSRF or General RF improved significantly with relaxation training. The capacity of PFPP to improve panic specific reflective functioning (PFRF) is powerfully illustrated by case material. Patient C, whose overall RF was high or marked at the beginning of treatment, moved over the course of 12 weeks of PFPP from a PSRF score of 6, between marked and ordinary to a score of 7, or marked. Although this improvement might appear minimal, the qualitative examples illustrate that while the patient initially showed some capacity to reflect on her mental states related to her panic symptoms, her responses were vague and amorphous, typically including phrases such as a scary lack of control thing. After 12 weeks of PFPP, she showed a much more precise and well elaborated capacity to reflect on her mental states.

Thus, this one point increase in RF shows a shift from not knowing about her conflicts over independence or her guilt about her success to a capacity to acknowledge and talk about her feelings of guilt about surpassing mother and her fears that success would separate her from mother and lead to abandonment. These qualitative examples illustrate that small increments on the RF scale may be clinically significant, particularly with higher functioning patients. The position of both knowing and not knowing can be reflected in the vagueness and amorphousness of some of the statements character-ized as between ordinary and marked RF, although the awareness of unconscious conflicts leading to articulated awareness lends a new dimension to understanding of the higher RF scale points. Thus, one must take into account the ways that unconscious conflicts may appear in speech patterns of higher functioning patients. This case illustrates that increased precision, richness and clarity of language in talking about mental states, which may mean only an increment of one to two points on the RF scale, may illustrate the lifting of the veil of repression which obfuscates language even in subtle and uneven ways. These findings also suggest the need for more differen-tiation of the upper scale points of the RF scale.

In sum, in their extension of the RF questions, Rudden and col-leagues have made a major contribution in refining and clarifying and operationalizing the RF construct. These investigations suggest that mentalization may fluctuate within the individual across dif-ferent relational situations, according to the nature of the self and object representations, unconscious conflicts or specific mental states that may be evoked. Their targeted measure of RF provides further evidence that RF is a measure of a synthetic ego function that seems likely to be affected by unconscious conflicts, in this case conflicts that underlie anxiety symptoms. Additionally, they provide empirical data to support the increasing evidence that mentaliza-tion is a multifaceted and variable process, a state like rather than a trait like process, one that may not be captured in a single over-all RF score. Rather, RF may fluctuate according to the activation of different unconscious conflicts or environmental triggers. In fact Rudden and colleagues' preliminary findings indicate that for higher functioning individuals with neurotic organization, RF may decline or even plummet when unconscious conflicts are activated; on the other hand, in neutral or nonanxiety provoking situations it may be well preserved.

Further investigations might study the extent to which RF may be influenced by aspects of the therapeutic relationship. Our longitudi-nal investigations of the treatment process and outcome of borderline patients in TFP suggest that even though borderline patients improve overall in their capacity for mentalization, the improvement appears to be a function of characteristics of the therapeutic relationship, including the level of the therapist's reflective function about the

particular patient. Surprisingly, the most efficacious patient therapist match was where the therapists' mentalizing capacity was only
slightly ahead of that of the patient. (Diamond et al., 2003). It was
also noted that the same therapist might show differential capacities to mentalize with respect to different patients, with the reflective
function ranging from low to high according to the patient under
discussion. Further investigations need to microanalyze all aspects
of the treatment relationship in order to more finely tune the inter-
relationship between RF and therapeutic efficacy.

The findings reported by Steele and Steele that the quality of parent's RF, even when measured during pregnancy, predicts the security
of parent child attachment in situations where mother has suffered
deprivation speaks to the importance of intervention programs that
target RF in parents. Slade has developed a comprehensive model
of child psychotherapy based on the theoretical model that many
behavioral and/or emotional difficulties in children are the result
of parent's inability to mentalize about the child's experience. Slade
recognizes that mentalization is not a unitary function. She suggests
that in some parents, the capacity to think in mental state terms may
be well retained except in relation to their child, who may become
the recipient of projections and distortions devolving from their own
insecure internal working models of attachment. Such disruptions in
the parent's capacity to mentalize about the child's mind can lead to
developmental derailments, affect deregulation, behavioral difficulties and symptoms that may then lead to further distortions in the
parent's understanding of the child's mental states. Consequently,
Slade has developed a comprehensive treatment model that sees
concurrent work with parents around their capacity or lack of it to
mentalize the child's experience as an essential aspect of child treatment. Through the connection with the model of the child's mind
in the mind of the therapist, the parents develop a more nuanced,
complete and differentiated understanding of the child's intentions
and affects.

In this model, the mechanism of change is in the therapist's capacity to form a coherent picture of the child's mind—one that connects
the disparate aspects of his or her disregulated behavior and chaotic
affects with internal psychological states, including wishes, impulses
and fears. The focus of work with parents is in the increased comprehension of the child's mind through identification with the therapist's capacity to mentalize about the child. The therapist explores

the factors that might interfere with this process, including aspects of the couple relationship, insecure working models of attachment vis-à-vis the parent's own early attachment experiences, and negative attributions deriving from these early experiences that interfere with the parents' capacity to understand the child's mind separate from them. Such therapeutic explorations allow the parents to express their anger and frustration toward the child whose mind has heretofore been opaque to them, with a goal toward helping them to mentalize rather than enact such negative feelings. The mentalization approach to parent-child treatment emphasizes the development of parents' conscious cognitive understanding of the child's mind; with less focus on unconscious factors, including their own conflicted identifications, fears, anxieties, and wishes, that might interfere with the parent's capacity to mentalize about the child.

Slade acknowledges that there are some parents for whom the process of projection of their own insecure or disorganized attachment models make it impossible for them to experience the child in any but the most negative and or pernicious way, and in such circumstances the parent–child therapeutic program is ineffective at best and harmful at worst, but does not elaborate on the dynamics involved in such RF refractory parents. It is possible that the nature of the object relations of the parents might interfere with mentalizing capacities. For example, in another study, Diamond and colleagues (Diamond & Doane, 1993; Doane & Diamond, 1994) found that parents who showed insecure negative attachment representations of their own same sex parent were not able to benefit from a family treatment program designed to target negative affective style; that is, overt hostility, intrusiveness and guilt induction displayed by parents in family interaction tasks with their severely disturbed adolescents. All of these factors have been found to precipitate relapses in severely disturbed adolescents. In other words parents who had persistent negative affective style in interactions with their adolescent children even after a year long course of family therapy, and who were not able to benefit from skills training or psycho educational approach, were those who showed evidence of polarized highly negative attachment representations. Research which indicated the extent to which mentalization about the child patient is discrepant with overall reflective capacity about self and other, and which explored the particular factors that appear to account for deficits in mentalization in the parent-child pair, with focus on the specific projective processes that may impede mentalization, would be a valuable extension of the current groundbreaking work.

In sum, the papers in this volume have made a major contribution to clarification and amplification of the concepts of mentalization and reflection function. The majority of the papers link psychopathology and the therapeutic process to developmental processes involved in the evolution of mentalization or reflective capacities. Although this developmental model is based in intersubjective early mirroring experiences, these papers, particularly those of Fonagy, Gergely and Unoka, and Yeomans and colleagues, provide a more elaborated model of representational systems. In so doing the majority of the papers contribute to a developmental and structural perspective on severe psychopathology, particularly borderline disorders, that counters the prevailing DSM classification criteria based primarily on symptoms and descriptive traits. Furthermore, the papers, particularly those by Yeomans and colleagues and Rudden and colleagues, illustrate the advances in the use of the RF scale to measure therapeutic change and the therapeutic process. One interesting finding is that while overall RF rating functions as an adequate measure of change for borderline patients whose RF score improved significantly over one year of TFP, it did not prove to be an adequate index of psychopathology and change in the panic disorder group. For the latter group, overall RF was well preserved despite the psychopathology, with reflective capacities declining significantly only around specific conflictual issues related to anxiety and panic symptoms.

These findings speak to the importance of expanding and refining the RF concept to encompass different aspects of symptomatology and psychological functioning. They also suggest that RF may function as an index to level of psychological organization (e.g., borderline vs. neurotic) with those in the borderline spectrum being deficient in RF overall, while those in the neurotic spectrum are deficient in their reflective capacities only around the dynamic conflicts that fuel their particular symptomatology. These findings call for a further refinement and expansion of the RF scale and of the concept of mentalization on which it is based.

References

Alien, J. (2003). Mentalizing. *Bulletin of the Menninger Clinic, 67,* 91–112.

Bartels, A., & Zeki, S. (2000). The neural basis of romantic love. Neurore-port, 11(17), 3829–3834.

Bartels, A., & Zeki, S. (2004). The neural correlates of maternal and romantic love. Neuroimage, 27(3), 1155–1166.

Bateman, A. W., & Fonagy, P. (1999). Effectiveness of partial hospitalization in the treatment of borderline personality disorder: A randomized controlled trial. *American Journal of Psychiatry, 156,* 1563–1569.

Bateman, A. W., & Fonagy, P. (2001). Treatment of borderline personality disorder with psychoanalytically oriented partial hospitalization: An 18-month follow-up. *American Journal of Psychiatry 158,* 36–42.

Behrends, R. S. & Blatt, S. J. (1985). Internalization and psychological development throughout the life cycle. Psychoanalytic Study of the Child, 40, 11–39. Translated and reprinted in Arbeitshefte Kinderanalvse.

Blatt, S. J. *Discussion of Affect Regulation, Mentalization and the Development of the Self by Peter Fonagy, Gyorgy Gergely, Eliot Jurist, & Mary Target.* New York, December 15, 2002.

Blatt, S. J. & Auerbach, J. (2001). Mental representation, severe psychopathology, and the therapeutic process. *Journal of the American Psychoanalytic Association, 49,* 113–159.

Blatt, S. J. & Auerbach, J. S. (2001). Mental representation, severe psychopathology, and the therapeutic process. *Journal of the American Psychoanalytic Association, 49,* 113–159.

Diamond, D., Stovall-McClough, C., Clarkin, J. F., Levy, K. N. (2003). Patient-therapist attachment in the treatment of borderline personality disorder. *Bulletin of the Menninger Clinic, 67*(3), 224–257.

Diamond, D. & Doane, J. A. (1994). Disturbed attachment and negative affective style: An intergenerational spiral, *British Journal of Psychiatry, 164,* 770–781.

Doane, J. A. & Diamond, D. (1994). *Affect and attachment in the family a family based Treatment of Major Psychiatric Disorder.* New York: Basic Books. Italian ed., Raffaello Cortina Editore, 1995.

Fonagy, P., Gergely, G., Jurist, E. L., & Target, M. (2002). *Affect regulation, mentalization, and the development of the self.* New York: Other Press.

Fonagy, P., Leigh, T., Steele, M., Steele, H., Kennedy, R., Mattoon, G., et al. (1996). The relation of attachment status, psychiatric classification, and response to psychotherapy. *Journal of Consulting and Clinical Psychology, 64,* 22–31.

Fonagy, P., Steele, M., Steele, H., Leigh, T., Kennedy, R., Mattoon, G. & Target, M. (1995). Attachment, the reflective self and borderline states: The predictive specificity of the Adult Attachment Interview and pathological emotional development. In S. Goldberg, R. Muir, & J. Kerr (Eds). *Attachment Theory: Social, Developmental and Clinical Perspectives,* Hillsdale, N.J: Analytic Press, pp. 233–279.

Fonagy P., et al. (1998). Reflective-Functioning Manual, version 5 for Application to Adult Attachment Interviews (unpublished, available from authors).

Gabbard, G. O. (2006). When is transference work useful in dynamic psychotherapy? *American Journal of Psychiatry, 163,* 1667–1669.

George, C., Kaplan, N., & Main, M. (1998). The Adult Attachment Interview Protocol, 3rd ed. Unpublished manuscript, Department of Psychology, University of California at Berkeley.

Høglend, P., Amlo, S., Marble, A., Bøgwald, K., Sørbye, Ø., Cosgrove Sjaastad, M., & Heyerdahl, O. (2006). Analysis of the Patient-Therapist Relationship in Dynamic Psychotherapy: An Experimental Study of Transference Interpretations. *American Journal of Psychiatry, 163,* 1739–1746.

Kernberg, O. (2004). Aggressivity, Narcissism, and Self Destructiveness in the Psychotherapeutic Relationship: New Developments in the Psychopathology and Psychotherapy of Severe Personality Disorders. New Haven: Yale University Press.

Kernberg, O., Diamond, D., Yeomans, F., Clarkin, J. & Levy, K. (in press). In E. L. Jurist, A. Slade, & S. Bergner, (Eds). *The Future of Psychoanalysis: Mentalization, Representation and Internalization.* New York: Other Press.

Jurist, E. (2005). Mentalized affectivity. *Psychoanalytic Psychology, 22*(3), 426–444.

LeDoux, J. E. (1996). *The Emotional Brain: The Mysterious Underpinnings of Emotional Life.* New York: Simon & Schuster.

LeDoux, J. E. (2002). Synaptic self: How our brains become who we are. New York: Viking.

Levy, K. N., Clarkin, J. F., Yeomans, F. E., Scott, L. N., Wasserman, R. H., & Kernberg, O. H. (2006a). Mechanisms of change in the treatment of borderline personality disorder with transference focused psychotherapy. *Journal of Clinical Psychology, 62,* 481–502.

Levy, K. N., Meehan, K. B., Kelly, K. M., Reynoso, J. S., Clarkin, J. F., Lenzenweger, M. F., & Kemberg, O. F. (2006b). Change in attachment and reflective function in the treatment of borderline personality disorder with transference focused psychotherapy. *Journal of Consulting and Clinical Psychology* 74:1027–1040.

Matte-Blanco, I. (1975). *The Unconscious as Infinite Sets.* London: Duckworth.

Matte-Blanco, I. (1988). *Thinking, feeling, being.* London: Routledge.

Main, M. & Goldwyn R. (1998). Adult attachment scoring and classifications system. Unpublished scoring manual. Department of Psychology. University of California, Berkeley.

Milrod, B., Busch, F. N., Cooper, A. & Shapiro, T. (1997). *Manual of Panic-Focused Psychodynamic Psychotherapy.* Washington, D.C.: American Psychiatric Assoc. Press.

Patrick, M., Hobson, R. P., Castle, D., Howard, R. & Maughn, B. (1994). Personality disorder and the mental representation of early social experience. *Development and Psychopathology.* 6. 375–388.

Roth, G. (2001). Das Gehirn und seine Wirkglichkeit Kognitive Neuorobiologie und ihre philosophisden Konsequenen. Suhrkamp.

Roth, G. (2003). Paper presented at a conference, the Lindau Psychotherapy Week, Lindau, Germany, April, 2003.

Stouvall-McClough, K. C. & Cloitre, M. (2003). Reorganization of unresolved childhood traumatic memories following exposure therapy. *Annuals of the New York Academy of Sciences, 1008,* 298–299.

9

Commentary

Mary Target

Introduction

This issue represents a timely focus on the background, development, current status, and future challenges of the concept of mentalization, which is operationalized as reflective function (RF). This concept is increasingly discussed as offering a possible and exciting way forward for psychoanalysis in this century.

A major reason for some to be enthusiastic about the concept of mentalization is that it is currently a hot topic in several neighboring disciplines, where it is the focus of considerable theoretical and research work. As well as philosophy, these disciplines include developmental and clinical psychology, and cognitive neuroscience, where mentalization goes under a number of related names: theory of mind, social cognition, mind-mindedness, and so on. Although some analysts believe that building bridges with other sciences of the mind is a waste of time (Green, 2000), for those who see the future of psychoanalysis as lying partly in exchange with other disciplines and in collaborative research (see e.g., Fonagy, 2003; Shapiro, 2003), mentalization is a vital integrative concept. In addition to its interdisciplinary relevance, mentalization is claimed to offer a unifying bridge for theory and technique across the clinical disciplines of psychoanalysis, psychoanalytic psychotherapy and other forms of talking therapy such as cognitive, family, parent–child, and group therapies.

There are, however, some objections to this bridge concept, within the psychoanalytic world. One concern is that mentalization is not a

psychoanalytic concept at all, because although it refers to a fundamental mental process outside conscious awareness, it is not framed
in terms of the dynamic unconscious. An alternative criticism comes
from those who believe the idea is fundamental to psychoanalysis,
but that mentalization is just a clumsy bit of jargon for something
that has been fully explained and conceptualized decades ago (e.g.,
by the French *école psychosomatique*, Bion, and Winnicott). Sometimes, curiously, critics voice both concerns.

It is certainly true (and regularly acknowledged by proponents
of mentalization as a useful concept) that mentalization as a mental capacity and process has long been recognised in philosophy and
psychoanalysis, as explained in this issue by Steele and Steele; Fonagy; and Bouchard and Lecours *inter alia*. What is new is the further
development of the concept especially by Fonagy and colleagues, in
two main ways: (a) as *the basis of a theoretical model* of clinical problems (especially personality disorders), of psychic development, and
of therapeutic technique and action in psychoanalysis, all of which
have been extensively elaborated within this specific conceptual
framework, and (b) to connect psychoanalysis to other contemporary
disciplines and to a broad and fairly deep empirical research base.

So *is* mentalization part of psychoanalysis? Yes, when psychoanalysis is understood in a broad sense. Mentalization as a process means thinking about what someone does, and what happens
between people (at least in emotionally important relationships such
as those involving intimacy or authority), in terms of psychological
meaning and motivation. Psychoanalysis clearly contributes unique
understanding of particular kinds of motivation (somewhat different kinds depending on the psychoanalytic theory being considered,
drive theory, object relations, self psychology, and so on). The theory
of stages of mentalization underlying the development of personality
and relatedness (Fonagy, Gergely, Jurist, & Target 2002) is psychoanalytic in that it concerns the unconscious foundations of mental functioning, which may be dynamically as well as descriptively
unconscious. It also draws strongly on earlier psychoanalytic models
as stated above. It is an account of how the early relationship with
parents, and relational trauma, may shape and distort emotional
and thinking capacities and hence later personality functioning,
the ability to understand self and others, and the ways in which a
patient behaves in the therapeutic relationship. Difficulties in mentalizing can therefore be thought of as a very important aspect of the

difficulties of our patients, particularly when the majority of patients we see have character and relationship difficulties as well as neurotic symptoms. Improving mentalization is a relevant feature of the outcome for many patients (see e.g., the papers in this issue by Slade, Rudden, Yeomans et al.). Building models of what happens between people in psychological terms, and playing this out in the transitional space of transference and countertransference so that it can be much more directly observed, understood and changed, are, of course, the currency of psychoanalysis as a process—and what often attracts us to our clinical work, and keeps us enthralled. In these ways mentalization is part of psychoanalysis, rather as attachment theory is: neither is encompassed by the other but they have common origins, continuing important areas of overlap with fertile interconnections in both directions.

All interpretations come from and express some variety of mentalization, whether they are reconstructions of development (why one became who one is today, how the patient's father was experienced by him as a child, etc.), elaborations of fantasies and dreams, or here-and-now interpretations of how the mind is used, the analyst is perceived, the analysis is used, and how this relates to the way in which the patient is living his life. Some would say that mentalization is the essence of the psychoanalytic process—mentalization focusing on dynamically and/or descriptively unconscious processes and attributions, in relation to emotionally important aspects of self and other (including of course the transference relationship), which over time strengthens this ego capacity more generally.

Still, it is sometimes said in psychoanalytic meetings that thinking in terms of mentalization is less useful to our work than using other psychoanalytic theories, and there is something important to be recognized and considered here. It may be that the developmental model, which aims to account for one aspect of psychopathology, contributing to understanding of limitations and distortions in thinking and feeling within a session, does not seem to do justice to the intensity and richness of a clinical experience, especially the most visceral emotional states and particularly in intensive and prolonged psychoanalytic work. The mentalization model may seem cognitive, academic, and lacking in the emotional rawness, irrationality, and immediacy of the unconscious. This perception may have arisen because presentations of these ideas have undeniably often emphasised the research base, and sometimes focused more on thinking than on feeling. This emphasis is not however inherent and may have been a result of trying to underline the distinctive features of the theoretical model, and its connections to empirical science, more than its continuing connection to its psychoanalytic roots. I suggest that the time has come for mentalization theory to be further developed to (a) elucidate the place of psychoanalytic understandings of the unconscious within the theory of mentalization (which is often more concerned with form than with content, and with bringing things into conscious awareness rather than with the organization of unconscious mental life), and (b) make it clear that while there has been an emphasis on capacities for symbolization and thinking, we are most concerned with the application of these capacities to emotional life and relationships.

This journal issue is a welcome opportunity for some of the key mentalizers to set out their stalls and to give us a sense of where the theory is going and to what extent it can be usefully applied clinically. It is a pleasure to have been asked to comment on this diverse and very stimulating collection of papers.* Each paper is, I think, very characteristic of its author(s) and should enable readers who are new to the topic to gain a good idea of the concept and its applications, in both research and clinical work. The opening section, which includes papers by Fonagy; Gergely and Unoka; and Bouchard and Lecours, sets the theoretical scene of mentalization. Howard and Miriam Steele's paper then furthers our understanding of the place of mentalization in the history of psychoanalytic theory and attachment research. Yeomans and colleagues, Slade, and Rudden and colleagues, round off the issue by describing innovative clinical research that builds upon the concept of mentalization.

I do not intend to summarize the seven papers, each of which deserves to be read in full; I focus most on those by Fonagy, Gergely and Unoka, because they extend the central theoretical foundations of mentalization, but they may be the least accessible for clinical readers, because of their scientific and cognitive emphasis. I also consider some more general points that often arise in analytic discussions of mentalization, and address specific issues raised by the other papers.

---

* The present author has contributed to the mentalization literature, so must declare an interest.

Peter Fonagy's paper offers a very useful, comprehensive exposition of his constantly evolving theory that the capacity to mentalize is a key determinant of self-organization, that this capacity is acquired in the context of early attachment relationships, and that disturbed attachment relationships may compromise the development of a child's social cognitive capacities. The paper takes a biological perspective, in which attachment relationships give children the opportunity to develop social intelligence, by stimulating and supporting the brain processes which underpin it. He introduces the work of the evolutionary biologist Richard Alexander, and the idea that social intelligence evolved not to deal with hostile forces of nature, nor to enable us to create lasting attachment relationships, but to deal with competition from other people (know thine enemy). Fonagy suggests that the capacity to interpret human behavior requires the capacity to mentalize, to name and understand affect, regulate arousal, and exert effortful control.

The paper discusses some intriguing findings on the neurobiology of attachment and mentalization, including the role of mirror neurons, the conceptualization of attachment as an addictive disorder, and the suggestion (from Bartels & Zeki) that activation of the attachment system suppresses mentalizing, surprising given that security of attachment promotes the development of mentalization capacity over time. Fonagy suggests that individuals whose attachment is secure will have less need to activate their attachment system, and so will be freer to practice mentalization. This suggestion is persuasive and fits with some other data (noted later) but I would like first to suggest an alternative reading of the Bartels and Zeki results, which is that because their study compared responses to familiar photographs, the stimulus for mentalization is absent (there is no 'demand' in the terms used in coding RF). The participant is simply looking at a photograph of a loved one and then at another of a friend. Why would attachment or mentalization in fact be activated by looking at such photographs, with no interaction, story, or situation that gives the viewer something to worry about or try to understand? If the participant sees a picture of her partner smiling into the camera or her baby looking cute, the participant would presumably not feel under pressure to come up with an explanation for the apparent contentment, but would simply enjoy it. If, however, she had been presented with an image, even a static one like a photograph, in which the loved one looked angry or sad, we might find that mentalization is more strongly activated in an attachment relationship than in others. We care what our loved ones are feeling, and if they are upset we very much want to know why. It would be easy to test this prediction, that mentalization would be more strongly activated the closer the relationship, and increasingly so where there is a problem or puzzle about these feelings. This would be consistent with my experience of coding RF in the attachment interviews of adults and children, that mentalization is strongest in relation to conflict, distress, and confusing behavior in emotionally important relationships.

Fonagy advances an important argument about the vicious cycle created by attachment trauma in hyperactivating the attachment system and shutting down mentalization, exposing the child to further attachment trauma, and retraumatization from within by memories of the trauma relived in the mode of psychic equivalence. (This is also clearly illustrated by the case of Andy, described vividly by Gergely & Unoka in their paper). In this section of his paper Fonagy implicitly addresses the accusation that he has put forward mentalization as a panacea (mentalize and all will be well, mentalize more and all will be even better). As he acknowledges, and as is evident from clinical experience and from coding research interviews from clinical populations, mentalization can be used for destructive as well as prosocial ends, to destroy or exploit attachment as well as to enhance it. We may assume that just as trauma by an attachment figure is worse than other trauma, this will be worse still if the abuser is also mentalizing (chooses knowingly to inflict mental suffering on the child). It is likely to destroy his trust not only in the abuser, but also in attachment and mentalizing—in being close to and needing another person, in thinking about what is in that loved person's mind, and in expecting comfort if the loved person has him in mind.

Gergely & Unoka's paper elaborates the basic tenets of the model of early affective self development worked out with Watson, Csibra, Fonagy, Jurist, Koos, and other colleagues represented in this volume, especially the Steeles and Arietta Slade. They present a case illustration to demonstrate the model's clinical usefulness. Gergely's painstaking commitment to precision in his descriptions of psychological mechanisms demands that the reader wrestle with dense and complex language. This can be alienating to clinicians who may dislike information processing models of mind, and feel that descriptions of emotional life and relationships in these terms are somewhat mechanistic. The clinical material and the examples of babies' experiences are very helpful here. I would like to urge readers of this commentary to make the effort to engage with the highly original ideas of Gergely, a brilliant experimental psychologist conversant with psychoanalysis, whose model of the development of relatedness can (with the help of Unoka) disinter some of the foundations of the states we meet every day in our consulting rooms.

Despite the academic language, Gergely & Unoka's paper should in fact help to dispel the common impression of mentalization theory as too cognitive. They show us how the cognitive capacities that eventually constitute mentalization crucially depend on the earliest emotional exchanges with the mother,* if the infant is to begin to develop recognition of his own emotional world and learn to differentiate and manage his feelings. There are key developmental concepts here, which I believe will stand the test of time as elements of this model of the developing emotional mind.

Gergely emphasizes the crucial role played by the caregiver's mirroring of the infant's emotions, both in regulating the infant's feelings and in helping him to acquire the capacity to do this for himself. The idea that mirroring must be contingent, congruent and marked in order to facilitate the development of the capacity for affect regulation is becoming increasingly widely known and has been described in several papers and a joint book with many clinical examples (Fonagy, Gergely, Jurist, & Target, 2002). Other concepts are also vital but less familiar, including the distinction between sufficiency and necessity in the mother's response to her baby's emotional signals. The baby implicitly asks: "Does she react when I express my feelings, and if she does, how sure can I be that it is *about* my feelings? That she is picking me up this time because I needed to be picked up, not just because she generally likes to carry me around?"

In the clinical situation one could think of parallel dilemmas: "How much is my analyst's gentleness/impatience/sleepiness in the session specifically about how I am being at the moment? Is he (a) no more likely to be like that when I am like this than at any other time [neither necessary nor sufficient], (b) like that whenever I am like this, but also at many other times [sufficient but not necessary], (c) only like that when I am like this, but it does not always happen even then [necessary but not sufficient], or (d) always and only like that

---

* Or of course other trusted attachment figure.

when I am like this [both necessary and sufficient]?" Let us imagine that, in the last case, the analyst is gentle in tone *only when* the patient is very distressed. The patient then gets a clear set of messages from the gentleness—she *is very distressed* at this moment (even if she did not fully know it), the *analyst knows* that she is very distressed, the analyst responds with gentleness *because he knows* she is distressed (and not for any other reason). This sharpens the patient's awareness of her own feelings, and strengthens her sense of the analyst's reliable, specific responsiveness. She knows both of them better and this makes her emotional world in general, as well as the particular analytic relationship, more predictable and understandable. Because the analytic relationship is likely to be experienced quite powerfully as a core part of the patient's emotional world, especially its unconscious depths, the sense that that relationship is feeling more coherent and understandable makes the patient's self, itself, feel more so.

Some readers might want to take issue with Gergely and Unoka's focus on observable interaction and rational inference, as though the emotional world and its capacities were built up simply through registering and internalizing the behavior of the more or less attuned mother. The fracturing of perceptions of reality, and the freezing of emotional processing seen in cases of trauma are there (exemplified both in the description of Unoka's case, and in the babies with disorganized attachment that Gergely and colleagues have extensively studied), but what about the more organized response of the developing mind to more subtle but systematic distortions? For example, what about the mother who responds reliably to her baby's distress (it is sufficient to get a caregiving reaction), but who also for her own reasons picks up the baby at many other times, even when this disrupts his internal states (of absorption in play, sleep, listening to his father's voice, etc.)?

Gergely and Unoka describe the predicament and defensive strategy of the avoidant baby and they refer in passing to the infant activating different emotional coping responses, which are automatic. But it may be worth emphasising that these responses (which are perhaps adaptive at the time they are developed, as Gergely & Unoka imply) become aspects of character and relating that often persist precisely because they are automatic and outside awareness. Much of what we deal with clinically, with more neurotic patients at least, is in this area of personality functioning. The person selects and distorts not only his behavior but also his internal awareness of his psychic reality. This may not necessarily be because his mother has not helped him to identify it, but because it has become painful to continue to identify it. The person may then defend against the pain of realizing what the experience is and what it means, even though it has been adequately differentiated. The process of mentalizing and knowledge of the emotional world are reasonably well-established, but particular contents have been excluded. Blaming oneself rather than being aggressive when dismissing the recognition of feeling angry, intellectualizing so that the emotional significance is detached from an idea, attributing one's own emotional response to someone else.... These are mundane, basic manoeuvres with which we are all familiar.

Gergely & Unoka give a touching example of the toddler turning from expressing anxiety or sadness at being abandoned, to saying "Mommy, I love you," and knowing at some level that this will get Mommy to pick him up.* This requires an internal shift, which is not a conscious pretence, but by means of which sadness, anxiety, or anger is transformed into 'loving sweetness.' We see very similar automatic transformations routinely in analytic sessions and it may help to link this to the paper's example. A male patient arrives for a session after a break in which he attended a conference in an exotic location; he looks very directly at his female analyst and then unusually makes a personal comment: "You must have been having a good time—you look wonderful!" Of course, there are many potential meanings to explore here on the overt level. The analyst may believe the patient meant what he said, under the sway of transference ('with whom have you been having a good time while I was away?', 'let me see if I can get away with flirting with you before we get back into role', etc). However, the analyst thinks she caught a fleeting look of concern as the patient first glanced at her. She knows that she is actually looking tired, that charm is one of his strategies for deflecting trouble, and that while he cares about her, he tends to fear being trapped with a needy woman. She suspects, therefore, that his immediate feeling was one of anxiety, leading to fear of what might be demanded of him, and retreat before these thoughts were registered. Further thoughts have probably been dismissed (who or what has been giving you a tough time? were you sad or jealous

---

* This is automatic and it is shocking to see—for example in the Strange Situation—how, at 1-year-old, the baby readily reverses his internal experience of anxiety (clearly measurable physiologically, as Gergely & Unoka report) into a falsely bright, self-sufficient even indifferent manner.

that I had abandoned you, and was having a good time while you were stuck here? I had better cheer you up or I will be punished). After habitual preconscious mentalizing along these lines, the analyst said in a sympathetically humorous way: "You felt you had better bring me back a present?" After a moment of double-take the patient laughed ruefully then said: "It is true...now I can see you are tired, maybe strained—working too hard!" This is of course only the beginning of digging for the emotionally real experience and what worrying thoughts led him to dismiss it and try something else. Of course if the analyst had taken the flattery offered as social gallantry, or as actually felt, then he would have remained 'out of touch' with his feelings of anxiety about the depressed or angry mother, fear of punishment for getting away and being lively and excited and proud, for being a man who can do those things, and so on...feelings which had led to depression and self-defeating behavior and ultimately to analysis. Only a light touch was needed at this stage of the work to prompt the patient to move beyond, "Mommy, I love you" to the more real, "Mommy, I don't like it that you are tired and might get irritated with me; I will have to pretend to be sweet."

Gergely and Unoka help us to see at the level of mechanisms and processes what this being out of touch means, and how and why treatment can help to reduce it. But the implication is that treatment needs to involve a sort of feedback loop—that is, the visibility of necessity and sufficiency in the contingencies between patient and analyst. This is of course a delicate thing within the boundaries of the patient–analyst relationship and the traditionally inscrutable face, voice and person of the analyst. More than in classical technique, to enhance mentalization, to help patients to be better in touch with more of their psychic reality, and to be more confident in their ability to deal with others' psychic realities, the analyst needs to be judiciously somewhat more readable so that the patient can get the kind of feedback about his states that helps him to elaborate and strengthen a realistic model of his mental life. Contingency and markedness are as crucial here as Gergely and Unoka have shown them to be in the mother's interactions with the infant. The feedback given has to be contingent on the material and marked as *about the patient*. The analyst's reality (tiredness) is not denied, but it is not the point or the focus of discussion by the analyst except in so far as it is part of the patient's mental world. Again as Gergely and Unoka describe with a parent, the analyst adopts a peculiar way of speaking,

parallel to motherese, marked as about the patient by a combination
of interest and detachment, warmth without need, encouraging
the patient progressively to own his states of mind, his awareness
of them initially borrowed but increasingly sure and free-standing,
independent of the analyst as a person, and eventually independent
even of the analyst as an analyst. Her recognition has become joint
recognition and then been absorbed into his self, a new, increasingly
automatic set of responses that are genuinely authentic to the patient,
no longer dependent on the analyst's reflection.

Bouchard and Lecours draw an illuminating comparison between
the Francophone tradition of theory about mentalization, including the work of writers such as Marty and de M'Uzan and the theories developed by Fonagy and colleagues which can help enrich our
understanding of mentalization. Bouchard and Lecours contrast the
French model of the psychogenetics of mental structures, with its
focus on mental elaboration of and defences against instinctual urges,
with the developmental and intersubjective approach. Whereas the
French analyze affect regulation in terms of life and death drives and
pressures, Fonagy and colleagues focus on preoedipal intersubjective relationships and the mother's (and analyst's) role in helping the
infant (patient) to develop more efficient affect tolerance and regulation within the dyad. This work necessitates the re-examination and
modification of more classicical conceptions. However, Bouchard
and Lecours argue that these contrasting views of mentalization are
not incompatible; in fact, both are required for a full account of its
complexity.

Bouchard and Lecours propose that intersubjective and relational
events, particularly those occurring in primary object relations, significantly modulate the drives to a far greater extent than previously
thought. They also argue that an integrative understanding of the
two traditions requires a discussion of three issues: the mentalization
of affective structures into drives, the mentalization of the object as
it relates to the agentive self, and a comparison of the nature of the
two primitive modes of thinking (psychic equivalence and pretend
modes) associated with poor mentalizing.

Their ensuing discussion identifies four key themes that are
shared by the different traditions of writing on mentalization: (a) all
highlight the undermining of mentalization by trauma; (b) all use a
concept of mental rejection as a vital adaptive and defensive mechanism for the infant and the traumatized adult; (c) all draw attention

to the persistence of primitive forms of thinking; (d) all highlight the presence of affect dysregulation. Bouchard and Lecours suggest that Fonagy and Target's approach indicates the need to modify classical Freudian approaches in order to acknowledge that the specialized apparatus responsible for the mentalization of the drives is itself reciprocally determined by the quality of primary object relations. On the other hand, although one may accept that affects are not inherently known but are discovered (through mirroring, appropriate differentiation (marking), and internalization), affective structures, insofar as they indicate the body's present situation, have to be seen also as inherently oriented and orienting. Calling for mental elaboration, they determine the direction and quality of mentalization.

The movement toward integration has not just been a Francophone phenomenon. A recent paper by Fonagy and Target (2007) extends previous thinking about the connections between attachment theory and psychoanalysis, focussing on the idea of the mind as embodied, and the rootedness of symbolic thought in sensory, emotional and enacted experience with objects. The paper also presents some speculations about the nature of language that emphasize the origin of internal working models and of representations in general in early sensorimotor and emotional experiences with the mother. It is argued that language and symbolic thought may be built on a foundation of gestures and actions, profoundly influenced by the experience of early physical interaction with the primary object. We anticipate that, although there are still many differences between the various psychoanalytic traditions, this development of our approach will to some degree bring us closer to French psychoanalytic theorising, which emphasizes the rooting of thought and mind in experiences of the body and drives, as very thoughtfully explored in this issue by Bouchard and Lecours.

The theoretical background is extended by Howard and Miriam Steele, who present an historical account of the conceptualization and stages of operationalization of mentalization as reflective function for research purposes. Steele and Steele were not only, as they wrote, in the right place at the right time, but they were also certainly the right people in the right place at the right time. Their leadership of the London Parent-Child Project and its waves of follow-up studies have been a model of systematic longitudinal study, collaboration, and networking. They have also been the inspiration for a new generation of researchers working on the boundary between psychoanalysis and developmental psychology. It is London's loss that these rare talents have been transplanted to New York. Their work on the development of the RF concept and scale, as well as on parent–infant and child attachment, very clearly described in their paper here, crucially underpins the empirical work which has followed, including the remaining papers in this issue.

A very important issue running through these papers and some of the wider literature is the question of whether mentalization capacity is required for analyzability. Another side of this question is whether the absence of mentalizing or antagonism to it, as seen in antisocial personality disorder, might defeat any form of psychological treatment. (See e.g., Steele & Steele's description of negative RF in the AAIs of violent offenders. I can confirm these observations from coding interviews from similar samples.) Steele & Steele suggest that adequate mentalization is a criterion of treatability within an analytic model, but that some forms of treatment, including the three treatment approaches described in this issue, attempt to address very substantial mentalization deficits. One part of the answer to this conundrum lies in the adaptation of treatment to address the mentalization deficit itself, thereby shoring up and developing the process, before expecting it to populate the mind with different content. All three clinically-focussed papers give excellent illustrations of how this may be done both by using expert knowledge of particular clinical populations and by specifically applying the concept of mentalization, sometimes developing it further in an attempt to apply it to each challenging group of patients.

The paper by Yeomans, Clarkin, Diamond, and Levy, for example, focuses on the mechanism of action of Transference Focussed Psychotherapy (TFP), a form of psychodynamic psychotherapy specifically modified for patients with borderline personality organization (BPO). Yeomans and colleagues use TFP in their studies of severely disturbed patients with gross limitations to their mentalization capacities. Similarly, Mentalization Based Therapy or MBT (see Bateman & Fonagy, 2004) has been developed to build the capacity for mentalization in severely borderline patients from a very low or negative base. Clinical and research investigations have shown increasing mentalization to be one of the mechanisms of change in TFP. Yeomans and colleagues argue persuasively that interpretation of the patient's experience of the therapist, of the transference (a technique used with great caution with borderline patients by Bateman and

Fonagy), is an important part of facilitating mentalization and of improving social functioning in such patients.* It would be interesting to see equivalent before-and-after mentalization measures from MBT patients, and to relate changes, as Yeomans and colleagues do, to the specific techniques used and closely monitored in TFP. In this paper, the vignette of Sara beautifully illustrates the importance of mutuality of influence if mentalization is going to increase in the patient through increasing integration of thinking and affect. The therapist (who nicely exemplifies what we have called the *inquisitive stance*, Fearon et al., 2006) explains one hypothesis, a model of the unconscious fantasies of self, object and relationship controlling the patient's interactions with the therapist, but then notices that she is more affectively involved in another model she has referred to. The therapist can see how the two relate but focuses first on the one which is more meaningful to the patient. It is only if the hypothesis means something emotionally to the patient that it is worth elaborating with her. I believe it is also very important here that the patient finds she can influence the therapist's mind as well as learn from his knowledge of her mind. By the end of therapy, she needs to feel some confidence in her own expertise as well as his.

The elegant and clinically rich descriptions of using a mentalization model of working with panic disorder (Rudden et al.) and with the parents of young children (Slade) bring up further points of general relevance to thinking about this model in relation to psychotherapy and psychoanalysis. It is a common observation, even in severe personality disorder and certainly in patients with trauma, relationship difficulties, and neurotic conflicts, that mentalization is in some areas quite good, even impressive. For some high-functioning patients seen in analysis (this may include candidates in training analyses), the idea of fostering mentalization may even seem irrelevant (Michels, 2006). However, I believe it is not.

There are some key points to make on these questions. One suggested by Steele and Steele, Yeomans and colleagues, and elaborated in some depth by Fonagy and Gergely and Unoka, is that mentalization is not a unitary capacity that a person either does or does not have. It is really a hierarchy of capacities, involving more or less

---

* Bateman and Fonagy have recently further clarified their position regarding transference interpretation in a letter in response to a recent paper by Gabbard in the *American Journal of Psychiatry* (see Bateman & Fonagy, 2007).

sophisticated ways of thinking about feeling founded upon more basic appreciations about the nature and content of mental reality. Trouble can arise with basic capacities or with more sophisticated ones which are breaking down in complex, heated situations, for example, in marital conflict, becoming a single parent, or learning to become an analyst. A second point made, for example in Rudden's paper, but also commonly observed and discussed among clinicians, is that mentalization may be strikingly uneven in different areas of the patient's mental life. Not surprisingly, it may be most lacking in the area of acute symptoms, such as thinking about panic experiences, or, in the case of parents, thinking about certain affects in themselves or their children (angry feelings, disappointment, fear of loss, sexuality). As Slade describes, it becomes much more useful (as well as more obviously relevant to the patient) to measure RF in the context of discussion of the currently difficult relationship, as opposed to through the AAI (in which it is measured in relation to the parents, mainly in childhood). Similarly, it is interesting and helpful that Yeomans and colleagues' TFP group measures mentalization in relation to the therapy relationship as well as through the AAI. Others of us have also tried to do this with different samples, which allows us to measure mentalization in different domains and to get a clearer understanding of where it works well and of what changes occur in treatment. For anyone, even those with a generally high capacity for mentalization, there are certain things that are harder to contemplate and to understand honestly.

Finally I would like to discuss briefly some common assumptions about mentalization and to refer to data which shed some light on them. One, shown by research and clinical experience to be misleading, is that limited mentalization is always a sign of poor mental health, or a risk factor. Here I refer to some studies from the Anna Freud Centre (AFC, Target & Fonagy, 2003). In our long-term follow-up study of children seen at the Centre, the highest RF was found among securely attached people who had had difficult family experiences (earned secure). Securely attached people who had had benign family experiences (unearned secure) had moderate or sometimes low RF, while insecure and unresolved people generally had low or very low RF. It may be that, while we know that secure attachment facilitates the early development of mentalizing capacity, this capacity is not elaborated as extensively in relation to attachment figures in favourable family circumstances. Note that reflective functioning has mostly been measured in the AAI which is restricted to family relationships. Preliminary studies of latency age children suggest that secure children may mentalize less about their families, but more about their peers, which is presumably an adaptive shift of investment in benign circumstances. This would be expected then in adulthood to result in an unearned secure classification with low average RF in the AAI. Some traumatized and/or personality disordered patients had negative levels (–1 or 0, see the final part of the Steele & Steele paper in this issue). This is consistent with the findings described in the Parent-Child Project (again, see Steele & Steele), that higher RF was only necessary to produce security in the next generation where the parents had had particularly adverse experiences. In the absence of deprivation, RF in the parent was not strongly associated with security in the child.

The suggestion is then that if there have been consistently disturbing or traumatic events or relationships in a parent's past, he or she needs to develop stronger mentalization to become secure and to have a secure child, but that in more favorable circumstances this is not necessary. There is then much less confusion, distress, and conflict to be processed, and less of a danger that such distracting preoccupations in the parent will interfere with their relationship with the child. It is vital, however, to distinguish the lower RF seen in these luckier, secure parents from the very low or negative RF seen in very insecure or personality disordered individuals. Secure parents with low to moderate RF are still likely to have secure children (who may in turn be less precocious mentalizers than other secure children with higher RF parents). One might speculate that they may not only have children with secure attachment, but also children who are happier despite their and their parents' less elaborated mentalizing capacities. Increasing mentalization above an average level can in this sense be seen as a way to overcome problems, something only associated with good mental health when there has been a substantial challenge which has required cognitive tools to help contain and process difficult emotions in self and others. There is reason in the resilience literature to assume that children who overcome adversity and become earned secure adults have had an adult in their life (e.g., teacher, grandparent, step-parent) who helped them gain this capacity for perspective taking, for recognising and thinking about their feelings and others' behavior.

In the same vein, drawing on the follow-up study already cited and on another AFC study (Ensink, 2003) of children and families currently referred for psychiatric assessment, it seems that, within clinical and subclinical samples, earned secure people may be reflective and functional, but they tend to be somewhat more vulnerable to depression than their unearned secure peers. The children who are most reflective about their families are also more worried about them, the less worried children tend not to think about their families that much. Perhaps these unworried children can afford to take their security and their own and others' thoughts and feelings more for granted. Similarly, when we compare treated children and their siblings who are followed up as adults, we have found that among the secure people, those who have higher RF (and remember their childhoods as having been more problematic) tend to have subclinical depressive affect. They have more accurate (negative) memories of their childhoods (we had access to extensive contemporaneous descriptions). Their capacity to mentalize has perhaps allowed them to process their negative memories, but their depressive realism seems linked to a sense of slight pessimism and an awareness of what might go wrong. The other side of this was that these higher RF secure people were more able to cope with major stresses in their adult lives, they were more prepared, perhaps saw it coming and understood what was happening more easily (the risk being that they see it coming even at time when it is not, hence the generally more guarded and gloomy, survivor quality to their interviews).

In positive circumstances having a rose-tinted view of the past and future may be more adaptive than having enough RF and vigilance to deal with whatever life throws at you. The downside might be that problems that do need to be appreciated and understood in good time might force other people in the family to carry anxiety, sadness, or anger for the sunnier, secure person, particularly if their rose-tinted optimism becomes denial. Those of us who become analysts are probably unlikely to be among the rose-tinted optimists; we have perhaps chosen to use our capacities for mentalization to develop depressive realism in ourselves and our patients. Like Freud, we may aim for ordinary unhappiness, or to achieve a kind of earned happiness: the appreciation of having overcome difficulties, of which we are constantly reminded by struggling with them continually on behalf of patients in our clinical work. The Kleinian concept of achievement of the depressive position, and its continued development in maturity, has relevance here although within a very different theoretical framework.

A concern sometimes expressed is that mentalization is really just intellectualizing about feelings. The Unoka case example of Andy, and many others in this issue and elsewhere in the literature of mentalization, should make it clear that mentalization is centrally concerned with appreciating emotional truth, allowing different perspectives but anchoring them in the evidence of actual feeling and direct experience, as well as in the capacity to imagine what could be different. People who use psychological ideas and explanations as culs-de-sac, to retreat from emotional reality, to manipulate or to justify inertia might be mentalizing in one very limited sense (using a cognitive capacity), but that is of course not the sense that we aim for in therapy, usefully differentiated by Elliot Jurist's concept of mentalized affectivity (Fonagy et al., 2002). The papers in this issue show us that analysts interested in mentalization aim to see that cognitive capacity recruited to the service of emotional depth, truth, contact and—with courage—change.

References

Bateman, A., & Fonagy, P. (2007). Re: Gabbard, G. O. (2006). When is transference work useful in dynamic psychotherapy? (letter). *American Journal of Psychiatry*.

Bateman, A. W., & Fonagy, P. (2004). Psychotherapy for borderline personality disorder: mentalization based treatment. Oxford, UK: Oxford University Press.

Ensink, K. (2003). Assessing theory of mind, affective understanding and reflective functioning in primary school aged children. Unpublished PhD Dissertation, University of London, London.

Fearon, P., Target, M., Fonagy, P., Williams, L., McGregor, J., Sargent, J., et al. (2006). Short-Term Mentalization and Relational Therapy (SMART): An integrative family therapy for children and adolescents. In J. Allen & P. Fonagy (Eds.), *Handbook of mentalizaiton based treatments*. London: John Wiley.

Fonagy, P. (2003). Genetics, developmental psychopathology and psychoanalytic theory: The case for ending our (not so) splendid isolation. *Psychoanalytic Inquiry, 23*(2), 218–247.

Fonagy, P., Gergely, G., Jurist, E., & Target, M. (2002). *Affect Regulation, Mentalization and the Development of the Self*. New York: Other Press.

Fonagy, P., & Target, M. (2007). The rooting of the mind in the body: New links between attachment theory and psychoanalytic thought. *Journal of the American Psychoanalytic Association* 55:2, 441–456.

Green, A. (2000). Science and science fiction in infant research. In J. Sandler, A.-M. Sandler & R. Davies (Eds.), *Clinical and Observational Psychoanalytic Research: Roots of a Controversy* (pp. 41–73). London: Karnac Books.

Levinson, A., & Fonagy, P. (2004). Offending and attachment: The relationship between interpersonal awareness and offending in a prison population with psychiatric disorder. *Canadian Journal of Psychoanalysis, 12*(2), 225–251.

Michels, R. (2006). Epilogue. In J. G. Allen & P. Fonagy (Eds.), *Handbook of Mentalization-Based Treatment* (pp. 327–334). New York: Wiley.

Shapiro, T. (2003). Commentary. *Psychoanalytic Inquiry, 23*, 367–374.

Target, M., & Fonagy, P. (2003). Attachment theory and long-term psychoanalytic outcome: Are insecure attachment narratives less accurate? In M. Leuzinger-Bohleber, A. U. Dreher & J. Canestri (Eds.), *Pluralism and Unity? Methods of Research in Psychoanalysis* (pp. 149–167). London: International Psychoanalytical Association.

Author Index

Subject Index

A

AAI. *see* Adult Attachment Interviews (AAI)
Abnormal perceptual illusions, 84
Abuse
    alcohol, 10
    cocaine, 10
Abyss, 114
Academic achievement, 135
Achievement, 135
Acting-outs, 109, 161–162
Activation, 60
Adaptive engagement, 92
Adolescents early development, 150–151
Adult Attachment Interviews (AAI), 135–139, 190–191, 249, 275
    rating scales, 142–143
Adults
    borderline syndromes, 106
    childhood attachment trauma, 35
    children playing with, 27–28
Advice, 89–90
    parents, 225
Affective experiences, 88
Affective freezing, 84, 87
Affective functioning, 57
Affective isolation, 91
Affectively supercharged moments, 227
Affective realm, 236
Affective-relational matrix, 106
Affective self disorders, 92
    analytic treatment, 57
Affective-sexual thinking, 110
Affective structures, 115
Affective subjectivity
    social interactive origins, 71, 72
Affect-mirroring, 58, 91
Affect-mirroring emotion displays
    mother-infant interactions, 70
    self-referential interpretation, 73
Affects

defined, 114
    dysregulation, 122
    inability to express, 92
    labeling and understanding, 7–8
    mentalization into drives, 114–115
    regulation, 7–8, 23, 241
Agency
    understanding, 26
Agentive self, 106
    development, 17–43
    mentalization of, 117–118
Aggression, 114
    paranoid, 164
Ainsworth, Mary, 135
Alcohol abuse, 10
Alexander, Richard, 6
Alien self, 34–35
Altruism, 13
AMBIANCE (Atypical Maternal Behavior Instrument for Assessment and Classification, Bronfman, Parsons, & Lyons-Ruth 1999)
    coding system., 22
Amygdala, 8, 9, 11
Analytic treatment
    affective self disorders, 57
Anger, 59, 89–90
    panic disorder, 187, 188
    preceding panic attacks, 89
Anna Freud Centre, 36, 153, 275
    child guidance model, 212
Anterior cingulate, 9
Anterior hypothalamus, 11
Anterior temporal cortex, 7–8
Anxiety, 114, 163
    infants, 15
    panic attacks, 198
    paranoid, 164
    PFPP, 190
Applied Relaxation Training (ART), 190
Approach avoidance, 60
Arnsten, Amy, 39

289